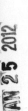

the Gospels:

THEIR ORIGIN
AND THEIR GROWTH

the Gospels:

THEIR ORIGIN
AND THEIR GROWTH

by Frederick C. Grant

HARPER & BROTHERS   PUBLISHERS   NEW YORK

Contents

CHARTS, DIAGRAMS, AND TABLES

Foreword

Most people are aware of the progress of physical science in our time. Far fewer realize that in the areas of literary and historical study, even in those of philosophy and theology, there also is progress, and that "time makes ancient good uncouth." Each generation requires its own interpretation, its own special approach to the great writings of the past, as historians and literary critics lead us to a closer and more intimate understanding of these classic works. This is no less true of the study and interpretation of the Bible than of the study of other literature.

Of primary importance, in the recent study of the gospels, their origin and development, is what is called Form Criticism. This should really be called Form History, from the German original, *Formgeschichte*. What it undertakes to do is to recover the traditions underlying the gospels, in the form in which they circulated during the oral period. Some persons view this as a purely negative and therefore dangerous method of study. But its positive values also are clear. It takes us back to the creative stage in early church history, when the gospel traditions were beginning to "crystallize" in writing, at first in brief collections or "sources," and then in the written gospels of Mark, Luke, Matthew, and John.

There was nothing automatic or mechanical about this process. It was the work of the church's teachers and evangelists, who—in a highly literate age, the opening decades of the Roman Empire— were simply setting down in writing the church's own oral traditions of "all that Jesus began both to do and to teach." These traditions were already, for the most part, circulating in a more or less fixed, definite form and even arrangement, for purposes of memorization and transmission, perhaps even for use in public worship. That is what tradition meant in the ancient world, especially in Oriental and Near Eastern areas: a fixed body of definite teaching. And if, as many of us hold, this process was divinely inspired and overruled, as was the activity of the early Christian movement as a whole, it was at the same time a perfectly normal procedure. God uses human instruments in the achievement of His purposes. Hence we may with a perfectly good conscience apply the methods of modern literary and historical research to the ancient literary and historical records of the earliest church—as we do to those of the church in every age. Only, it must be recognized that Form History is a branch of literary criticism, not of historical. The analysis of literary structure or form does not take the place of historical criticism, any more than it takes the place of textual criticism, i.e., the study and comparison of manuscripts, or of philology, which is the study of words, grammar, and syntax. It does not entitle one to take a short cut and announce forthwith that this or that piece of tradition is "authentic" while some other is "spurious." All tradition is significant. The form critic's motto must be: "Gather up the fragments, that nothing be lost." Even sayings which are weakly attested in the manuscripts—for example, those in Luke 9:55, 22:20, 23:34—belong *somewhere* in the tradition, and are not to be discarded. Their historical value must be assessed upon other grounds than those of Form History.

This book had a predecessor, written a generation ago. It was entitled *The Growth of the Gospels*. It undertook to survey what was then their current study, chiefly during the period from 1900 to 1930. That small work became a war casualty, when its plates were melted down for metal. This was no great loss, since the progress of modern research would sooner or later have made necessary a more thorough, more up-to-date statement.

Certain parts of the present book incorporate material from its predecessor, but only after complete revision. The point of view and the results here set forth are those of the present generation, not those of the days, now so remote, of the period between the two world wars.

F. C. G.

CHAPTER I

The New Approach to the Gospels

During the past sixty years, and especially since about 1920, a new and distinctive view of the gospels has arisen. In contrast to the more or less traditional view, which stressed the name, character, and date of each author and viewed the gospels as literary creations, "biographies" of Jesus, the newer view emphasizes the importance, value, and character of the underlying oral tradition which provided the material used by the evangelists. This tradition was a "social" possession, the common property of the early Christian churches, and was not limited to the "recollections" of a few individuals—though of course it rested, ultimately, upon the memories of individuals, "eyewitnesses and ministers of the word," the earliest preachers of the gospel (Luke 1:2; cf. Heb. 2:3). The significance of this view is obvious. The memories of a few individuals might be mistaken—since human recollection is notoriously fallible—but the testimony of a group, even if anonymous, is more likely to have been verified, criticized, supported, culled, and selected during the course of the first generation of early church evangelism. The possibility of fabrication, by one or two individuals, is completely ruled out. A book like the Quran is definitely one man's book—the suras dictated by the archangel Gabriel to the Arab prophet Mohammed. But the New Testament is a widely "social" production, with many contributors, including many who were and will forever remain anonymous. Although the tradition was no doubt modified in the course of transmission, its basic trustworthiness is beyond doubt; for it rests, not upon one man's recollections—say Peter's—or those of two or three persons, but upon the whole group of earliest disciples, whose numbers are reflected in the hundreds referred to by Paul (I Cor. 15:6) and the thousands described in Acts (2:41, 4:4). The early church did not grow up in isolation, in some corner

(Acts 26:26), but in the full glare of publicity, in the great cities of the Roman Empire.

On the other hand, in the light of this renewed emphasis upon tradition, the purposes of the four evangelists have been studied with much greater care. As a result, their distinctive aims stand out today as never before. Not only are the aims of the four evangelists better understood, but also the character and purpose of the underlying gospel sources, and the aims of their compilers— these are now much better understood than in the nineteenth century, say, or at any time prior to 1900. It is even possible to distinguish "sources of sources," i.e., component groups of material which went together to form such sources as Mark, Q, L, and M. And these primary sources, i.e., the "blocks" or "sequences" of traditional material which are found here and there in the gospels, have each a distinct character and purpose of its own. Q is largely made up of sayings of Jesus. As a body of teaching, it was doubtless used in the instruction of converts and others, and perhaps also in the early church's services of worship. L contains many parables, and numerous anecdotes from the ministry of Jesus. This material was probably used in preaching, but it need not necessarily have been a single, unified document. "St. Luke's notebook" may describe it well enough. M is more formal and didactic, and is much more deeply concerned with the Christian interpretation and observance of the Jewish Law than any other document in the New Testament. It looks more like a manual of instruction for use within the church than a propaganda writing or a collection of materials used in preaching. Mark is a gospel addressed to, and used in, a martyr church, that at Rome in the days of Nero when the blessed apostles Peter and Paul laid down their lives in witness to the faith—and when every member of the Roman church "stood in jeopardy every hour" and might be called to offer a like testimony and seal it with martyrdom (Mark 8:34–38). Of the later gospels, Luke (together with its second volume, the Acts of the Apostles) is an apologetic work, addressed to the outside world, especially to the world of Roman officialdom, and designed to prove that Christianity was not only nonsubversive but as a sect within Judaism was positively entitled to the same consideration at law which the mother-religion enjoyed, i.e., the right to be let alone. Matthew is a well-organized literary, perhaps even liturgical, work, with the life of Jesus and his teaching arranged under five main subject divisions, for purposes of study, teaching, and memorization. The Gospel of John, finally, is a dramatic presentation of the life, ministry, death, and glorification of Jesus for purposes of both instruction and worship within the church, and for inter-pretation and propaganda outside. It is concerned with issues which had arisen in the gentile Christian world of the late first or early second century, when a theory known as Docetism was spreading here and there—a theory which attempted to do honor to Christ but only by making him unreal, a phantom, the tem-porary manifestation of a divine being who could neither suffer nor die.

Thus it is largely the background and the character of the gos-pels and their sources which shed fresh light upon their purposes. More clearly than ever before, it is obvious that the gospels—and indeed all the writings contained in the New Testament—were "church books" from the very start. They were written by mem-bers of the church, for reading within the church, to meet the needs of the church; they both presupposed and also made use of the traditions, the ideas, the language, and the doctrines of the church. There was nothing here resembling a literary movement or a school of philosophy. These writers were the protagonists, the propagandists, the missionaries, the teachers, the preachers and devoted advocates of a new religious faith, and many of them paid for their devotion with their lives. But their writings, chiefly the epistles and the gospels, were not the sole religious—or sacred—literature of the new sect. Fundamentally the early church was an offshoot of Judaism, and in the Greek-speaking congregations out-side Palestine and Syria the Greek Bible, i.e., the Septuagint, the Jewish translation of the Old Testament (to which were added the fourteen apocryphal books, found only in Greek), was also the sacred book of the Christians. The "New" Testament, i.e., the twenty-seven selected books of the early Christians, was simply a supplement to the Greek Bible—its supplement and also its climax.

This fresh approach and principle of interpretation is now so well established that many recent works on the gospels simply take it for granted: the New Testament is the church's book, the gospels belong within and to the early church, and therefore they must be interpreted as "church books." Thus one of the most re-cent works on Mark takes full account of its probable use as a liturgical book—its sections or pericopes being correlated with and appropriate to the successive seasons and festivals of the early Chris-tian-Jewish calendar. This is the thesis of Archbishop Philip Car-rington's pioneer work, *The Primitive Christian Calendar* (Vol. I, 1952). Although the theory has not been widely accepted (see W. D. Davies' "Reflections" on the book in *The Background of*

the New Testament and its Eschatology, ed. by W. D. Davies and
D. Daube, 1956, pp. 124–152), it nevertheless brings out a large
quantity of relevant data pointing toward the use of the gospel in
the church's liturgy. It is of course reasonable to assume that the
gospels, and their component pericopes and earlier sources, were
used not only in preaching and teaching but also in public worship. For the early Christian liturgy was like the Jewish; essentially
it consisted of passages from scripture, introduced and accompanied by prayers, blessings, hymns, and exposition of scripture.

Other examples of the liturgical interpretation of the gospels
may be seen in Professor George D. Kilpatrick's *The Origins of the
Gospel According to Matthew* (1946) and the late Benjamin
Wisner Bacon's *Studies in Matthew* (1930) and *The Gospel of
the Hellenists* (1933). Bacon held that the discourses in John
were intended to expound, from the Christian point of view, the
inner meaning of the great Jewish festivals: Passover, Pentecost,
Tabernacles, Hanukkah, Passover once more. It is probable that
still more suggestions of reference to the Christian-Jewish festivals
can be identified in John, as for example to Rosh ha-Shanah, Yom
Kippur, perhaps even Simkath Torah; the subject will repay careful investigation.

The study of the text of the gospels has received much attention
since 1900. For a time it appeared that the "Western" type of
text—i.e., that which underlies Codex Bezae, the Old Latin and
the Old Syriac versions, and was used by many early church writers,
especially in the second century and in Egypt—had much help to
offer in the recovery of the original Greek text lying behind all the
"families" and types of manuscripts. Thus the late Kirsopp Lake,
in his essay, "The Text of the Gospels," in the volume *Studies in
Early Christianity*, edited by Shirley Jackson Case in honor of
Professors Bacon and Porter at Yale (1928), set forth the view
that the Western text was bringing us far closer to the autographs.
It was the day of Friedrich Blass's hypothesis of two editions of
Luke and Acts and the era of the old "Bezan Club" among English scholars. But J. H. Ropes's edition of Acts in Foakes Jackson
and Lake's *The Beginnings of Christianity* (Vol. III, 1926), with
its decided preference for the "Neutral" rather than the "Western" text; A. C. Clark's edition of Acts (1933), with its detailed
study of interpolations, repetitions, omissions, homoeoteleuta
(similar ending lines, explaining both), in the light of similar
phenomena in classical manuscripts—especially those of Cicero;
Adolf Jülicher's explanation of the Western text as the result of
many copyists' combination of effort and carelessness (see his

Einleitung in das Neue Testament, 7th ed., 1931, Pt. III); above all the publication of the Chester Beatty Papyri (1933–34), which exhibit a type of text much closer to the so-called "Neutral" than to the "Western" type, though they come from a very early period—the gospels from ca. A.D. 250–300—all this cumulative influence has tended to confirm and support the critical text of Westcott and Hort (1881). Thus the translators of the *Revised Standard Version of the New Testament* (1946), without agreeing in advance upon Westcott-Hort as their standard, and insisting, instead, upon the duty of examining each significant variant as it came before them in the course of their labors, nevertheless ended by accepting the Westcott-Hort text in the vast majority of cases. (See *An Introduction to the Revised Standard Version of the New Testament*, 1946, ch. V, "The Greek Text of the New Testament," by F. C. Grant; see also K. W. Clark, "The Effect of Recent Textual Criticism upon New Testament Studies," in Davies and Daube, *The Background of the New Testament*, 1956, pp. 27–51.)

It is probable that the present-day student of the New Testament has a better equipment of tools for his task than anyone hitherto—even the great scholars of the past. The latest editions of Nestle's Greek Testament (the 21st in 1952) or the Greek-Latin editions of A. Merk (7th ed., 1951), J. M. Bover (3d ed., 1952), H. J. Vogels (3d ed., 1949), or the new edition of A. Souter (2d ed., 1947), all of them based on a text formed in large part by Westcott-Hort, all of them far removed from the late medieval Textus Receptus, and all giving a good selected apparatus of the variant readings of ancient manuscripts, versions, patristic citations, and modern editions—with such a Greek Testament in hand, and new editions of the Septuagint within easy reach, and also the new edition of Walter Bauer's New Testament Lexicon open before him—the latest is the American translation by Professor W. F. Arndt and F. W. Gingrich (1956)—the present-day student enjoys advantages which would have been the envy of any New Testament scholar in earlier times, from Irenaeus and Origen to the twentieth century.

Another subject of continuing interest, and a problem now nearer solution as a result of many years of study, is the chronological order of the gospels and their interrelations. The view advanced in this book is that the true order is Mark, Luke, Matthew, John. This is the order of the symbolic figures in Rev. 4:7—lion, ox, man, eagle—which Irenaeus (ca. A.D. 180) understood to mean the four evangelists. It is also the order of the gospels in the famous mosaic in the Tomb of Galla Placidia at Ravenna (ca. A.D. 440), and in the medallions of the Sala della Presentazione in the nearby Accademia at Venice. It is the order followed by practically all artists and by many interpreters since Irenaeus. To me it seems more probable than ever. (I first set it forth in the first edition of this book, in 1933.) Not that the relative dating of Matthew and Luke makes any very great difference, i.e., whether one places Matthew first, then Luke, or vice versa; for the two gospels were clearly independent of each other. It is their common dependence on Mark which is of fundamental importance for the interpretation of the Synoptic Gospels.

Similarly the independence of the Fourth Gospel, i.e., its nondependence upon any and all of the synoptics, but only, and then to a limited extent, upon the old pre-synoptic tradition—this conclusion seems inescapable, in the light of present-day researches, and is of fundamental importance for the interpretation of the Gospel of John. Hans Windisch's formulation of the inquiry, Was the Gospel of John designed to supplement, to correct, or to supplant the synoptics, must be answered in every case, No! The Gospel of John, like each of the others, was intended to be *the* "gospel" of the church or group whose tradition it enshrined or recorded. Luke is the only possible exception to this rule; and yet Luke-Acts certainly relies upon a distinct body of tradition, not identical with any other save for the use which its author made of a large part of Mark. Mark contains the Roman tradition, Matthew (presumably) the Antiochian, John the Ephesian—or perhaps the Alexandrian, as many writers now hold. Luke's tradition is South Palestinian, Judean, Caesarean, Jerusalemite, Antiochian, and to this the author has added an extensive collection of material on Paul, in the second half of the Acts. These views of the origins and interrelations of the gospels are not those of any one man or school, but represent a wide consensus among present-day New Testament scholars.

It may be thought that the views here advanced are too radical. Using the word in the true sense, however, it may be replied that no criticism (if we are to undertake criticism at all) can be "too radical," i.e., go too deeply into the roots of problems, and unearth them in their full entanglement. Only on the old and now antiquated view that scripture is verbally inspired and inerrant can opposition to thoroughgoing historical and literary criticism maintain itself. To me it seems that the counterview, viz., that the New Testament is really "the church's book," that "the church came before the New Testament," that behind the literature, the documents, there moves a living and continuous and still-vital stream of creative spiritual life, and that the sources have significance primarily as they are related to that onward-moving current of spiritual energy—this view not only safeguards the rights of historical criticism but also provides an intellectually defensible position for faith at the present day. Men feared the results of destructive criticism in the seventies and eighties of the nineteenth century; but higher criticism has come to stay and Christian faith has survived the ordeal—is, in fact, the stronger for the change in attitude that criticism has wrought. A church, or a faith, that has lived with the New Testament for eighteen centuries and more is not likely to suffer greatly from still further changes in its outlook as a result of free historical investigation of the process by which its sacred book came into existence.

One may still find unhappy examples of industrious Bible study of a perverse and fruitless kind. We are told which is the longest verse in the Bible, or the shortest, or the middle verse (do the computers include the Apocrypha?), or the middle letter (which surely cannot be the same in different editions), or the proper combination of Daniel's "prophecies" (viewed as predictions still awaiting "fulfillment") with those of Ezekiel, and of both with those found in the Book of Revelation, thus forming a scheme of coming events at the end of the world—the harmonization of the seventy weeks with the 1,290 days and the "time, times, and half a time" of the apocalyptic chronology. Most persons probably recognize the futility of this kind of "study." But is it really much worse than the kind which gets no further than the dates and authorship of the books or of their sources, and rests content if it can be shown that I and II John are by the same author, or that Ephesians was written by Paul, or that the date of the Apostolic Council in Acts 15 can be fitted into the chronological scheme presupposed by the letters of the apostle, or that the Epistle to the Hebrews is basically Pauline?—and which assumes that these conclusions, set forth in advance of any research, are matters of orthodoxy, to be defended at all costs as a vital part of the Christian faith? These are interesting questions, but they are not very close to the fundamental purpose of Bible study. True, they are on a level some flights above biblical numerology, but even so they are not very fruitful religiously. It is only when the study of the Bible and its underlying sources, the date and the process of compilation of its component books, their authorship and provenance, is related to and serves the ends of *the religious understanding of holy scripture* that its full value can be seen. The true importance of the Bible lies in its religious thought and teaching; its true value is to be seen in the application of this teaching to life. Such literary studies as are reported and examined in the present volume are really subservient to this greater end. Otherwise, we might as well be making up or solving "biblical" crossword puzzles, or counting the letters in the King James Bible, or debating such purely "secular" dates as that of the Battle of Magnesia or the Fall of Nineveh.

But most persons study the gospels with one sole purpose in view: for further light upon the life and teaching of the One who was himself the Light of the World. It is not a purely literary or historical problem, or set of problems, that confronts either the ordinary reader of the gospels or the technical student. One may study the chronological sequence and date, the sources and the technique of Shakespeare's plays, without one's ethical or religious presuppositions and convictions being affected. Not so the reader of the gospels. We are fully convinced that no study of the gospels, conducted under the generally accepted canons of modern historical and literary criticism, even the most "radical" and up to date, those of the school of form criticism or, better, form history, will remain fruitless of positive results for Christian faith or prove inimical in the long run to Christian convictions. It is a part of the long story of criticism that some of the church's doctrines have had to be reformulated again and again, as a result of "the assured results of criticism" or of the progress of physical science or of changes in philosophical outlook; but it has not been wholly loss —gain, rather—that this was so. Bibliolatry has ceased to be dominant in the Protestant world, where it once flourished and where, indeed, it reached its climax; its place has been taken by a saner, more wholesome, more constructive, a more ethically and religiously satisfying conception of the biblical literature and of the history behind the literature. It remains for the church to absorb the new viewpoints and press on at its age-old task; I for one cannot see how even the most radical criticism (if it be sound criticism) can permanently upset or really injure the faith which is rooted deep in man's experience of the Eternal—a present experience, and no mere echo of some ancient authority, however venerable. "The foundation of God standeth sure." The new light upon the gospels which has come from their critical study during recent years has only increased the certainty that behind them stands One who, while he "spake as never man spake," nevertheless spake as man.

The historical origins of the Christian faith are still no doubt in many respects quite obscure, and probably must ever remain so. As William Sanday once remarked, we shall never have an account such as the morning *Times* or *Telegraph* might have given of affairs in Galilee in the closing years of the third decade of our era. But would such an account bring us much nearer to the goal of our quest than the gospels as we have them now—the final product of the tradition, at first wholly oral, then partly written, of the Christian churches in the first and second and perhaps (to some extent) even the third generations of the new faith? A purely external observer and objective recorder of those events might easily have missed the many-splendored thing; it took long years of selective and interpretative experience in "the Way" to bring out the full significance of "all that Jesus began both to do and to teach." And it may be that the experience of men will make it possible, even today at this remote stage of history, for still more light to break forth from the life and the sayings of Jesus. In lieu of the storybook life of Christ, which modern historical and literary criticism has now rendered impossible; in lieu of final answers to a multitude of questions, Where? When? Why? Under what circumstances? In whose presence? On what journey? and so on— we are forced back to a situation not wholly dissimilar to that in which the church stood once before, at the very beginning of the gospel-writing period, when only scattered anecdotes, sayings, or brief collections of sayings, together with a short account of Jesus' passion, comprised the Christian believer's knowledge of the life, ministry, and death of the Lord. And as then Paul could write, "Even though we once regarded Christ from a human point of view, we regard him thus no longer" (II Cor. 5:16), so now it is the *spiritual* Christ, the Lord who is the Spirit (3:17), who appears before us and beckons us to follow him. In a profoundly true sense it is not—and never has been—the historical Christ, the Jesus of history, who is the redeemer of men and the hope of the world, but the spiritual Christ, the risen and exalted Lord of the church's faith. The two should never be set in opposition, as by the ancient Gnostics (who denied the earthly "man Christ Jesus") or the modern "Jesus of history" school (who ignored his eternal, transcendental, divine nature). Modern New Testament study fully recognizes this theological element in the gospels and in the earliest proclamation of the Christian faith. These are not merely records of the apostolic age and its beliefs, but essential manifestoes of the church's saving message, the Good News about Jesus Christ.

Someone has said that with advancing years men's prejudices harden into convictions, their convictions into dogmas. This is true of generations as well as of individuals. One wonders why it is that ever since the days of Koheleth and Sirach, so many persons have been inclined to identify either dogmatism or skepticism with maturity. For there is really nothing dogmatic about it, and personal preferences do not count. Our task is not simply to note verb-endings or list peculiarities of style, but to fit together a whole scheme of historical development, especially one of religious thought and practice, and to find the proper places in this development for the writings before us. The New Testament writers did not date their books, or give the place of writing, or—except for Paul—even sign their names! And it is only after decades of study that this hypothetical reconstruction of the development of early Christianity and the growth of the church, its rites and practices, its ministry, its literature—and its use and understanding of this literature—begins to take very definite form. Nor is it a matter of skepticism. For the positive reality of the early Christian faith and hope, its tremendous impact upon the ancient world as a force quite new and never before experienced in the old run-of-the-mill nationalistic cults and religions—all this now stands out more clearly than ever, as a result of the past two generations of New Testament study and research. Judaism with its saints and martyrs, its high morality and its holy books, its pure and spiritual monotheism and its one and only temple devoid of statues or idols, had already deeply impressed many of the best minds in the pagan world. But here was something that went even beyond Judaism—like it, but more evangelistic, more missionary, and bent upon converting the world before the Day of Judgment. The objective reality of this early Christian spiritual power, its immense drive and transforming earnestness about the things of God—here is something that steadily grows upon one as one studies the New Testament. And this is the true *Sitz im Leben* of the gospels and of their underlying traditions—Greek books and their sources, written, handed down, copied and recopied in the Greek-speaking gentile churches of the Mediterranean world in the second half of the first century and/or early in the second. No one can even catch a glimpse of this vast, panoramic, dramatic movement of living religion and remain skeptical, either about the truth of Christianity in the first century or about its future in the twentieth.

CHAPTER II

The New Testament the Church's Book

Modern historical and literary criticism of the New Testament is returning to an old and, to many persons, a familiar theological position. As often happens, it is returning to an old position—but with a difference in approach and emphasis. And it is this difference in approach and emphasis that marks and measures the real progress made in the course of a century and more of modern New Testament research.

(1) The old position is this: the New Testament is *the church's book.* Its existence, its preservation, its transmission in manuscripts and in printed editions and in new translations, its interpretation, its original aim and purpose and outlook, the reason for its existence as a whole, are quite inexplicable apart from its production and eventual canonization by the church. Two centuries and more of Rationalism, ending soon after the close of the eighteenth century, though an indispensable preliminary stage in the genesis of the modern critical view of the scriptures, tended to obscure and ignore this fact. The New Testament books were often treated as individual creations, and their writers as isolated authors, working outside any social group or possessing only a tenuous connection with the group, and from quite private and personal motives —though the motives were sometimes supplied, hypothetically, from the needs of early Christian propaganda. This antiquated view still survives and occasionally finds expression in works which reflect far more the independence and individualism of modern religious thought than the actual conditions under which the New Testament writings appeared. But just as the Old Testament has come to be recognized as inexplicable apart from the social-religious milieu in which it arose—a changing *milieu,* ranging over ten centuries of social development and change—so the New

Testament has come to be recognized as inexplicable apart from the religious movement which gave it birth and the church or religious community for which it was written. In spite of the errors and exaggerations of the "Tübingen school" of New Testament interpretation, in the middle of the nineteenth century (i.e., early in the "critical" period which followed the era of Rationalism), it is clear that this was one contribution of real value: the New Testament documents were brought into closest relation with the tendencies and movements of the early church, i.e., the church of the first and second centuries. Not "in lonely isolation, fancy free," but in living contact with the labors and ambitions, the hopes and fears, the faith and convictions of the church were these documents produced. As we view it today, the New Testament is quite indissociably and inseparably the church's book. The Tübingen movement had much to do with bringing this view into clear recognition and general acceptance.

Today, the school of form criticism emphasizes even more strongly the dependence of the gospels upon the traditions of the church and its needs. But form criticism is not alone. All modern historical study of the New Testament makes it clear that these twenty-seven sacred books came into existence and survived, i.e., were preserved, as *the Christian supplement to the Old Testament*, which was already accepted and used, in the Greek version, throughout the early gentile churches. These Christian writings were viewed as bringing to a climax and conclusion the long story of salvation, i.e., the narrative of God's dealings with mankind from the beginning of history down to the "last days," the coming of Christ, his rejection, death, and resurrection, and his prospective speedy return to hold the Final Judgment. The earliest Christians did not think of their sacred books as forming a "New" Testament (or the documentation of a new Covenant) distinct from the Old: the two were one and the same and continuous. "The Law, the Prophets, and the Psalms" (Luke 24:44)—or, better, as the third class, the "Writings"—were perfectly familiar to all Jews, including the Christian Jews in Palestine and elsewhere, and also to all converted proselytes, who already had been attached to the Jewish synagogue before their conversion to Christianity. When the early Christian writings appeared—Paul's epistles, which were read publicly at the assemblies for worship (Col. 4:16), came first, then other writings, epistles, homilies, and gospels—they were looked upon as proper additions, supplementary to the lections from the Law and the Prophets which were read each week in both Jewish synagogue and Christian church. More than this, the standards of Christian behavior, as well as belief, were derived from both the Jewish Old Testament and its new Christian supplement—which was also a kind of Appendix, like the Greek books found only in the Septuagint, not in the original Hebrew, and later misnamed the "Apocrypha." When the early gentile Christians "searched the scriptures" (John 5:39, Acts 17: 11), they were studying the Old Testament—though it was not long before Christian writings, in addition to the Christian oral tradition, provided the required guidance in such a search.

Paul had no idea that he was writing "scripture" when he dashed off his heated epistles to the Christians in Corinth, Galatia, Philippi, and elsewhere. They were simply "occasional" writings, intended to meet an immediate and pressing need, and were in reality only substitutes for a personal visit accompanied by appropriate administrative action (I Cor. 11:34b, II Cor. 13:10). But the church treasured these letters, read and reread them, and finally made them canonical—a process which most of us view as the result of a divine overruling. The gospels, similarly, were not at first viewed as sacred writings—the freedom with which they were copied, altered, revised, and edited during the first two centuries makes this perfectly clear. They were looked upon simply as the writing down of the traditions concerning Jesus' life, teaching, miracles, controversies, death, resurrection, and glorification—the traditions, that is, as they circulated in the various churches, chiefly the larger centers at Antioch and Rome, and perhaps at Caesarea, in Achaia, or at Ephesus, or Alexandria. What was sacred was not the "form of words," however "sound" (II Tim. 1:13), but the contents, the meaning, chiefly the sayings of Jesus. Only later did the written gospels come to be viewed as sacred, i.e., inspired, and more or less infallible. The earliest title was "The Gospel, according to . . . Mark, Luke, Matthew, or John"; i.e., "the Gospel" was the book containing all four (this was sometime in the middle of the second century), and the individual writing was only this "gospel," or message of good news, according to one evangelist or another. There was no talk of any gospel "by" So-and-so, or of the gospel "of" such-and-such a writer. These books, like all "traditional" books, were anonymous—and only a few lingering traces of personal authorship survived. Thus it was nearly a century, from ca. A.D. 68, when Mark was written, to ca. A.D. 150, when the fourfold Gospel Canon appeared, before the gospels became really sacrosanct, and took the place of the "living and abiding voice" of tradition for which Papias, the bishop of Hierapolis in Phrygia about A.D. 140, had maintained his preference (Eusebius, *Church History*, III. 39. 4).

(2) The new emphasis and approach to this old and, indeed, traditional position is as follows: Whereas for many centuries the church maintained its claim to exercise a sole and exclusive authority in the interpretation of the New Testament, interpreting it in strict accordance with the later formularies of the faith and, in fact, not infrequently in terms of far later theologies, *that right is now challenged*, where it is not ignored, throughout the Protestant world—everywhere, in brief, outside Roman Catholicism and the narrowest circles of Protestant Fundamentalism. It was not many generations ago that orthodox Protestants clung as tenaciously to the Calvinistic, or the Lutheran, the Evangelical, or the Anglican interpretation of scripture as the majority of Roman Catholics today cling to the Tridentine or the Thomistic interpretation. The day of historical criticism was not yet; no one dreamed of its coming. The only key or clue to the interpretation of scripture was the one provided by the traditional, orthodox faith— though each bibliolatrous heterodoxy was completely, and sometimes complacently, orthodox in its own eyes. This was a natural enough position, and one that was widely accepted. "The church to teach, the Bible to prove" was the old High Anglican view. The received faith held a position of general acceptance, within the particular communion, comparable to that of "the assured results of modern science" in the minds of men generally at the present day. It was the authentic summing-up of Christian experience, of the presuppositions of all Christian history, and of the Christian revelation; and it was not so much logically posited—let alone defended—as the prius of correct interpretation (since the principle was simply unchallenged) as it was simply taken for granted, much as men now take it for granted that the earth is round, moves about the sun, and has a history reckoned by geological aeons of time. Moreover, this position appeared to be historically justified. Had not the true faith vindicated itself in the days long ago, in alliance with and in dependence upon the New Testament, as against the vagaries of Gnosticism and the mythologizing tendencies of an Arius and a Marcion? Was not the church's faith— i.e., the orthodox, or "received," faith or system of doctrine—far more historical, far more consonant with the actual and demonstrable or documented past, than the whims and fancies, the hallucinations and the speculations of the sects?—the "sects" being viewed consistently, even by Protestants, as outside the church. In the broad, general sense this was indubitable, certainly in the

minds of the majority. Orthodox Christianity was identifiable with
the religion of the New Testament; Montanism, Arianism, Sabel-
lianism, Monarchianism, Monophysitism, and the rest, in spite of
affiliations with certain phases of New Testament Christianity, and
strong emphasis on isolated texts, were not so identifiable. And
who can doubt that, in the main, this view is still a sound and
fruitful one? It takes no prolonged examination of the history of
doctrine to discover the sanity and security of this position in its
general outlines, as far as it concerns the ancient church.

But the modern historical study of the New Testament and of
the Bible generally has profoundly modified all this, certainly in
its detailed expression. The gravest danger implicit in the old position—it was all but unavoidable—was that the later formulations
of the faith, and the later technical theological details, should be
read back into the New Testament: predestination, the seven
sacraments, supra- or sublapsarianism, the Anselmic or the Origen-
istic theology of the atonement, or Episcopacy or Presbyterianism
as the sole principle of church order. Each has claimed to find its
antecedents and vindication in the scriptures. The exaggerated
emphasis upon hard-and-fast formulation of doctrine, in Roman
Catholic and in Protestant scholasticism alike, and the exaggerated
view of scriptural inspiration held by many Protestants, equally
tended in this same direction and produced similar results. But
today the method of scholars is quite different. *Room is left for
growth,* for development and evolution, in doctrine, in ecclesiastical organization, in world view, even in ethical outlook. It is not
expected that modern or even medieval standards or statements of
doctrine will be found, either explicit or implicit, in the New
Testament. On the contrary, it is now assumed that the state of
doctrine, organization, and ethics must necessarily have been different at a stage some generations and centuries earlier than that
in which they are found in any period of history. The claim of
unchangedness, of sameness, of identity, is at once under sus-
picion. *E pur si muove*—history still moves, always moves, and
nothing, however sacred, ever continueth in one stay. It is only
God Himself, not men's thoughts of Him, who changes not. Even
the divine revelation, since it cannot be a revelation unless it is
understood by those to whom it is addressed, or for whom it is
intended, is inevitably bound up with this ever-changing, never
static universe in which we live, and with the words of men (in
whose language God must speak) which constantly change their
meanings.

Hence when we turn to the New Testament we do not expect

to find a fixed and definite system of doctrine, or a fully articulated scheme or plan of church organization. Quite the contrary: we expect to find—and we do find—anticipations, suggestions, foreshadowings of later developments; but we find them in the midst of much else, suggestions that were never followed out, tentative and experimental solutions that were destined to be overlooked and forgotten in the onward-moving development of the church's life. But in the light of a genuine faith in the divine mission of the church and in the real guidance of men by the Holy Spirit, this seems perfectly natural. The study of church history in its earliest period—including that of the New Testament—from the modern point of view finds in it real evidence of inspiration and revelation, evidence which is just as real as anywhere in history. The living God speaks through living men. The oracles of God are not delivered in baskets of scrolls or in jars hidden in some cave or inscribed openly on tablets of stone, but from the lips of living men or written out of their burning hearts and active minds. The growth of the church, its literature, its liturgy, its faith, its hope, its awareness of its mission, its organization, its doctrine (which means its teaching), its interpretation of scripture (the Old Testament, first of all), its hymns and its devotional practices —all this was perfectly natural and to be expected in a divinely founded human society. Since historical criticism is inevitable— it is now applied to every institution and every literature coming down out of the past—it is clear that such a faith is the only possible one for intelligent students at the present day.

Thus the emphasis and the approach have changed; but the fact stands out clearer than ever—the New Testament is the church's book. Its contents were produced for the church's edification, enlargement, defense, encouragement, or consolation. Its suggestions of possible future development were suggestions made within the church, for the development of the church. Its tentative statements of doctrine in new terminology—where they are tentative— were statements of the church's doctrine, of the common consensus of believers: even the least normative of them, in the later sense, were set forth in the belief that they were true to the church's experience and would be acceptable as such—e.g., Paul's doctrine of faith, or the Logos Christology of the Fourth Gospel. The New Testament is not even a "traditional book" in the sense in which Gilbert Murray applied this term to the Old Testament in brilliant illustration of his theory of the "rise of the Greek epic" (Rise of the Greek Epic, 2d ed., 1911, Lecture iv); for the New Testament is no product of a long, slow growth covering seven to ten centuries, or representing a wide social whole like the nation of Israel. Much of it belongs to the literature of "social control" in a relatively small group; and it grew up within a century at most—most of it came into existence in the course of two generations.

The proper historical approach to the study of the New Testament is thus by way of church history, viz., in its earliest period. Curiously enough, this is quite apparent even in the first great history of the church, by Eusebius of Caesarea, who wrote early in the fourth century. Allowing, as we must, for his personal bias and for his doctrinal and ecclesiastical predilections, he nevertheless sets the New Testament in its proper main perspective, as the literature of the origins of the church and of the church's formative age, as the church's own book; and it is he who preserves the most important and most germane traditions of its authorship and significance. Even where he is in error, it is evident that he has tried to get at the truth (as he tells us at the beginning of his *Church History,* I. 1. 3–8). The canons of historical criticism which he followed, fairly high for his day, were not the highest; and the tools and materials available to him were not wholly adequate. Such as they are, however, they are in most cases the best that he had—and, by consequence, about the best that we have for the case in hand. For the New Testament is the earliest of early Christian literature and contains practically all that survives in the way of written documents from the first two or three generations of the church's life. It is, of course, not all one uniform book, but a collection. It represents not one sole dominating view, but a variety of views, so that one can trace with considerable accuracy the different directions in which Christian thought and feeling advanced, as well as—with some limitations—the geographical and numerical expansion of the church, and also the stages in the earliest development of the church's theology and ethics, worship and organization.

As the literature of a movement and of a community, the New Testament grew up in *a series of groups of writings.* It seems extraordinary, at first glance, that this is so; but it is the general rule in literary history. No great writer works in isolation; and certainly no ordinary writer does so. There were plays before Shakespeare, and after. Greek Tragedy is a clustering galaxy of stars. Dante was not the only canzonist of his time; and there was not one Victorian or New England poet—there were poets.

We may distinguish six such groups of writings within the New Testament:

(1) The *Epistles of Paul*—the earliest group, and these, indeed, separable into three main groups written some years apart.

(2) The *Synoptic Gospels*, incorporating earlier documents or blocks of oral tradition and resting upon a steadily growing body of evangelistic preaching (*kērygma*) and of church teaching (*didachē*) which reached back to the earliest days of the church's history and to the events and the Person recorded.

With these is naturally grouped the Acts of the Apostles, as the continuation of the Third Gospel and as the record of the beginnings of the church.

(3) The *Apocalypse of John*, apparently isolated, but really one of a large number of Jewish and Christian apocalypses, and almost certainly containing earlier Jewish as well as Christian material.

(4) The *Pastoral Epistles*, perhaps based upon earlier epistolary writings, and, indeed, quite possibly upon a fourth group of Pauline Epistles; but considerably modified to meet the situation toward the close of the first century—or possibly even later.

(5) A group of *Catholic Apostolic writings*, ascribed usually to apostles, but showing clear affiliations with such extracanonical writings as the Didache, I Clement, the Epistle of Barnabas, etc., whose point of view is that of the turn of the century and of the early second century, when, in the growing crisis of the times, especially the conflict with Gnosticism, an ever-stronger appeal was being made to apostolic authority. The New Testament group is but the earlier representative—or subgroup—of a class of writings more usually associated with the apostolic fathers and apologists. As attributed to an apostle, even the "Apocalypse of John" may be numbered in this group.

(6) The *Johannine Literature*, i.e., three epistles and a "gospel" (the Apocalypse belongs above in another classification, and shares with these writings no more than the author's name, which was a common enough one in Jewish and early Christian circles). The outlook and aim of the Johannine "epistles" are different from those of the Pauline, the Pastoral, and the Catholic Apostolic group; while the "gospel" in no way belongs in the same category as the synoptists, nor yet with the Apocryphal Gospels—the earlier of which were far closer in purpose, outlook, and style to the synoptics than to "John"—but is a unique book of the early second century, designed to be a twofold *apologia* for the church's faith, repudiating both the Gnostic misinterpretation of the Christian religion and the Jewish "misunderstandings" and countercharges against its propaganda.

One might go on and name the types of literature produced in the church down to the time of Constantine and Eusebius—

apologetic, exegetical, polemic, historical, hortatory, disciplinary, legislative, liturgical, devotional, personal and biographical, epistolary, theological—and show how some of these elaborated types were already emergent in the New Testament; and how these likewise appeared as a rule in groups, one writer apparently provoking or inspiring others to write, and the church preserving the best, or at least the most useful, of their productions for posterity —and this at a time when the possession of Christian writings was often a dangerous and sometimes an indictable offense. But enough has been said to make it clear that the writings contained in our New Testament were all produced within the church, by the church (i.e., by its members), and for the church (i.e., designed to serve its purposes and meet its needs). They were all "church books" from the start. (a) The gospels presupposed the common .tradition of Jesus' words and deeds; and even Luke's gospel, which is dedicated to Theophilus and might appear therefore a less impersonal writing, makes use of a wider range of traditional (written or oral) material than either Mark or Matthew. (b) The Epistles of Paul were obviously addressed to Christian communities, and were occasioned for the most part by problems that arose within these communities. They took the place of personal visitations—a poor substitute, in Paul's view: "The rest will I set in order when I come" (I Cor. 11:34). It is significant that the only personal letter in the collection, apart from sundry postscripts and conclusions to the other epistles, is a mere note, in length, and could easily have been penned on one side of a scrap of papyrus: I refer, of course, to his letter to Philemon. (Deissmann gives a number of examples of letters of similar length in ch. iii of his *Light from the Ancient East,* 1908; English translation, new ed., 1927.) It is the most personal letter in the New Testament—the formal addresses of "the elder" (II–III John) do not bear comparison—and it is almost the briefest. (c) And as for the later groups of writings, Revelation (addressed explicitly to "the seven churches"), the Pastorals, the Johannine literature, and the Catholic Apostolic group, it is obvious at once that these are all embraced within the designation "church books." Over them all might go the motto: "No scripture is of private interpretation" (II Pet. 1:20). There was no biography for its own sake, no fiction with which to while away idle hours (unknown to most early Christians!), no ambitious objective historical writing addressed, like the work of Thucydides or Polybius, to the educated world (Luke's aim is clearly different), no poetry or drama (save the solemn lyric rhythm of many of Jesus' sayings, come down out of Jewish-Christian tradition, and one or two snatches of simple early hymns), no philosophy or dialogue: none of the major literary forms of the classical age or of the contemporary Graeco-Roman world is represented in the New Testament. Not only the gospels but even the epistles, for the most part, belong to *Kleinliteratur*, and reflect both the practical needs and the lowly social status of the Christians, and also the originally oral form of the Christian tradition. As time went on, Christians endeavored to write dialogues, poems, and romances; but they were not altogether successful, nor did the church look with entire favor upon such undertakings, even when their motive was doctrinal or ethical—e.g., asceticism. During the early centuries life was too dreadfully earnest a matter for dalliance with such "light literature," inevitably redolent of pagan associations—feelings, ideas, moral and religious standards. The general attitude is comparable to that held in evangelical circles toward the reading of novels, say around 1900; and probably for a precisely similar reason—one having its roots in the social attitudes and prejudices of the middle class, as well as in the "sound religion and morals" of that same class. Certainly, nothing in the way of "popular literature" was even thought of in the period of the New Testament. There are stories in the gospels (the Gerasene swine, Salome's dance, the marriage at Cana, etc.) which have their secular interest, but the evangelist's use of them is clearly apologetic and theological.

The New Testament was the church's book; and nothing merely personal, or merely literary, was included within it by the toiling, struggling, outwardly oppressed but inwardly triumphant believers in Christ who stood in jeopardy every hour for their faith in him.

GROUPS OF EARLY CHRISTIAN WRITINGS

50	I–II Thessalonians	
51	Galatians (perhaps 55)	
55	I–II Corinthians	The Pauline Epistles, in three groups
56	Romans	
59–61	Philippians Philemon Colossians (Ephesians?)	
68	Gospel of Mark	
90	Gospel of Luke	Synoptic Gospels and Acts
95	Acts of the Apostles	
95–112	Gospel of Matthew	
95	Apocalypse of John	

ca. 95	Hebrews I Peter Jude James	A "Catholic Apostolic" group
96–98	I Clement	
100	I–II Timothy Titus	The Pastoral Epistles
100–125	Gospel of John I–II–III John	Anti - Gnostic writings
110–115	Epistles of Ignatius Epistle of Polycarp	
125 135	Quadratus' Apology Papias' Exposition of the Oracles of the Lord	
135	Epistle of Barnabas Teaching of the Twelve Apostles = The Didache	Late "apostolic" writings
135	Shepherd of Hermas (or earlier, ca. 100?)	
140	Aristides' Apology (or earlier)	
140	Marcion's Antitheses Valentinus' Gospel of Truth	Gnostic works
150	II Peter	Apocryphal; based on Jude
ca. 150	The Fourfold Gospel Canon II Clement	
155	Justin's Dialogue Justin's Apology I	Apologetic works
161 170 ?	Justin's Apology II Tatian's Oration Epistle to Diognetus	

The purpose of this chart is not to display a final chronological scheme, since the dates are in many instances either uncertain or only approximate. But even with an approximate dating it is clear that the early Christian writings appeared for the most part in groups. These groups may reflect not only stages of authorship, but also primitive collections of writings, in the earliest period in the history of the Canon. On either view, they reflect the growing interest of the church.

CHAPTER III

Why We Have Gospels

*T*he old High Anglican view expressed in the formula "The Church to teach, the Bible to prove" had at least this justification: the church came before the New Testament, and the latter is to be studied as the church's own book, as the church's formal selection from its own earliest literature of those writings which were useful for edification, for admonition, and for the maintenance both of the orthodoxy of its teaching and of its contact with history. The New Testament provided the historical substantiation of the church's position, the "proof" of the divine origin of the Christian message and way of salvation. Both of these motives, orthodoxy and historicity, were at work in the period when the New Testament arose as a sacred collection sometime in the second century. The books of the New Testament were thus not only the Christian supplement to the older sacred books of the Jewish synagogue, which had been read from the beginning in the church's services of public worship (especially in the Greek version, the so-called "Septuagint"); they were also the strong bastion of defense against the Gnostic misinterpretation of the gospel.

Gnosticism is the modern name for a type of religious speculation which deeply influenced the Christian church in the second century. Its beginnings are usually traced—as they were by the church fathers—to Simon Magus of Samaria (see Acts 8:9-24), though its most eminent and most influential teachers, men like Basilides and Valentinus, belong to the period A.D. 130-150. The question is still debated whether or not Gnosticism existed outside the church. Similar movements were to be found there—e.g., the one which produced the Hermetica, a group of writings from the second, third, and fourth centuries A.D. attributed to Hermes Trismegistus, probably originating in Egypt and surviving now in

Greek, with one long tractate (the *Asclepius*) in Latin. The Jewish features in Gnosticism are undeniable, and may go back to "fringe" groups in the Judaism of the first century, or even to Simon the Samaritan. Tractate I of the *Corpus Hermeticum* ("Poimandres") clearly reflects Genesis ch. 1 in the LXX. The probability is that "Gnosticism" is the correct name for this type of thought so far as it affected Christianity, but that back of the Christian heresy lay a whole tidal movement of syncretistic theological—or, better, theosophical—speculation which affected the religious outlook of men throughout the Near Eastern and Mediterranean areas. Its basic principles were dualism and syncretism. It took for granted the old Greek (Orphic and Pythagorean) distinction between mind or soul and matter, with its view of the body (*sōma*) as the tomb (*sēma*) of the soul. It also endeavored to find a place within its epistemological, cosmological, or phenomenological system for all the "essences" and "powers" (Wisdom, Nous, Spirit, Desire, etc.) celebrated in the various religions of mankind—i.e., the gods, interpreted as types of existence, experience, knowledge, or creative activity. In this respect, Gnosticism shared the allegorism and syncretism of the Stoics, who interpreted the gods as physical phenomena. It also shared to some degree the fatalistic views associated with popular astrology, i.e., the whole deterministic view of the human soul's unfortunate "fall" into the realm of matter, where it is subject to physical force and necessity, the power of the "elements," the stars or their animating spirits. The whole material universe was viewed as the offspring of a downward-tending "passion" of once-pure ethereal beings, lost in love of their physical counterparts or even of their own reflected image in earth or water (the downward-tending elements; fire and air ascend). Creation itself is evil; so is birth; so is "generation" (i.e., procreation); so is marriage—here the metaphysics of this strange creed produced its ethics of abstinence and universal celibacy. Salvation, on this view, is not release from sin or reconciliation with God, but release from enslavement to evil, i.e., from imprisonment within "this present evil world" of matter. This can take place only by the soul's realization (i.e., knowledge, *gnōsis*) of its own true nature, heavenly origin, and divine destiny, and of the falsity of the pretended claims of the senses, their report upon the material world as real and substantial, their promise of happiness in sensory (not to say sensual) enjoyments. It is a religion of "salvation by knowledge," i.e., knowledge about eternal realities. This knowledge is not discovered by the soul or mind engaging in lonely speculation or research, but is a revealed body

of truth, which must be brought by the divine teacher or—in
Christian Gnosticism—by the Saviour or Redeemer, who descends
the long ladder that reaches down from the topmost realm of pure
being to this dark dungeon of matter, and there rouses the drugged
and blinded soul, bidding it rise and follow its Guide upward to
the region of light. (See further p. 160.)

Quite obviously, if this type of philosophy had come to prevail
in the Christian church, the whole historical foundation of the
gospel would have been swept away, and a shifting, kaleidoscopic
system of metaphysical "essences" would have taken its place.
Hence the urgency of the crisis reflected in John and I John, and
even in earlier New Testament writings (e.g., the Epistle to the
Colossians), as the invasion of Christian teaching by this strange
philosophy first began to make headway. Against the claims of this
"gnōsis, falsely so called" (1 Tim. 6:20) the church made a three-
fold appeal to history. (1) The baptismal creed, to which every
Christian must subscribe; the oldest form of what is still called the
"Apostles'" creed denied one or another Gnostic tenet in almost
every clause. God is the Creator, not some secondary being, a
demiurge in league with the powers of darkness; God is the all-
ruler, the pantokratōr, and dualism is a baseless theory; Christ is
God's Son, not one of the subordinate aeons; he was born, suffered, died, and rose again—the whole Docetic-Gnostic theory of
the fleeting apparition of a phantom deity, who left this realm of
matter before the first nail was driven into the cross (so that the
Romans only crucified a corpse)—this theory is fantastic and
impossible, a travesty of the history recorded in the gospels; finally,
Christ will come again as judge of all mankind, the living and the
dead—a doctrine as old as Christianity, but for which there was
no room in Gnosticism. (2) A second line of defense against the
Gnostic error was the appeal to the open and public "tradition"
of the teachers (i.e., bishops) in the great centers of church life,
Jerusalem, Antioch, Ephesus, Alexandria, Rome. Each bishop
knew what his predecessors had taught, all the way back to the
apostles, and none of them had taught Gnosticism. This "apostolic succession" of true teaching guaranteed that the orthodox
faith was now held by their successors. (This is a very different
conception from the modern theory of the "validity of orders"
guaranteed by a "tactual" succession; the theory may be true, but
it is not the original doctrine of apostolic succession.) Finally, (3)
the apostolic teaching as set forth in the creed and guaranteed by
the open and well-known succession of the church's teachers is
reinforced by appeal to the apostolic writings—the New Testa-

ment. Every one of these books was written, presumably, by an apostle or by a friend of the apostles—i.e., by one of the "apostolic men" (Eusebius, *Church History*, II. 17. 2)—and therefore sets forth the pure, original teaching of the church. This original teaching of the church was, quite demonstrably, *not* Gnosticism. Even though John had used quasi-Gnostic language in combating the view, and earlier still Paul had used a phrase which seemed to open the floodgates to it (Rom. 8:3, the "likeness of sinful flesh"), Gnosticism was not the Christian gospel, but something else, and very different. The theories of secret channels of tradition, by which Christ's esoteric teachings had come down to the Gnostic writers, or by which Gnostic gospels, books of Acts, epistles and apocalypses could be defended as sources of information superior to the "public" gospels read by the church at its services of worship—all such theories were refuted by appeal to the books which had been known and read by all Christians everywhere and always, from the apostles' time to the present. Hence the great stress upon the *apostolic* origin of the New Testament books.

Thus the apostolic creed, the apostolic succession of the church's teachers, and the collection of apostolic writings, bascially the contents of the New Testament, were the three main defenses against the new movement which threatened the very existence of the church and its faith. Among these writings none was more important than the little Johannine collection, one gospel and three epistles named for John the apostle and "beloved disciple"—the very one claimed by the Gnostics as the apostolic representative and champion of their views (see the apocryphal *Acts of John*, *passim*, especially §§ 89, 96, where John testifies that Jesus' body was sometimes tangible, at other times not).

But the question arises, both from the older point of view and from the more modern, Why do we have *gospels?* How did the Christian tradition come to be written down in this particular form? Other religions have nothing of the kind, and the data for the lives of their founders are usually recovered only from documents of much later date, relatively to religious origins, than our gospels, and often in most scattered and inconsequent form. The origins of Mandaeism, for example, are buried in the phantasmagorian mists of the sacred legends enshrined in the *Ginza*; the life of Zoroaster is gone almost beyond recall—it is uncertain even in what century to place his appearance; the anecdotes told of the rabbis were only *disjecta membra*, affording almost no material for an account of their lives; while the founding of Judaism, in the days of Nehemiah and Ezra, is one of the most debatable fields in religious history; the legends of Buddha are late, and there is no consistent life of the founder; and the nearest approach to a gospel, the *Life of Apollonius of Tyana* by Philostratus, may quite possibly have been modeled on the Christian gospels, as a sacred *Euaggelion* in the interest of a revived and platonized paganism, under Septimius Severus and Julia Domna, at the beginning of the third century. How, then, did it come to pass that the church has provided itself with gospels?

The question has been approached more than once from the point of view of literary history, but without an entirely satisfactory solution. Such analogies as we find in Plutarch's *Parallel Lives*, or in Suetonius, or in the popular *Lives of the Sophists, Lives of the Philosophers*, and so on—popular in the late classical period— do not go very far. Xenophon's *Memorabilia of Socrates*, upon which some scholars have laid considerable stress, is far too old an example, too individualistic in its outlook and aim, to provide an exact parallel—though Justin Martyr and others in the early church did not scruple to apply the term "memoirs" (*apomnē- moneumata*) to the evangelic writings. (Justin's purpose was doubtless merely to suggest to educated readers the general contents and purpose of the gospels, not their literary classification.) On the contrary, the gospels were not biographies, or memoirs, or even memorabilia, written by individuals as accounts of the life and teaching of Jesus; they were compilations of traditional material handed down within the church, handed down orally and then later written out and compiled, in the interest of the church and for its purposes of edification, worship, discipline, or defense. The purely literary interest was neither paramount nor primary. The name of the author or compiler is only accidentally retained, so to speak, or is added as an afterthought—as in the second century when the gospels were being collected into a group, and separate names were required to distinguish them one from another, and when, nevertheless, the title of the group as a whole was "The Gospel," while the several books bore only the legend, "according to" Mark, Luke, Matthew, or John.

It is the origin of the gospels that explains their literary uniqueness. They are not biographies written by *literati* for the reading public of their day, like the *Lives* of the Caesars, the Sophists, the Grammarians, or the Philosophers. Nor were they written for a school, to be studied by the followers of a philosopher, like Porphyry's much later *Life of Plotinus*. They are, rather, the literature of a movement; and when we consider in what environment that movement arose, it is not surprising that they contain so little; the surprising thing is that they contain so much, in the way of a narrative of the life of our Lord. For the Jews, as a rule, made little attempt to cultivate biography: neither prophet nor wise man, scribe nor later rabbi, was the subject of an extended and continuous biographical account. All the more surprising is it, therefore, that the early Christian church did actually produce a class of literature which belongs in a general way under the category of biography. And it is surely significant that the first impetus in this direction was felt at Rome—not in Palestine or Syria, but far away in the Hellenized West, in the literary and political capital of the empire. It was only long after Mark was written and brought to Syria that the Gospel of Matthew appeared—a new edition of Mark, with much other material incorporated; while Luke (and even Proto-Luke, if we accept that hypothesis) was equally a gentile writing; in its final form (as the Gospel of Luke) it owes much to the Marcan outline of Jesus' public life. Such a collection of sayings and parables as we find in Q, or of sayings, parables, and anecdotes as we find in L, is probably Palestinian in origin, and is still far from both the finished gospel form and the Graeco-Roman public biography.

But the question is not, Why did the church produce biographies of Jesus?—since the distinction must steadily be borne in mind between our gospels and the Graeco-Roman type of biographical literature; the question really is, How did it come to pass that "gospels" came into existence? So important was the gospel form that it was retained not only by John—when a more didactic, apologetic form of composition might conceivably have served his purpose better—but also by the still later writers of apocryphal gospels. The answer to this question requires a wide consideration of the factors affecting literary production of any kind in the early church.

It goes without saying that the earliest evangelical narratives were oral. The whole problem—and the proposed solutions—of *Formgeschichte* lie within this area. The existence of oral tradition is not only a basic presupposition of the written gospels (see once more the Preface to Luke-Acts), whose form and contents can by no means be explained otherwise; but we actually have evidence of the existence of this tradition in the period prior to the earliest of them. Not only does the earliest preaching of the Christian message, reflected in the opening chapters of the book of Acts, imply the repetition of teaching about Jesus, his words and "mighty works"; but in a famous passage in I Cor. 15:3, St. Paul reminds his readers that he "delivered to them first of all [or as of first importance] what he also had received"—viz., the tradition of the Passion and Resurrection of Christ. And it was the testimony of the "eyewitnesses" referred to by Luke which doubtless became their message as "ministers of the word." Such a late reference as that in the Pastoral Epistles to the "form [or pattern] of sound words" (II Tim. 1:13) probably involves something more than a bare formula like the inchoate creed of I Corinthians, "Jesus is Lord" (I Cor. 12:3). In fact, the material found in Q and L, and in certain of the stereotyped narratives of Mark, must certainly be reckoned with as part of the "catechetical" subject matter of the first two generations.

The delay in writing down this material, which seems so unnatural to modern readers, accustomed to ubiquitous printed communications and records, is to be accounted for in several ways. That is, it was not just one but several factors in combination which made writing unlikely and delay inevitable.

(1) In the first place, *the earliest Christians were not a literary, not even, for the most part, an educated group*—as we should define "educated." "Not many wise, according to worldly standards, not many powerful, not many of noble birth [are called]; but God chose the foolish things of the world, that he might shame the wise . . ." (I Cor. 1:26 ff.). They were the humble, the simple, the poor, and some of them were no doubt illiterate. God chose to reveal Himself to "babes"—"little ones" is an interchangeable synonym for disciples in the important central section of the Gospel of Mark (9:42; cf. Matt. 11:25). Their very language, when they did come to write, was, as Adolf Deissmann conclusively showed (chiefly in his *Light from the Ancient East*), the language of the masses; not illiterate, but certainly nonliterary. Education, in the first century, was still in large measure the possession of the aristocracy and of the well-to-do, in spite of the exceptions—Epictetus, for example, who was born a slave, but lectured daily on the Stoic classics at Rome and Nicopolis. When the Christian church established itself in Rome, it was probably among the slaves in well-to-do households, perhaps including the imperial (Phil. 4:22), and among the Jews in their scattered neighborhoods, chiefly in Trastevere, the Campus Martius, and the Subura, i.e., near the centers of trade. The earliest gospel (Mark) shows what rugged, homespun Greek was used; and with it tally the spelling and grammar of some of the early epitaphs.

(2) Added to this, for the still earlier period of the preaching of the gospel in Palestine, was *the custom of the oral transmission*

of religious teaching (that of the Tannaite scribes and rabbis is strictly in point), and it is obvious that the motive for writing down an account of our Lord's teaching would not emerge very early—in fact, not until special circumstances rendered it necessary, while the continuous narrative of his life would come later still, if at all. As we have seen, the motive to provide the latter arose in the gentile church, and was first carried into effect by non-Jews. There were many religious teachers in the Graeco-Roman world whose teachings never were handed down in written form but only orally, and so eventually left only the faded impression of a general point of view and a few scattered sayings—often out of their original context, and hence difficult to interpret.

(3) A third factor was *the cost of materials*—perhaps not prohibitive for the ordinary person, but certainly for the penniless. Not without reason are the nonliterary papyri found buried in the sands of Egypt mere scraps and fragments, for the most part, and along with them broken bits of pottery—the ostraca—upon which the natives scratched their missives, records, and accounts. Even literary writers took account of the length of their "tomes," or "cuts," of rolled papyrus upon which books were to be inscribed. As William Sanday and others have argued, the standard size of a "tome" probably had something to do with the length of the Gospels, Acts, Romans, and the Epistle to the Hebrews. Nothing seems cheaper than paper and ink at the present day. But in the ancient world the cost of writing materials, for the production and reproduction of books, was really no inconsiderable item, certainly for the poor among whom the gospel first spread abroad in the world. It is surely significant that the first writing which purported in any sense to be a "life" of our Lord (the Gospel of Mark) came from one of the book-distributing centers of the ancient world—though it apparently was intended for use within the church rather than for public and general circulation.

(4) Another factor, and one that had a very real bearing upon the production of written narratives of the life and teaching of our Lord, was *the prevalent expectation of the Parousia*—the "coming" of the Lord in glory. If "the end of all things" was at hand; if any day might be the last; if every event of importance in popular rumor or report might be of significance for the approaching end—then it is clear that those who shared such views would be in no frame of mind to write records of the past. Above all, if the Lord, who tarried only for a time in heaven until his final manifestation in glory, was already and continuously in communication with his church, through the messages of prophets and the

activities of workers of miracles; if, in brief, the life of Jesus upon
earth was only what he "*began* both to do and to teach" (Acts
1:1), the continuation of his work being just as real in the present,
leading up to "greater works than these" (John 14:12) shortly to
be accomplished, then it is clear that the motive to write down
his life and teaching was destined to come only slowly into the
church's consciousness, and to become operative only after the
primitive apocalyptic enthusiasm had begun to wane. And it is
significant, I think, that the mood reflected in Q, Mark, and L is
not quite the same flaming apocalypticism that we discover in or
infer from some of the other sources. While the eschatological
temper continued at white heat, there was neither the mood nor
the motive to write an account of Jesus' life. The kind of book
the apocalyptic mood produced is to be seen, rather, in the
Apocalypse of John, in IV Ezra, II Baruch, and the other apocalypses. The Gospel of Matthew, I believe (like the Apocalypse of
John, though they are by no means related), represents a revival
of apocalypticism, in a particular locality and under special circumstances, sometime about the beginning of the second century.

(5) Finally, there was *the difficulty of collecting data*. How
could the ordinary Christian find the time to go about collecting
data for the life of Christ, or for the earliest period of the church's
life—as Hegesippus certainly did in the second century, and as
Luke doubtless did in the first? By the time the need for written
records had come to be felt—upon the death of those who had
been "eyewitnesses" as well as "ministers of the word"—the
church had spread far beyond the borders of Palestine; and even
within Palestine it had been "scattered" more than once, as a result of persecution. With but few exceptions the primitive disciples had been disbanded; Peter had gone "elsewhere" (Acts
12:17)—presumably to Antioch, and then to Rome; and the tradition of a dispersal of the apostles is probably not to be credited
entirely to later inference from Acts 8:1, where "except the
apostles" sounds like a gloss. Moreover, in Galilee, the scene of
Jesus' own ministry, the church seems never to have taken deep
root, though it is inconceivable that there were no early Christians
in Galilee. There are, in fact, Christians in Galilee today, who
claim that their ancestors have been Christian ever since the time
of Jesus. But it is difficult to describe many of the Galilean traditions as in any sense *local* traditions (e.g., the day in Capernaum) or legends (e.g., the Gerasene incident); the gospel
narratives simply do not bear upon them the impress of any particular locality, and the later evangelists faced a real problem in

trying to adjust their materials to a topographical framework. The topography was as difficult to determine as the chronology; the two were of course closely related. Quite obviously the underlying sources suggest the strain and tension of ostracism and persecution suffered by those who handed them down—expulsion from the synagogue, derision and excommunication at the hands of their neighbors. And the woes pronounced upon the towns where Jesus did his "mighty works"—Chorazin, Bethsaida, Capernaum (Luke 10:13–15)—are scarcely understandable if we suppose them to have been centers of Christian missionary work in the generation following our Lord's death. It is as communities that they are condemned; it is certain, therefore, that as communities they had rejected the gospel (cf. Luke 9:53, 10:10). Even Nazareth, where Jesus grew to manhood, had been cold and unresponsive and lacking in faith: "He could do no mighty work there . . . because of their unbelief" (Mark 6:5, 6).

It is significant that the early ecclesiastical tradition connects the writing of the first gospel (Mark) with the death of Peter—the living voice of the martyr apostle was silenced, and "afterwards," so Irenaeus says, Mark wrote down what he remembered of Peter's testimony (Eusebius, Church History, V. 8. 2, 3).

Thus it required time for the need to be felt, and it required also individuals to undertake the task of gathering the available material. This material, in Mark's case, was doubtless the tradition current in the Roman church. However, it is still true that, although communities provide tradition, conserving it and handing it on, they do not write books—these are the work of individuals. But, as we have seen, the motive for any kind of historical writing was not present from the first; it was slow in appearing, and hence delay was inevitable. The strange thing is not that our gospel records are so incomplete; the wonder is that we have any at all! Only exceptional circumstances and requirements could give rise to written records of the life of Jesus; otherwise, there was nothing in the situation to give occasion for them. And yet it became inevitable, after a time, that written accounts should appear. Over against the motives for delay just noted, operative in the first generation, there were others, destined to become effective in the second and third generations.

(1) We have already noted the growing consensus of scholars that the gospels were intended, originally, for use within the church. Their early liturgical use in addition to the Old Testament, in lections appropriate to the Christian-Jewish "ecclesiastical

year"; their pointed applications of Jesus' teaching to the needs and life-situations of Christian readers and hearers; their arrangement of Jesus' sayings and of incidents from his life in groupings by subject, e.g., in triads, or in "catenas" or sequences strung together by similarity of words, a device useful in memorization if not always in interpretation; the addition of homiletical "tags" at the end of the parables, especially in Luke, which now read like brief notes added by early Christian preachers or teachers; the emphasis laid upon esoteric interpretation, especially in the earliest gospel (e.g., Mark 4:11, 13:14)—a feature impossible in a work intended for publication and general circulation—all these features combine to indicate that *the gospels took the place of the original oral tradition*, and came into use as the period of its transmission solely by word of mouth came to a close. Presumably this was at a time when the first generation of Christians were dying out— "after the deaths of Peter and Paul," as the old Western tradition states it. The gospels were a substitute for oral testimony, but only because they were based upon it, contained it, and were, essentially, only its crystallization in writing.

(2) Another motive for writing was *the edification of new converts*. The arrangement of the material, and the subjects chosen for emphasis already suggest this—especially, in Mark and Q, the strong central emphasis on *discipleship* and the duty of loyalty to Christ, in life and death. Since the gospel meant more than simply repentance, which was only the first step, and involved a new "way" of life, it was necessary that the teaching of Christ—conceived first of all, no doubt, as a guide to the disciples—should be set forth in explicit terms. And even though this might for a long time be sufficiently presented in stereotyped oral form, it was inevitable that eventually it should be written down, not least as a guide for the instructors themselves. As modern Jewish scholars have shown, even in such an obviously oral compendium as the Mishnah, which was drawn up ca. A.D. 210 for school purposes, as a textbook of law, but based upon the oral traditions of the earlier rabbinic authorities, there are traces of a beginning of written notes or memorabilia which were made as early as a century before its final compilation in writing. And if the teaching of Jesus came to be written down in this way, it was inevitable that incidents from his life should follow; since much of his teaching was embedded in incident, conversation, controversy, or narrative. Moreover, the Passion Narrative, which was the earliest consecutive account to be narrated in fixed sequence, could not avoid taking its place as the final chapter in the earthly life of Jesus. The stories

of the Resurrection, on the other hand, described in various ways how he "entered into his glory" (Luke 24:26). It was the Passion Narrative, without doubt, that provided the original nucleus of the gospels.

(3) A third motive, offsetting one we have already noted among factors explaining the late appearance of the gospels, was *the delay of the Parousia*. To understand this, it is not necessary to come all the way down into the second century, when we meet with the question, "Where is the promise of his coming?" (II Pet. 3:4), and find Christians stumbling over the problem of the death of an apostle whom they had expected to survive until the coming of the Lord (John 21:23). For even earlier than this there were those whose love had "waxed cold," whose loyalty had broken down under persecution, who had come to question "the time of the end" and required to be told that it was not for them to know, since "that day and hour" lay solely within the Father's authority (Matt. 24:12, Rev. 2:4, 3:16, Acts 1:7).

As delay succeeded delay and the end was discovered to be "not yet," and as the repeated postponement of the expectation weakened its hold upon men's minds—"hope deferred . . . maketh the heart sick"—the old motive lost force. It was necessary now to gather up the teaching of Jesus, even on this very subject, and to study it afresh. New interpretations were introduced. "The gospel must first be preached unto all the nations" before the end could come (so Mark, in 13:10). "The times of the Gentiles [must] be fulfilled" (so Luke; see 21:24). The Gentiles must first be evangelized, even before Israel itself could be saved—now that the nation had rejected the Messiah and called down his blood upon themselves (so Matt. 27:25).

Hence the delay in the Parousia operated in a twofold way: it removed the inhibition upon writing which had operated while apocalyptic messianism was at fever pitch; and it made necessary both the further conservation of Jesus' teaching and of the narratives of his life, and likewise the fresh study, perhaps the reinterpretation—i.e., a truer interpretation—of his actual words. We can see this motive at work in even as highly apocalyptic-eschatological a gospel as Matthew, where the exalted view of the Parousia is no more obvious than the problem of its delay.

(4) Still another motive is to be seen in *the nascent historical and biographical interests of certain individuals*, chiefly the author of Luke-Acts, though the motive is not wholly lacking in Mark or in Matthew, or even in John. (a) In Mark it takes the form of an attempt to show that Christianity is grounded in actual history;

i.e., Jesus, the Lord of the church's faith and worship, had already been Son of God, Messiah, and Son of Man while he walked upon earth, and therefore had been exalted to God's right hand, and was rightly the object of the church's adoration and highest hopes. Even the Roman centurion at the cross had testified, "Truly this was a Son of God" (Mark 15:39). The term was pagan—"Son of God" was the highest conceivable title for a divine being who had come to earth, or for a "divine man" on the way to apotheosis. This term the gentile church had taken over and Christianized, even, apparently, before the time of Paul's epistles. (b) For Matthew it took the form of a demonstration of Jesus' messiahship from Old Testament prophecy—both in prediction and by prototype—so that if the Jews would but read their scriptures with the clue now afforded them, they would find them fulfilled in Christ. (c) And for John it took the form of a proof (especially against Docetists and Gnostics) that Jesus during his earthly life was really human, really walked in Galilee, thirsted and wept, and died a human death. (Mark had found it necessary to prove that Jesus was divine, John that he was human!) Thus the historical or biographical motive, though not strong, and far from primary, was really present and operated with increasing force as considerations steadily accumulated leading to the conservation of all that could be learned regarding the actual life of Jesus upon earth, in addition to his teaching. But the biographical motive was constantly influenced—as we have seen—by the theological.

It is generally assumed by New Testament scholars that the gospels were written in Greek, not Aramaic. Indeed the whole New Testament was a Greek collection of books, from the start— as Professor Goodspeed has always insisted, and rightly. The argument that Papias' statement, "Matthew collected the oracles in the Hebrew dialect" (Eusebius, Church History, III. 39. 16), refers to a gospel is nothing but special pleading (see p. 65), while the interpretation of gilyōn in the Mishnah Yadaim 3:4, as meaning "gospel," would never in the world have occurred to any ancient Jewish scholar (see p. 70). It was in the Greek-speaking gentile world outside Palestine, where the historical and biographical interest was strongest, that our four gospels and book of Acts were written.

(5) Another motive was one which sprang into prominence as a result of the controversy with Jews and heretics. The extent and importance of this we shall see when we come to consider separately the Gospels of Mark, Matthew, and John; here it is sufficient to note that the simplest answer to the calumnies of "the Jews" regarding Jesus' birth and resurrection (as in Matt. 28:15)

was to state the facts as they were believed to have occurred, or as they could be inferred from the Old Testament. And if some of the scribal and Pharisaic attacks were still leveled against Jesus' disciples rather than against Jesus himself (as in the question of fasting, in Mark 2:18–22), it was sufficient to state the answer the Lord himself had given, long before, to this very charge. Or if apostasy threatened the church (as in Matt. 24:10–12), it was enough to state that the Lord himself had foreseen and foretold it.

(6) Still another motive, one that took on special significance in the days of Nero and again in those of Domitian, and was probably not absent for long at any time during the interval, was the apologetic or defensive one: viz., to set Christianity in the right light in the eyes of the governing class and of Roman officialdom generally. It is quite clearly at work in the two Lucan writings— especially in Acts; and it certainly had a bearing upon the form taken by the Passion Narrative almost from the start, where the responsibility for Jesus' death is shifted from the Romans to the Jews. Obviously, Jesus had been put to death as a disturber of the peace and an insurgent, if not an active revolutionist. The placard over his cross had read, "The King of the Jews" (Mark 15:26). Furthermore, his followers had been conspicuously involved in the tumults and disturbances that sprang up wherever their missionaries went. It was, of course, possible to view Christianity as a sect within Judaism—and therefore deserving the special toleration accorded the practice of that ancient religion; and Luke clearly chose this opening for a defense. But at best the Jews were a turbulent lot—as Roman officials well knew, sometimes to their cost (e.g., Acts 17:13, 18:2, 14–17, 19:33, 20:3, 21:27, 23:12); moreover, when the Jews themselves came to "cast out the name" as evil, it was necessary for other defenses to be set up. These we can see still standing in the accounts of our Lord's words regarding the tribute money (Mark 12:13–17) and, especially, in the accounts of his trial and crucifixion. And there are still other evidences: the healing of the centurion's servant, for example, certainly a friendly deed done to a Gentile (Luke 7:1–10), and the "two swords" of the disciples on Passover eve (Luke 22:35–38)— an utterly insignificant arsenal for a band of revolutionists!

(7) Another motive was no doubt that of missionary propaganda. The gospels contained—i.e., wrote down and thus preserved —the early Christian proclamation (kērygma) as well as the early Christian teaching (didachē). Out in the broad Mediterranean world, outside Palestine, the use of the written word was increas-

ingly recognized, in our period, as a medium for the dissemination of religious teaching. The Epistles of Paul, "occasional writings" at best, and really letters in their primary intent, had easily become in the apostle's hand a means of reiterating his teaching and missionary preaching in Corinth, Galatia, Thessalonica, Philippi. Nor were other teachers unaware of the value of the written address—the published "discourses" of contemporary philosophers and the *diatribes* of Cynic and Stoic teachers are examples. It was inevitable that such a medium should be adopted in time by the Christians, and such writings in the New Testament as Hebrews and the Epistle of James or the noncanonical epistles of Clement and "Barnabas" and the one addressed to Diognetus make clear its use; as time went on, the use became more widespread, though it never was entirely severed from the community. All along, the missionary was a man, not a pamphlet, and the instruction of those who were to preach and teach the gospel by word of mouth remained more important than the formation of a tract-distributing society.

(8) Still another motive may be seen in the purely *literary interest*—we have no other name for it—of such a writer or writers as gave us the incomparable passage, "Consider the lilies . . ." (Matt. 7:28–33) or the parable of the good Samaritan (Luke 10:29–37) or the Lucan Infancy Narrative (Luke 1:5–2:52) or the story of the walk to Emmaus (24:13–35) or the sublime High Priestly Prayer in John 17. These are pure prose-poetry of the highest order. Not that the religious motive was secondary in the writing down of such passages; but it is clear that a standard of literary beauty, quite on a par with the highest flights of Old Testament poetry and prophecy, was set up for some of those who recorded the teaching of our Lord.

Furthermore, the implications of the Prologue to Luke-Acts (Luke 1:1–4) make it clear that in the course of time the church really made an attempt to interest educated circles, and to put forth writings comparable to the finest prose narratives of the Hellenistic-Roman world. The "social" rise of the Christian movement led at an early date to a taste for fine literature—though it is not uniformly visible either in the New Testament or in the writings of the postapostolic age. But the Epistle to the Hebrews, a homily constructed more or less in accordance with the rules of Greek oratory, tells us much about at least one phase of early church thought and interests. So does the Epistle to Diognetus— wherever it belongs, perhaps late in the second century. So does Clement of Alexandria with his mass of classical quotations.

(9) Other motives also were at work, such as *the liturgical*—a motive almost certainly affecting the form, and to some extent the contents, of Mark, of Matthew, and perhaps also of John. This motive, the origin of which goes back to a much earlier period than we used to assume, survived for a long time and showed its influence in the later preservation of the gospel form, even in the late second, third, and fourth centuries when apocryphal gospels were being produced.

(10) Another motive—perhaps one of the earliest of all—was *the encouragement of Christians in persecution* and, indeed, as in Mark, faced with the clear probability of martyrdom—"he that endureth to the end, the same shall be saved" (13:13).

(11) Still another motive was the formulation of a kind of *incipient canon law*—far in advance of the guidance of converts noted above, and destined to be still more highly developed in the *Didache*, later on, in the *Apostolic Tradition*, the *Didascalia*, and the *Apostolic Constitutions*, but already recognizable in our Gospel of Matthew.

(12) Another was the motive of *philosophical apologetic*, as in John, where Paul's identification of Christ with the Logos, "in whom all things consist" (Col. 1:17), is carried through consistently as an interpretation of Christ as the revealer, indeed as the theophany or manifestation, of the Father.

There were no doubt still other motives at work in the production of the gospels; but these twelve are sufficient to make it clear that the production of biographies, in the modern sense, or even in the ancient classical sense, was only one among many and, indeed, probably an extremely minor one. "Why we have gospels," then, is a question to be answered only after a consideration of the various, indeed, quite numerous, motives that were actually operative in the production of the writings that bear this name. As we have seen, the term "gospel," used in describing a book, is a late one. For it seems clear that one phase of that vast flood of fresh creative spiritual life which swept into the world with the coming of Christ was the production of a new literary genre, not anticipated by anything that had gone before, and only faintly analogous to other literary creations of the Hellenistic age. It is a literary type which can be interpreted only in the light of the peculiar needs and aims which the gospels were meant to satisfy. And these needs, let us repeat, were exclusively the needs and requirements felt *within the church*. For the gospels are pre-eminently "church books" from beginning to end, and throughout the course of their production, from the earliest sources underlying the synoptics to the finished Gospels of Luke, Matthew, and John. In form, they are the natural result of the effort to set forth "what Jesus both did and taught," in order to meet the church's need for such records in its teaching, worship, discipline, missionary propaganda, controversy, political and philosophical apologetic.

Why gospels resulted from this process, rather than diatribes, exhortations, epistles, apocalypses, codes, liturgies, hymns, mystic meditations, or other forms of religious literature; or, rather, why gospels resulted *in addition*—and sometimes even prior—to these other forms (all of which are represented in the New Testament and the other early Christian literature) is wholly bound up with the purposes and motives that went to their production. That these motives were operative, and at so early a time in Christian history, must be a reason for thankfulness on the part not only of devout believers but also of the literary historian and the historian of religion. Without the gospels, our knowledge of the historical Jesus would be only a magnificent, perhaps even sublime, but nevertheless mysterious x, an unknown quantity even though it were obviously one of the highest order. What Ludwig Lewisohn said of Goethe is true in even fuller measure of our Lord. If we possessed only scattered groups of his sayings, as in the so-called *agrapha* (unwritten sayings), or pronouncements, parables, criticisms and reinterpretations of the Law, we should of course realize that here was a master spirit, one of the few "whole" men in all history. But fortunately we have much more: a large and varied body of tradition—in fact, four main bodies of tradition—thus not only preserving the scattered sayings which they gather up and mount like jewels in a setting of narrative, but also conveying to us the very spirit of the Teacher, his times, his background, the ethos of his place and period in the changing panorama of the world's history.

THE INTERRELATIONSHIP OF THE SYNOPTIC GOSPELS

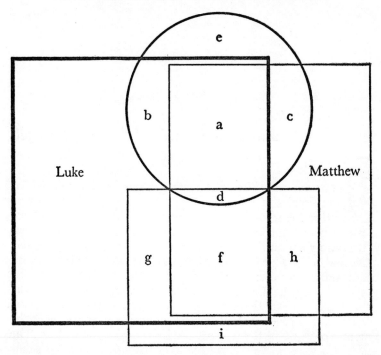

The large heavy square at the left = Luke (1,149 verses)
The thin square at the right = Matthew (1,068 verses)
The small square at the bottom = Mark (661 verses)
The circle = Q (ca. 242 verses)

    a = material from Q found in both Luke and Matthew
    b = material from Q found in Luke only
    c = material from Q found in Matthew only
    d = material in Q with parallels in Mark
    e = material in Q not used in any gospel, hence now lost
    f = material in Mark used in both Luke and Matthew
    g = material in Mark used in Luke only
    h = material in Mark used in Matthew only
    i = material in Mark not used in Luke or Matthew

Material in Luke not found in Mark or Q includes L, the Lucan Infancy
  Narrative, and other special Lucan material

Material in Matthew not found in Mark or Q includes M, the Matthean Infancy Narrative, and other special Matthean material

Method in the Study of the Synoptic Gospels

*I*t is not surprising that many persons unfamiliar with the
intricacies of synoptic study have the general impression
that the reconstruction of such basic documents as Q and
L is purely hypothetical, subjective, and arbitrary. To some readers
it may easily appear that these earliest sources exist only in the sen-
sitive and suggestible imaginations of higher critics. Indeed, I have
heard well-educated clergymen remark that they prefer to take the
gospels as they stand, as the church has received them, and as the
church has handed them down. And it is notorious that many
preachers, and some religious educators, treat the gospels as if the
synoptic criticism of the past hundred years were nonexistent. The
underlying assumption seems to be that synoptic criticism is solely
the concern of specialists, and that it either results in further and
somewhat superfluous support of the traditional view of Christian
origins—support which the gospels do not greatly need—or else
needlessly brings in question the traditional view, in which case it
may be suspected of rationalistic and antiorthodox motivation. It
may be well, therefore, to point out how few, simple, and objective are the steps in the process by which the main outlines of the
earlier sources are recovered and how directly the process leads to
the all but inevitable hypothesis of their existence.

It would be going over ground already well trod to undertake
to establish the priority of Mark. This practically everyone takes
for granted at the present day. Even those who are committed
theologically to the priority of Matthew find it necessary to posit
an original Aramaic version whose ultimate translator made considerable use of the already existing Greek gospel of Mark. Modern
"harmonies" of the gospels take Mark's priority for granted—
works like Albert Huck's (*A Synopsis of the First Three Gospels*
[in Greek], 9th ed., revised by Hans Lietzmann; English ed. by

F. L. Cross, Tübingen, 1936; or *Gospel Parallels,* based on Huck
but using the Revised Standard Version text, by Burton H.
Throckmorton, 1949), or the one by E. D. Burton and E. J. Goodspeed, using the Greek text of Westcott and Hort (1920), or their
parallel edition in English, using the American Standard Version
text (1917). The great advantage of Huck's edition is the fuller
apparatus of variant readings, parallels, and Old Testament references; that of Goodspeed's is the arrangement of the text in corresponding sense-lines opposite each other, so that one can
recognize the identities at once. The freshness and directness of
Mark's narrative, which the ordinary reader can recognize for himself; the simpler explanation of Matthew and Luke's dependence
upon Mark as against the more involved one of Mark's derivation
from either Matthew or Luke, or from both; the often divergent
modifications introduced by the later writers in their adaptation
of Mark's material, more easily explicable upon the hypothesis of
Mark's priority than upon that of a conflation of materials drawn
from Matthew and Luke resulting in a vivid and characteristic,
stylistically unified narrative—all this evidence points unmistak-
ably in the direction of the priority of the Gospel of Mark.

At the least the priority of Mark will not be questioned by anyone who has worked through Mark and the Matthean and Lucan
parallels, word by word, phrase by phrase, underlining the words
and phrases and whole sentences in Matthew and Luke which, on
this hypothesis, have been taken over from Mark. And, to be perfectly frank, no one has the right to condemn the hypothesis who
has not thus worked it out fully in laborious detail and on the
basis of the Greek text. This is the first task which should be set
every advanced student of the synoptics. The following is a simple
and easily followed plan:

(1) Go through Matthew and Luke and mark the exact equivalents to Mark by underlining the words in *unbroken* black lines
(breaking the lines only to indicate inversions in order), and underlining in *dotted* black lines words and groups of words which
are similar and represent only slight grammatical changes (person,
case, tense, voice, mood, or number). This is laborious and minute
work; but it is worth all the trouble—one gains a grasp of the
problem and of the proposed solution which nothing else can
supply.

(2) The next step, for those who wish to test the "Urmarcus"
hypothesis (this is the hypothesis that Matthew or Luke, or both,
used an "edition" of Mark differing from and presumably earlier
than the one in our New Testament), or to gain a clear view of

the Matthean-Lucan omissions from Mark, or to study the question of later additions to the text of Mark, is to go over Mark and underline (again in black, and following the same rule for broken and unbroken and dotted lines) the material which Matthew and Luke have drawn from this common source. One can readily find the passages listed in Sir John Hawkins' *Horae Synopticae* (2d ed., pp. 114–149) or in Canon B. H. Streeter's *Four Gospels* (English ed., pp. 195 ff.); but the student will have a much surer grasp of their significance if he works through the Gospel of Mark in the manner just described. Nothing can take the place of that firsthand acquaintance with the text which will result from the minute and exacting work, carefully and accurately done, which this task involves.

A few words should be said at this point about the textual apparatus supplied at the foot of the page in the standard Greek Harmonies. Huck's volume originally was designed to accompany H. J. Holtzmann's Commentary on the Synoptics in his *Hand-Kommentar*, first published in 1889. Very naturally it followed the text which Holtzmann presupposed—a text based largely on Tischendorf, and reflecting, accordingly, a marked preference for the readings of the Sinaitic ms., *Aleph* (now often referred to as S), which, it will be recalled, Tischendorf himself had discovered in 1844. Burton and Goodspeed, on the other hand, presuppose the text of Westcott and Hort—whose preference for the agreements of B and *Aleph*=S (i.e., the so-called "neutral" text) was their primary canon in restoring the text. One does not go far before discovering that Huck and Goodspeed—or Tischendorf and Westcott-Hort—are in slight disagreement; and that neither of them agrees entirely with the popular manual edition of Nestle, whose text represents (at least in the earlier editions) a mechanical averaging of the texts of Tischendorf, Westcott-Hort, and B. Weiss. There is nothing extraordinary about this; but the student should be warned that the possibility of textual assimilation is nowhere greater than in the Synoptic Gospels, and that the variants at the foot of the page are constantly to be reckoned with. As a rule, *proclivi lectioni praestat ardua*—the "harder" reading, among the divergent variants, has the right to first consideration—and sometimes even a vagrant reading (if I may be allowed the expression) has the strongest right: a reading which recurs in unexpected places has a strong right to favorable consideration. For example, the omission of the definite article before John's title in Mark 1:4, in AD . . . min is trivial enough; but it seems more characteristic of Mark's rugged style than the reading of S B; and it has no equivalent in Matthew or Luke (Matthew and Luke have the definite article before "John"). But Mark's style calls for the title "the Baptizer," and this is the reading followed in the new Revised Standard Version. (The earliest title was presumably "the Baptizer"; later, as head of the movement known to church history, John was "the Baptist." Mark uses both titles.) Or take Mark 1:7: does the second *mou* belong in the text, or is it derived by assimilation from Matthew? The manuscript B and the Alexandrian church father Origen both omit it; but then both B and Origen may represent to some degree a grammatical revision of the earlier text. These are fairly simple cases. But take Mark 2:22, which is quite involved, especially in the versions, and where some mss. add, "But new wine in new wineskins" (S* B 102). As Cuthbert Turner pointed out in Gore's Commentary, this carries on the thought of the first part of the verse ("No one pours new wine into old skins"). The verse form is perhaps the one known as *chiasmus*, where lines 1 and 4 are parallel, and also lines 2 and 3 (see my arrangement in Harper's Annotated Bible Series). But v. 21, the first half of the double parable, is not chiastic, and so we are left without any absolutely certain conclusion, on either textual or stylistic grounds. Verses 22 d, e, may be only a parenthesis or an aside—quite in Mark's moralistic manner, however, and not necessarily the work of a later scribe. Some other manuscripts (ACL . . . versions) add the verb "is poured," no doubt assimilated from Luke, and not really required by the language of Mark, whether or not a parenthesis intervenes between the first and last parts of the verse, and whatever the original conclusion. The significance of such a textual addition—or omission, whichever it is— will appear more fully in dealing with the common material of Matthew and Luke outside Mark. For if the final words, "New wine in new wineskins," belong to Mark, the agreement of Matthew and Luke in using them is no greater than their agreement throughout the whole preceding passage—and throughout the following passage as well. On the other hand, if the words do not really belong to Mark, as Hort's and Huck's square brackets suggest, then we have here one more of the Matthean-Lucan agreements against Mark, i.e., a common addition in a Marcan context, requiring special consideration from the synoptic student. Coincidence is ruled out; conflation is possible, but improbable; perhaps the words represent a stray echo of Q—the great non-Marcan source common to Matthew and Luke—though it is strange that no other traces of Q exist in the immediate neighborhood. More probable than all these conjectures is the hypothesis that the

words once belonged to Mark, but were later lost out of the text
—perhaps by some early copyist who failed to see their connection
with what immediately preceded, especially since the sentence
lacked a verb. This was before ACL and the versions—or one of
their Greek ancestors—had added *blēteon*, "is to be poured."

This brief excursion into textual criticism has been inserted at
this point in order to show the necessity of taking the variant readings into account, as one proceeds to examine the use of Mark by
Matthew and Luke; they are also important for the reconstruction
of Q. (There are of course many more variants than those usually
cited in editions of the text or in commentaries. Hort, Huck,
Nestle, and other editors give only a selection of the more important ones.) They must not be ignored. Literary criticism begins
with textual criticism, and the student should accustom himself
to examine *the entire text*, not just the readings preferred by the
modern editors. In its totality, the "text" of course includes the
variants.

(3) The third step in the construction of one's own apparatus
for Synoptic study is to go through the passages in which Matthew
and Luke are parallel to one another, *outside Mark*, and underline
in the same fashion, but now in *red*, words and groups of words
which they have in common—with unbroken lines for exact
equivalents and identical order, broken lines for a different order,
and dotted lines for the same words used in different grammatical
constructions. The results will be astonishing, to one who has supposed Q to be a figment of the critic's imagination! Page after page
will show hundreds of words in common, many of them arranged
in exactly the same order and given in the same grammatical form,
sometimes whole blocks of passages appearing in the same form
and order in Matthew and Luke. For example, the Preaching of
John the Baptist in Matt. 3:7–10 closely parallels Luke 3:7–9; the
Temptation Narrative in ch. 4 exhibits the same phenomenon; so
does the Mission Discourse in Matt. 10 and Luke 9–10. Assimilation of Matthew's text to Luke's, or Luke's to Matthew's, is out
of the question, on such a scale as this. Oral tradition, whatever its
place in the original formulation of the narratives, is insufficient to
explain it. Only a common documentary, i.e., written or stereotyped oral, source will account for the multitude of minute agreements, and we may as well call it Q (i.e., *Quelle*, "*Source*") as
anything else.

(4) The next step is to carry this process back into the Marcan
narratives, and underline (also in red) the agreements of Matthew
and Luke *in Marcan contexts*—a not inconsiderable number of

such agreements appearing as we go along, and each demanding its explanation, from the point of view of thorough source-criticism. Many of these are doubtless merely stylistic, e.g., Matthew and Luke's preference of *eipen* to Mark's *legei*, for the same procedure can be observed in passages where they do not happen to agree in thus revising Mark; others may be due to assimilation of text; others demand still other explanations. Some of these agreements—Matthean-Lucan "contacts," as the late Professor Easton called them—can hardly be explained otherwise than as evidence of Mark's use of Q, especially in passages forming "doublets," i.e., the second use of the same material in one gospel.

(5) A further step is to isolate and examine these *doublets*, noting (and underlining, preferably now in a third color, e.g., blue) words and phrases, order of words, and turns of thought and expression that suggest the influence of oral or documentary source materials not contemplated by the two-document hypothesis in its ordinary form. These doublets are found where Matthew and Luke have incorporated material from Mark or from Q which later appears in almost identical form when they are both copying the other document—for example, the well-known sayings on divorce and adultery, which are found in Mark 10:11 = Matt. 19:9; Matt. 5:32 = Luke 16:18; one passage being obviously Marcan, the other obviously Q, according to the general two-document hypothesis. Now, either the sayings are variants handed down separately in Mark and Q, both being drawn from oral tradition; or, as the identities of language suggest—and they are identities in Greek, not Aramaic—the version in Mark is dependent upon Q. The latter is no doubt the simpler hypothesis, and the one which seems to be gaining ground at present. In other words, Mark knew and presupposed Q, and from time to time he supplies evidence of this, quoting a number of sayings which presuppose an acquaintance on his own and his readers' part with that document. We shall examine these passages in more detail later.

(6) It will be evident by this time that there is still a fairly large mass of material in both Luke and Matthew, but chiefly in Luke, not assigned either to Mark or to Q. It is possible to maintain, with some authorities, that Q was much more extensive than the sum total of passages which Matthew and Luke agree in selecting from that document (see diagram, p. 39). Bernhard Weiss's reconstruction of Q, e.g., went far beyond the limits of this sum total of parallel passages, contrasting markedly with Adolf Harnack's severely restrained reconstruction (English tr., *The Sayings of Jesus*, 1908; still the best book to use in beginning the study

of Q). Indeed, it seems impossible to deny that some passages, particularly when found enclosed within blocks of Q material, and closely resembling the adjacent material in both style and thought, must have belonged originally to that document. It is easier to explain their omission by one gospel (either Matthew or Luke) than their insertion at this point by the other. Further evidence was, of course, afforded by the Matthean-Lucan contacts in Marcan passages: B. Weiss even went so far as to suppose that whole narratives, found in Q, underlay the Marcan version. In Weiss's view, Q was not so much a collection of the sayings of Jesus as an embryonic but fairly well-developed gospel. Another form of the hypothesis was that of Professor B. W. Bacon, who used "Q" to indicate the mechanically established parallels in Matthew and Luke, outside Mark, but preferred another symbol, "S," for the source from which these passages were derived—the latter a much more elaborate document. Finally, we should note that still others, like the late Professor F. C. Burkitt, prefer not to think of Q as a specific document at all, but merely as a convenient designation for a whole mass of stereotyped oral, or perhaps written—or perhaps partly written and partly oral—sayings and narratives upon which Matthew and Luke drew in addition to their use of Mark. According to this theory, Q material is to be found in different form and with varying content in different places in Matthew and Luke. It seems more likely that Q was written down *after* the translation of its contents (chiefly Jesus' sayings) into Greek, rather than during the period when the tradition was still in Aramaic.

On the other hand, Professor B. S. Easton, following the lead of Bernhard Weiss, and with him Canon B. H. Streeter and others, found in the additional or "peculiar" material of Luke sufficient indications of unity and homogeneity in outlook, in subject matter, in method of treatment, and even in style, to warrant the differentiation of still another document, which they designated as "L" (for obvious reasons). Weiss and Easton even went so far as to attempt to establish a special vocabulary (as Harnack did for Q) as a criterion or touchstone for indicating the presence of this source. An obvious difficulty in the way of establishing this vocabulary is the question of the original source of Luke's Nativity and Infancy Narrative (ch. 1–2). If it belonged to L, it certainly must provide a large part of the hypothetical vocabulary—since it contains, excluding the prologue, a total of one hundred and twenty-eight verses. But the provenance of Luke 1–2 is uncertain; Easton assigned it to L, while Streeter set it at one side as of uncertain origin, though inclining to agree with Torrey that it rests on a Hebrew original—in any event a written document (see *The Four Gospels*, pp. 266 ff.). In his book on *The Historical Evidence for the Virgin Birth* (Oxford, 1920), Dr. Vincent Taylor advanced the theory that Luke 1:34 f. (the reference to the Virgin Birth) was added to the gospel at a late stage in its composition, in fact on the very eve of its "publication," and in the final draft. The main difficulty with this earlier hypothesis is that vv. 36 f. do *not* continue the thought of v. 33 without interruption, but presuppose vv. 34 f. The hypothesis was later modified or supplanted by that of "Proto-Luke," which began, according to Streeter and Taylor, with Luke 3:1. But the still later view of the late Martin Dibelius, in his *Message of Jesus Christ* (1939), assumes that Luke 1-2 is composite, a weaving together of two different strands of legend, the Birth of John and the Birth of Jesus, the latter itself composite, with three distinct motifs: Mary, the Shepherds, Simeon. Obviously this material is not of the same type or quality —or "form"—as that in the main body of "L." The reason why some scholars think that the Infancy Narrative originally existed in Hebrew (not Aramaic) is that it can be retranslated into that language with the greatest ease. Others hold that Luke was a good stylist, knew the Septuagint thoroughly, and could write in the style of the historical and poetic books of the Greek Old Testament without difficulty.

However, Easton's vocabulary of L is not entirely vitiated by this uncertainty of the source of Luke's Nativity Narrative, since it may be checked with the one given by Sir John Hawkins, who lists the usage of Luke 1-2 in a separate column. The striking agreement of the diction and style of Luke 1-2 with that of L, evidenced by a comparison of Hawkins' and Easton's tables, may be interpreted in one of at least two different ways. Either Luke 1-2 belonged to L—which must then have been a "gospel" rather than a sayings document, particularly if it included Luke's peculiar matter in the Passion Narrative—and its place in L is Easton's *Q.E.D.*; or, in agreement with Easton's contention that many of the peculiar beauties of Luke's gospel in reality belong to L, these characteristic words and phrases are no more than the marks of Luke's own authorship of the whole (including the editorial revision of material taken over by him from Mark, Q, and other sources). A third possibility is that the Lucan Infancy Narrative, and likewise the Lucan Passion and Resurrection Narratives, formed no part of the document L, but were cognate or related sources—perhaps handed down in the same circle or locality as that which provided the material in L. The document L, then, was not a primitive gospel, complete with Birth and Passion Narratives (in one respect it would thus be more complete than Mark), but was mainly a "sayings" document like Q, and was probably compiled for a similar purpose. It may be said, of course, that in the end we shall have to abandon the precise form in which Weiss, Easton, Streeter, Taylor, and others have reconstructed L, and fall back upon the hypothesis that this was no more than a somewhat loose, though fairly homogeneous, collection of material which Luke gathered from various sources (the main source probably being found in Caesarea?), wrote down for himself, or rewrote (if already in stereotyped oral or written form), constantly used in composing Proto-Luke (if such a document existed), and retained in his full and final draft of the gospel that bears his name. But this is saying no more than that if L was not a document it was the next thing to one; all it lacked was a compiler to write down the material a little in advance of Luke! For my part, as I have said, I believe that L was probably nothing more than the contents of Luke's notebook.

At any rate, the close student of the gospels must reckon with the possibility of such a document—or fairly homogeneous body of traditions; he will readily grant, after going over the text as carefully as we have suggested, that the area within which it is to be sought is a strictly delimited one (viz., Luke's "peculiar" material), and that its existence is no merely subjective theory, sprung from idle fancy or the love of multiplying sources; and he will be the first to admit the unusual difficulty attending its recovery—we have no parallels in another gospel by which to check and control its precise extent and original form. In both these respects it resembles Luke's other sources, in the book of Acts, viz., the so-called Jerusalem and Antiochene material in the first half, and the "we-sections" in the second.

(7) The same, more or less, is to be said of Streeter's hypothesis of the existence of a fourth document, which he labels "M" from its presence amid the peculiar matter of Matthew (*The Four Gospels*, ch. 9). That is, we must reckon with the possibility. It is impossible to say whether or not its separate existence can be established—its vocabulary is so indistinguishable from that of the gospel as a whole. Canon Streeter did not, so far as I know, make any attempt to reconstruct the document. It may turn out that M is no more than an algebraic symbol for the peculiar flavor and tendency, or interests, of the author of Matthew, who, like Luke, was not limited to the two main documents now generally recog-

nized but made use of everything that came to his hands, suited his purpose, and satisfied his tests of authenticity. These "tests," of course, varied, as between the two authors concerned, Luke and the author of "Matthew." On the other hand, A. M. Perry's demonstration of a structural order in M points to a document, as in Matt. 5:17–48, 6:1–18, 7:6 (?). (The central section of Q, as also of Mark, was on discipleship; that of M was on the new interpretation of the Mosaic Law.) It is, of course, possible that M is a later form of Q, edited and arranged by Matthew, or by the school of Christian scribes or teachers which he represents, for catechetical purposes, i.e., memorization, and was made the basis of the discourse material in Matthew's enlargement of Mark to form the five "books" of this pre-eminently ecclesiastical gospel. (See p. 143.)

The student will now have, by the process of isolation and segregation described above, a clearly defined and objective grouping of the basic materials of which the gospels are made, the data upon which the various theories of gospel sources and origins rest and which they are designed to explain. Of course, the student may go no further than step one, or two, or three; but even so the work we have suggested is worth doing, for it will familiarize him with the details of agreement and divergence in the synoptics as nothing else can. But it must also be stated, as strongly as possible, that this objective isolation of the various strands of basic material in the gospels is the real basis of any sound synoptic theory—this, and not the easy impressionistic guesswork that too often follows a casual reading of the first three gospels.

(8) Finally, it will be asked, What is left?—after the more or less mechanical isolation of Q, the somewhat hypothetical identification of L, and the still more hypothetical isolation of M? The answer is clear: We have the editorial additions, revisions, and introductions to their source material, the transitions or sutures made by Matthew and Luke in connecting up their paragraphs and working them into a well-knit whole; and the small residuum of possibly oral or "floating" written traditions which they have derived from the "eyewitnesses and ministers of the word" to whom, in the last analysis, all our evangelic material is to be referred. As a final step, we should transfer all this underlining to a copy of Nestle or Westcott-Hort or Souter (preferably in a wide-margin edition with room for notes) in consecutive form, so that we may see how the writers of the gospels used their material as they went along. So important is all this more or less mechanical labor that one may even hazard the apparently uncharitable judgment that

until a student has gone through with it his opinions on fine literary questions in the gospels are not likely to be of much value. The good "Chart of Synoptic Relationships" prepared by Allan Barr (Edinburgh, 1938) is a very useful guide, but not a substitute for the detailed examination described above.

The resulting conception is not that of two, three, or four sources only, but of many, combining in the course of time into two, three, four, or more, and ultimately going back, for the most part, to the original "eyewitnesses," and handed down by the many "ministers of the word" during the first two or three Christian generations. Eventually they grew into the great blocks of tradition which were worked into the later Synoptic Gospels—and into such parts of the Fourth Gospel as may be referred back to earlier historical sources. Instead of a Two- or a Four-Document Hypothesis, then, what is really required is one that may be called a Multiple Source Theory. The basic documents are more than four in number—how many we cannot say with certainty, though the main sources of Matthew and Luke are in each case at least three. If the gospels or their sources had been the work of only one or two men, or even of four, we should doubtless have far more consistency of narrative, far greater unity of impression; but we should miss "the many-splendored thing," the variety and vitality, the freshness and charm of this manifold human testimony to the great deeds and events, the sayings and teachings which they record. Once more, the gospels are "church books"; they enshrine a collective tradition, not simply the "recollections" of two, three, four—or a dozen —individuals. They are a social possession and inheritance, and their testimony has the broad foundation of a multitude of witnesses, chiefly the teachers and preachers of the early churches in Palestine and elsewhere, headed by the original apostles who were the first "eyewitnesses and ministers of the word" at the very beginning of the Christian movement.

A MULTIPLE SOURCE THEORY OF GOSPEL ORIGINS

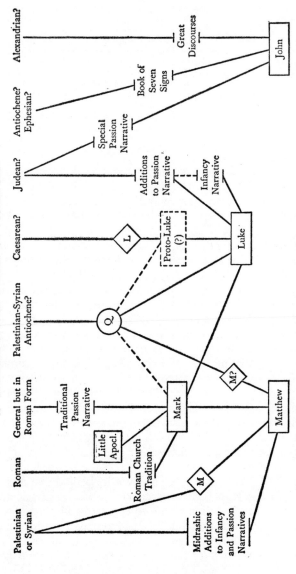

In addition to the main sources noted above, there were also no doubt many oral traditions still in circulation in the period during which the gospels were written—and even later, as the words of Papias (in Eusebius' *Church History*, III. 39, 4) suggest. Some of these undoubtedly existed in "blocks" or small collections, and in fairly fixed form.

CHAPTER V

The Gospel Before the Gospels

n an earlier chapter the attempt was made to outline the motives that led to the writing of the gospels. Both the delay in their appearance and the form taken when they finally appeared are to be explained by the conditions, external and internal, of the early Christian movement. Now, it must not be supposed that these conditions, or motives, came into existence all at once at a particular time and universally throughout the church. Some of the motives—e.g., the apocalyptic—were in operation a long time before the gospels were written. If this is so, then it follows without doubt that the tendencies or interests which determined the selection and affected the formulation of the material in the gospels affected also in some degree the selection and formulation of the tradition in its earlier oral form and in the earliest stages of writing, i.e., the compilation of the documents upon which the gospels are based. This is one of the major presuppositions of *Formgeschichte*, and with it no historical student will be inclined to quarrel. The materials themselves bear only too patently the marks of purposeful selection and formulation. Obviously, many other things Jesus both said and did "which are not written . . . but these are written that you may believe" (John 20:30 f.).

In other words, we can project backwards, behind the gospels, what we see in the gospels themselves, viz., a process of selection, revision, and reinterpretation. The whole Bible illustrates what Julius Bewer called the principle of "progressive interpretation"; the careful comparison of the gospels enables us to see the principle at work upon the data of the early evangelic tradition. A good example is the request for a sign from heaven (Mark 8:11–13, and parallels). In Mark the request is flatly refused: "No sign shall be given to this generation." But in Luke 11:29 and in Matt. 12:39,

16:4, therefore probably in Q, the clause is added, "except the sign of Jonah," the great preacher of repentance to the Ninevites: see Luke 11:30–32, Matt. 12:41, 42. And in Matt. 12:40 is inserted still another interpretation, as a third step in exegesis: the death and resurrection of the Son of Man will be like Jonah's descent into the whale and his later release—a favorite story in the early church, as the catacomb paintings show. Another example is the "progressive interpretation" of the "desolating sacrilege"—the Abomination of Desolation—in Mark 13:14 and parallels. In the original Little Apocalypse underlying the Apocalyptic Discourse in Mark 13, it presumably referred to Caligula's proposal to erect his own statue in the temple at Jerusalem, an early Christian-Jewish interpretation of the oracle in Dan. 9:27, 12:11 (LXX, Theodotion), where it originally referred to Antiochus IV's offering of a pagan sacrifice—an unclean animal, a pig—upon the altar of the Jerusalem temple to Zeus Ouranios, as Baal Shamayim. But in Luke 21:20 the interpretation is the siege of Jerusalem in A.D. 68–70, and in Matt. 24:15 it is Antichrist standing in the temple court at the end of the world. Each identification represents a different stage in the interpretation of the obscure oracle. Form criticism means, among other things, the projection of this principle backwards to the period between the original utterance and the earliest gospel sources. The same principle applies also to the narrative material in the gospels. The motives and methods which led to the amplification, revision, and reinterpretation of Mark's narratives by Matthew and Luke were probably already operative in the period of the oral tradition before Mark. The same is true of the narratives in John, which presumably have undergone a longer process of reinterpretation, whose earlier stages are now unknown and can be reconstructed only by hypothesis.

It ought to be clear by now (1) that form criticism is not a new and difficult kind of research, intended as a substitute for source analysis, synoptic study, textual criticism, or historical reconstruction, but only another branch of literary criticism, on a par with textual criticism, literary analysis, the study of style, vocabulary, sources, genres, composition, arrangement, and the like. In fact the study of any ancient book usually involves several steps in literary criticism; and wherever tradition is presupposed, there "form criticism" of some sort is required. It ought also to be obvious (2) that the various "forms" or categories of tradition described by the form critics, e.g., paradigm, apothegm, or pronouncement story, miracle story, parable, gnomic saying, "I-saying," biblical interpretation, controversy, legend, "myth," passion story, and so on, *all* have their *Sitz im Leben,* their true function and reason for existence, within the church itself. If the books of the New Testament, especially the gospels, were the church's books from the very beginning, and if the gospel sources were compilations made by the church for its own use, then certainly the old tradition which underlay these sources was church tradition —the peculiar possession of the early Christian group—from the outset and all along the way.

The other major assumption of form history, the one, in fact, which gives the school its name, is not quite so self-evident. It is assumed that general laws prevail in the formation and development of tradition, and that it is possible by classifying the types of material thus handed down to arrange them more or less in evolutionary sequence. Thus in the gospels short, pithy sayings of Jesus came before the long and involved allegories, exhortations, or expositions of the Law. But would anyone assign special priority to such a commonplace and perhaps proverbial saying as "The measure you give will be the measure you get" (Matt. 7:2) or attribute chronological precedence to "He who has ears to hear, let him hear" (Mark 4:9, etc.) in contrast to the parable of the soils, the reply to the charge of collusion with Beelzebul, or the exposition of the laws governing oaths, adultery, or nonresistance? There is undoubtedly some truth in the principle, and it is capable of a general application; but it is not nearly so certain that we can apply it in every case. Nor is it a sure inference from this general principle that the more thoroughly elaborated or extended units in the tradition must necessarily, one and all, have been developed out of far briefer sayings or anecdotes. Nothing seems more unlikely than that the original nuclei of the gospel tradition were brief, proverbial, sententious sayings of the kind we read in Pirqe Aboth, for example, or in the Wisdom literature. After all, Jesus was a prophet, not a "wise man" or scribe; and extended discourse rather than epigram or proverb was characteristic of the Hebrew prophet. Furthermore, the gospels are full of parables, many of them unique, most of them characteristic, which undeniably for the most part go back to Jesus himself; the contrast afforded by those few which the tradition itself provided (the amplified form of the parable of the wicked husbandmen in Mark 12:1–11, for example, or the classic description of the Last Judgment in Matt. 25:31–46, or the parable of the tares in Matt. 13:24–30) is clear and definite, and in some cases painfully so. The parables are obviously as authentic as anything we have in the gospels—the sayings are no whit "earlier" or more authentic. Nevertheless,

Formgeschichte has done this great service at least, it has made it evident that the gospel tradition is ultimately resolvable into separate units of narrative, discourse, saying, parable, interpretation of scripture, controversy—each of which had its characteristic use in primitive Christian preaching, teaching, and worship.

Valuable as this principle of analysis is, then, it is difficult to follow it all the way, i.e., to a hypothetical reconstruction of the "evolution" of the tradition. But we need not rest here with the conclusion that nothing further can be done in tracing back the development of the gospels. For, instead of breaking up the gospels at once into their primary oral components, and then attempting to reconstruct out of them the development of the tradition, a better method is surely to work backward from the finished gospels to their underlying written sources, and then on this basis to construct a hypothesis of the oral traditions that preceded them. It is much the same method that archaeologists follow. If an ancient town wall or house is to be removed in the course of excavation, the structure is first laid bare, exactly measured and recorded, so accurately in fact that the wall may be removed ten thousand miles and re-erected in a museum. Only after these careful studies of the actual structure have been made is the wall razed, the ground cleared, and the research carried on to the preceding historical stage. The process thus goes slowly backward, inch by inch, from stage VII to stage VI, from VI to V, and so on, down possibly to Sub-I or Sub-II. Everyone recognizes that it would be fatal to begin by removing the entire site at once, and then attempt to reconstruct "genetically" the whole process of development. In the study of the evangelic tradition the only proper mehod is to begin by reconstructing as far as possible the immediate sources out of which the gospels are built. This also is a kind of form history, though it is not the method which has been most prominent in works of that school, nor is it in any sense peculiar to any one school. Rather, the method grows out of the efforts at source analysis of the gospels which have been characteristic of modern gospel study generally. Indeed, it was suggested as long ago as 1910 in a little book entitled *The Growth of the Gospels*, by Sir Flinders Petrie, representing a brief and—it must be confessed—not altogether fruitful excursion of that veteran Egyptologist into the field of New Testament criticism. In it he outlined, on the basis of the then-common analysis of the gospels into "Double Tradition" and "Triple Tradition" (roughly equivalent to the elements derived from Q and Mark respectively), a method of study of "blocks" of tradition, the little groups and

sequences of narratives, sayings, or parables, embedded en bloc
in the gospels.

These "blocks" are apparent enough in Q and L, in the Passion
Narrative of Mark, in Luke's Infancy Narrative, and elsewhere—
certainly in the long consecutive sections taken over from Mark
by Luke, and even by Matthew. But even within Q and L, and
certainly within Mark, there are structural blocks which can only
represent sequences or groupings that obtained in the oral tradition prior to the writing down of these sources, and which no
doubt greatly assisted their writers in the arrangement of material.
It is astonishing how "structural" is the arrangement of these
sources; far from being heterogeneous collections of material, Q
and L show a real grouping of their contents—not an exhaustive
grouping, and not motivated by what can justly be called either a
historical or an artistic principle, but none the less a real subject
grouping, apparent here and there in the documents. This subject
grouping is most fully developed, of course, in the later Gospels
of Matthew and John; but it is very evident also in Mark, and is
to be seen even in Q and L (and also, consequently, in Luke). Of
course, the arrangement of L may be due, at least in part, to that
of Q, with which it is associated (whatever we make of the Proto-
Luke theory; see p. 128).

Now, it may naturally be suspected that the student has himself
supplied the grouping; and reads-in his own conception of what
ought to be the order of the sources. In reply it can only be said
that the right method is to follow the rules as strictly as possible
in reconstructing their form and order (see ch. IV), and then,
only then, to examine them for the evidence they themselves af-
ford of their inner structure. For example, one might think with
Streeter that Q *ought* to have contained an account of Jesus'
baptism, as an appropriate beginning of that document. But the
evidence, except for two minor contacts between Matthew and
Luke (the verb for the rending of the heavens and the obvious
epi in place of Mark's *eis* in v. 10), is all in favor of the Marcan
original—to which Easton assigned the narrative. And the first
thing to do is to examine the literary data, not the historical probabilities. As the medieval logicians insisted, "Hypotheses are not
to be multiplied beyond what is necessary."

The problem of the source of the Baptismal Narrative is one of
the most delicate in the gospels, and the evidence is so fine that
it must be weighed in the apothecary's balances. (a) Antecedently,
one would expect an account of Jesus' baptism and call to precede
the Temptation Narrative in Q—where the assumption is uni-

formly made that he thinks of himself as the Son of God. More-over, (b) something of the sort is required to make sense of the opening sections of Luke—or Proto-Luke, for those who accept that theory. Apart from the Genealogy, whose curious conclusion (Luke 3:38) seems to imply Jesus' sonship as asserted in 3:22, the opening verse of Luke 4 requires not only a visit of Jesus to the Jordan, where John has been preaching and baptizing, but also the coming of the Spirit, recounted in the Baptismal Narrative. The same is true of 4:14. Furthermore, (c) as a Jewish writing, con-taining the words of "a prophet mighty in word and deed," Q (or L, for that matter) could not dispense with an account of Jesus' Call. The same would be true a fortiori of a record of the words and deeds of the Messiah.

On the other hand, if a choice must be made between Luke and Mark as to originality of narrative, Mark's account (1:10, 11) is greatly to be preferred. It is straightforward, simple, and clear. Luke's account is obviously rewritten—it is loaded with participles and infinitives (compare the style of 3:1, 2). Moreover, Mark's eiden, retained by Matthew, looks more original than Luke's eidei; so that if the narrative stood in Q, Mark's wording is probably closer to the original than Luke's! In other words, if Q underlies Luke 3:21 f., it cannot be recovered from the Lucan narrative as it stands—which would be a phenomenon almost unique in this gospel. It may be so. And if so, i.e., if Luke's combination of the Marcan narrative (which was, accordingly, based on Q) with his own earlier (Q plus L) narrative has so greatly disturbed the orig-inal reading, we are not very likely to recover it now from Luke. What stood originally at this point in Luke (or in Proto-Luke) we can only guess: perhaps some account of Jesus' participation in John's activity, together with the narrative of his Call—recounted possibly, as some scholars think, in the words of the old Western variant based on the Psalm (2:7), "This day have I begotten thee." That is, omitting the participle derived from Mark, bap-tisthentos (which is incidental and circumstantial in the Lucan narrative, in any event; cf. Mark and Matthew), it read somewhat as follows: "It came to pass, while all the people were being bap-tized, that Jesus was praying; and the heavens were opened, and the Holy Spirit descended upon him, and a voice came from heaven, Thou art my Son; this day have I begotten thee." Thus no account was given (in Proto-Luke, Q, or L) of Jesus' baptism, any more than of John's own at the beginning of his ministry. The Baptismal Narrative was, accordingly, derived from Mark, with only a bare possibility that Mark drew it from Q. It is perhaps worthy of note that there is no account of Jesus' baptism in the Fourth Gospel, though it is clearly implied (1:32).

In the following reconstruction of Q and L, I have followed Luke not only in order but also in wording (where questions of wording arise to require a choice). It is generally recognized that the Lucan order of Q is preferable to that of Matthew, since Luke is not possessed with the systematizing enthusiasm of Matthew. It is not so generally recognized that Luke's wording is to be preferred—the usual formula runs, "Prefer Luke for the order of Q, prefer Matthew for its wording." But the conviction has steadily grown stronger, as we have studied the use which Matthew and Luke made of Mark, that Luke as a rule (to which there are, of course, certain obvious exceptions) exercises far greater care in following the exact wording of his source in relating *the words of our Lord.* This is not true of their settings, which he often enough rewrites. But the sayings of Jesus he alters far less, to say the least, than he does the narrative. (Q and L, of course, are made up almost exclusively of sayings and parables.) Matthew, on the other hand, does not scruple to introduce later exegesis into the very formulation of Jesus' words. I prefer, therefore, to follow Luke's wording of Q wherever possible. As for L, it seems to me not unlikely that Luke has dealt as faithfully with the order and wording of this material as he has with Mark and Q—certainly in transcribing the words of Jesus. It is therefore not mere lack of an additional "control" or "check" upon L (since Luke alone makes use of this source) that leads us to have confidence in its present order. Where Matthew goes out of his way to regroup his material by subject, Luke takes special pains to retain it as it stands and to provide suitable topographical or other setting for the separate units. This was the more possible in that Mark and Q, and even L, have a grouping of material that is now and then strikingly similar; have even common subject headings, one might almost say: and this is a phenomenon no one could possibly have anticipated in advance of the actual reconstruction of the two latter documents. It would seem then that here also we have an indication of the state of the material prior to the writing down of the sources. The subject groupings, as well as the contents of the "blocks," suggest a common use made of the material by the church's teachers and evangelists in the first generation. These were groupings that Mark was no doubt familiar with long before he put pen to paper—especially if he had known and used, and therefore remembered at least in a general way, the material contained in Q. And I should not be greatly surprised if the grouping antedated Q, as part of the "pedagogy" of the early church, to which Professor Easton, Archbishop Carrington, and others have drawn attention. It is significant that some groups—the Baptist's preaching, the controversy with the scribes over Jesus' works of healing, the admonitions to the disciples, the warnings drawn from the impending fate of Jerusalem, for example—reappear in L as well as in Q and Mark. Nothing should surprise us less than that these early documents overlapped here and there. One can almost hear the "teachers" of the early church at their task, as they turn over these brief but infinitely precious pages of their "manuals" for the instruction of converts!

The Contents and Structure of Q

The ministry and message of John the Baptizer.

Luke 3: [2b], 3a, 7b–9 John's preaching of repentance (cf. Matt. 3:1–10).

3:16, 17 John's prediction of the coming Judge (cf. Matt. 3:11, 12).

The ordeal of the Messiah.

4:1b–12 The Temptation (cf. Matt. 4:1–11).

Jesus' public teaching.

6:20–49 The Sermon on the Plain (or Mountain; cf. Matt. 5:3–12, 39–48; 7:12, 1–5, 16–27; 10:24, 25; 12:33–35; 15:14).

The response to Jesus' preaching.

7:2, 6b–10 The centurion's faith (cf. Matt. 8:5–13).

7:18b, 19, 22–28, 31–35 John's emissaries; Jesus' words about John (cf. Matt. 11:2–6, 7–19).

9:57b–60, 61, 62 Various followers (cf. Matt. 8:19–22).

The mission of the Twelve.

10:2–16 The mission of the disciples (cf. Matt. 9:37, 38; 10:7–16, 40; 11:21–23).

[10:17b–20 The return of the Twelve.]

10:21b–24 The rejoicing of Jesus (cf. Matt. 11:25–27; 13:16, 17).

Jesus' teaching about prayer.

11:2–4 The Lord's Prayer (cf. Matt. 6:9–13).

[11:5–8 The parable of the friend at midnight.]

11:9–13 Constancy in prayer (cf. Matt. 7:7–11).

The controversy with the scribes and Pharisees.

11:14–23 The charge of collusion with Beelzebul (cf. Matt. 12:22–30).

11:24–26 The story of the unclean spirit (cf. Matt. 12:43–45).

11:29b–32 The warning contained in the "sign of Jonah" (cf. Matt. 12:38–42).

11:33–36 Jesus' sayings about light (cf. Matt. 5:15; 6:22, 23).

11:39b, 42, 43, [44], 46–52 The controversy with the scribes and Pharisees (cf. Matt. 23:4–36).

Jesus' teaching about discipleship: the duties of disciples when
persecuted.

12:2–12 The testimony of disciples among adversaries (cf. Matt.
10:26–33; 12:32; 10:19, 20).

12:22–31 On freedom from care (cf. Matt. 6:25–33).

12:33b, 34 On treasure (cf. Matt. 6:19–21).

12:39, 40, 42–46 Three parables on watchfulness (cf. Matt.
24:43–51a).

12:49–53 Messianic divisions (cf. Matt. 10:34–36).

[12:54–56 Signs of the times (cf. Matt. 16:2, 3).]

12:57–59 The duty of speedy reconciliation (cf. Matt. 5:25, 26).

13:18–21 The parables of the mustard seed and the leaven: the
steady growth of the Kingdom despite opposition (cf. Matt.
13:31–33).

13:24–29 The narrow way (cf. Matt. 7:13, 14; 7:22, 23; 8:11, 12).

13:34, 35 The fate of Jerusalem (cf. Matt. 23:37–39).

14:11 = 18:14 On self-exaltation (cf. Matt. 18:4; 23:12).

14:16–23 The parable of the great supper (cf. Matt. 22:1–10).

14:26, 27 On hating one's next of kin, and on bearing the cross
(cf. Matt. 10:37, 38).

14:34, 35 The saying on salt (cf. Matt. 5:13).

15:4–7 The parable of the lost sheep (cf. Matt. 18:12–14).

[15:8–10 The parable of the lost coin.]

16:13 On serving two masters (cf. Matt. 6:24).

Sayings about the Law.

[16:16–18 The Law and the Prophets until John; on divorce
(cf. Matt. 11:12, 13; 5:18, 32).]

17:1, 2 On offenses (cf. Matt. 18:6, 7).

17:3, 4 On forgiveness (cf. Matt. 18:15, 21, 22).

17:6 On faith (cf. Matt. 17:20b).

The coming Parousia.

17:23, 24, 26–30, 34, 35, 37b The Parousia (cf. Matt. 24:26–28,
37–39; 10:39; 24:40 f., 28).

19:12, 13, 15b–26 The parable of the entrusted talents (cf. Matt.
25:14–30).

[22:28–30 The apostles' thrones (cf. Matt. 19:28).]

Uncertain passages are in square brackets. See the Introduction
to *Matthew*, in Harper's Annotated Bible Series. The total of
verses and parts of verses is *ca.* 242, counting 14:11 = 18:14 but
once.

It is to be observed that the document as a whole, including the
main, central section of Q, has to do with *discipleship*, i.e., the
duties and responsibilities of Jesus' disciples. This is exactly what
we should expect it to contain, if it was the kind of document and
was compiled for the purpose that we assume. It was a guide to

catechists, a manual for the newly converted, a statement of the Christian way of life—a handbook of "the Way"! It was not, as used to be held, a tract for missionary use; instead, its purpose was mainly catechetical.

Following the Sermon, which was an illustration of Jesus' general teaching, and the centurion's faith, an example of his healing activity, and the account of John's emissaries, describing or implying the effects of Jesus' ministry of teaching and healing and stating the messianic question to which it inevitably gave rise, we find the series of sections on discipleship: various followers and would-be followers, the mission of the Twelve, prayer, the duty of Jesus' disciples in the midst of controversy and persecution. The presence in it of the account of Jesus' controversy with the scribes and Pharisees is not surprising: for this was still a live issue and had a real bearing upon the conduct of the disciples in a similar situation. "If they have called the master of the house Beelzebul, how much more will they malign those of his household!" (Matt. 10:25).

The Contents of L

15:11–32	The story of the prodigal son.
16:1–12	The parable of the clever steward.
16:19–31	The story of the rich man and Lazarus.
17:7–10	Slaves do not claim either thanks or wages.
17:12–19	Jesus heals ten lepers, and only one thanks him.
17:20 f.	The Kingdom of God comes without observation.
18:1–8	The parable of the widow pleading for justice.
18:9–14	The story of the Pharisee and the tax collector.
19:2–10	Zacchaeus welcomes Jesus.
19:40	"If these kept silence, the stones would cry out."
19:42–44	Jesus foretells the destruction of Jerusalem.
22:31 f.	Jesus prays for Simon.
[22:35–38	The two swords.]
23:27–31	"Daughters of Jerusalem, weep not for me."

Uncertain passages are in square brackets. (See the Introduction to *Luke*, in Harper's Annotated Bible Series.) The total of verses and parts of verses is *ca.* 264. (If the material peculiar to Luke's Passion and Resurrection Narratives is added, the total must be increased by 64, making 328. But it is unlikely L included these later sections.) Q, as we have noted, totals 242 verses and parts of verses. The two sources were therefore comparable not only in subject matter but also in length.

It is clear that Q and L, each of which differs noticeably from the Gospel of Mark, have different outlooks and, in fact, distinct theologies. The apocalyptic-eschatological element, which dominates almost the whole presentation in Mark and Matthew, and is conspicuous enough even in Q, is almost absent from L. The picture we derive from L is not that of the transcendent "Son of Man" appearing upon earth as his own forerunner, so to speak, announcing his own impending advent (or "return") in terms of even stronger certainty than John the Baptist had used, and gathering together a group who were to be his faithful followers and witnesses until he himself returned in glory. Instead, L presents us with a prophet who is almost something of a rabbi, or teacher, a first-century Jewish prophet, with a band of disciples who followed him about, including even several women; with friends here and there throughout the country, in whose homes he is more than once a guest (rather than "the Son of Man who hath not where to lay his head," Matt. 8:20 = Luke 9:58, Q); who travels about healing the sick and teaching a gospel of pure and simple faith in God, having but slight relation to the future as conceived by the apocalyptists; and who, as Luke went on to relate, was put to death on a trumped-up charge, which at this distance in time is somewhat hard to make out but which seems to have involved political activity of some sort—or the threat of it. If we had only L to guide us, and lacked Q and Mark, it may be doubted if anyone would ever have supposed that Jesus was an apocalyptist, or thought the end of the age immediately at hand (the "prophetic," nonapocalyptic eschatology of L centers in the impending fall of Jerusalem), or claimed to be either the Jewish Messiah or the Son of Man; or that he was condemned by the Jewish leaders or the Roman procurator on some such charge. Its fidelity to early Palestinian tradition is obvious. Needless to say, there is not the slightest trace of Pauline influence upon it. Nor is there any trace of the institutionalism so apparent in the much later Gospel of Matthew. Thus neither later Palestinian nor contemporary gentile (or "Hellenist") ecclesiastical developments have left any mark upon L. Like Q, it is a thoroughly "primitive" document; in some respects it would seem to be even more primitive.

Another indication of early date is the interest in women. Neither the rabbinic-minded author of Matthew nor the Roman Mark would have understood such an interest. Luke, however, found it in his source—i.e., in this particular source, L—and retained it. In view of the scandals to which the presence of female attendants upon prophets and religious founders gave rise in the Hellenistic world, and considering the obviously apologetic purpose of Luke, it is the more remarkable that he retains this feature —one which was accordingly doubtless authentic, and was also perfectly normal and required no explanation in a Jewish environment at the time of Jesus. There was considerable difference between the charity and hospitality of the Jewish housewife, whether at home in the Galilean village or on the community-pilgrimage to the Passover, and the dangerous religious devotion of the Hellenistic votary and prophetess—as the church of the second century learned to its cost. The material in L carries with it the atmosphere of a different world from that of the empire generally with its mélange of religions; it is the atmosphere of strict and thoroughly moral Jewish piety.

CHAPTER VI

The Order of the Gospels

The chronological order of the writing of the gospels, their sequence in composition, is not necessarily that in which they are now found in the New Testament. In fact, other arrangements are apparent in some of the ancient lists of New Testament books and in some of the ancient manuscripts. Professor Edgar J. Goodspeed has printed several of these at the end of his excellent little book, *The Formation of the New Testament* (1926; see pp. 189 f., 191). The order of Codex Bezae is Matthew, John, Luke, Mark. Different orders have been followed not only in manuscripts and canonical lists, at different times, but also by artists and theologians. For example, the order of the reliefs on the hanging cross above the altar at Trinity Church in Boston appears to be based on an artistic or theological evaluation of the gospels, with John at the top, Matthew at the base, Luke at the left, Mark at the right.

The present New Testament order seems to be the one suggested by the theory of Augustine, viz., that Matthew was the earliest gospel, written in Hebrew and then translated into Greek, and that Mark was only a Greek abridgement of Matthew. Augustine in fact described Mark as "the follower who trudged in Matthew's footsteps and abridged his work" (*tamquam pedisequus et breviator eius videtur*; see his work *On the Agreement of the Evangelists*, I. 2. 4). This accounts for Matthew and Mark coming first in our New Testament. That John was the latest and last, according to the Muratorian Fragment and several other ancient traditions, is well known. This leaves only one place for Luke, i.e., third, between Mark and John. But Augustine's theory was only a literary man's guess, based upon casual study of the Latin translations, not upon any ancient tradition. In fact it contradicts the Greek tradition, already cited, from Papias to Irenaeus (see p. 31), according to which Mark was dependent upon Peter, not Matthew, and was written without reference to any earlier gospel or gospels. Eusebius, in his *Church History* (III. 39. 16), cited another statement from Papias, comparable to the one on the origin of Mark: "Matthew compiled the *logia* in the Hebrew dialect, and each person interpreted (= translated?) them as best he could." This statement is often understood today to mean that Matthew wrote the gospel in Hebrew (or Aramaic) or that he compiled the sayings of Jesus (i.e., Q); some nineteenth-century scholars even went the length of referring to this common source of Matthew and Luke as "the Logia," or "L," or used the Greek capital letter *lambda* as the symbol. But it is pure carelessness to interpret *logia* as "words" or "sayings." For two thousand years the ancient Greek language used *logia* as a term for oracles, divine utterances or messages, or prophecies. *Logia* and *logoi* were two entirely different words; it was only later on, in early Christian writings, when Jesus' sayings were occasionally referred to as the "oracles of the Lord," that the term *logia* was applied to them. That Papias did not confuse *logia* with sayings is clear from the next to preceding section in Eusebius (§ 14), where the *logia kuriaka*, the subject of Papias' exegesis (§ 1), are described as the oracles of the Lord, precisely as in the Old Testament prophets. On the whole, it seems probable that Papias meant just what he said; the Hebrew *logia* were the Old Testament prophecies of the Coming One, a collection of the kind embedded in the Gospel of Matthew. Papias, at least, would not have used the term *logia* in referring to the finished Gospel of Matthew or to any other gospel. (See p. 144.)

Unfortunately, many of the early "traditions" of gospel origins were derived, as Kirsopp Lake once observed, not so much from apostolic tradition as from postapostolic guesses. Hence the survival of traditions which do *not* accord with the views which were generally accepted later on and, especially, with Augustine's hypothesis, deserve far more consideration than they have usually received. For example, the order presupposed by the pre-Irenaean identification of the gospels with the four beasts in Rev. 4:7 is important, not only because it identified the gospels with these particular beasts—why in the world should Mark be a lion, Luke an ox?—but because it preserved what was then still known to be the order of composition of the gospels. Irenaeus' exposition in his work *Against Heresies* (III. 11. 8) is forced, the figures not naturally suggesting the significance attributed to them: The lion (Mark) suggesting regal power, the ox (Luke) the sacrificial and sacerdotal office of Christ, the man (Matthew) the human nature of Christ, the flying eagle (John) the Spirit flying in the church and manifesting grace. If the order had been another, Irenaeus could have found good reasons for the identifications: but this was the order as it came to him in the traditional identification of the apocalyptic beasts with the four evangelists. The order here is noteworthy in that it does not correspond with the order which Irenaeus cites elsewhere (e.g., III. 1).

Of course this is part of the ancient mythology underlying the Apocalypse of John, of which Archbishop Carrington and others have written. Layard found at Nineveh a winged lion of alabaster. It was presumably one of the four astral gods which—or who— were also identified with the four cardinal points of the compass —a view reflected even in Irenaeus, where he insists (as against Valentinus' new *Gospel of Truth*) that there cannot possibly be any more gospels than the traditional four, as there are four winds, four main directions, and so on. According to ancient Assyrian lore, i.e., the astral theology which so greatly impressed the Western world in the Hellenistic and early imperial age (about which Franz Cumont and Martin Nilsson have written at length), Nergal was represented by a winged lion, Marduk by a winged bull, Nebo by a human being, Ninib by an eagle.

Revelation 4:7 modifies the description in Ezekiel 1:10—in the direction of Irenaeus' interpretation. But Irenaeus' only concern is with the perfect symbolism. Four, and no more, Plato's perfect number, is the number of the cardinal directions, as we have noted. He is not interested in the *order*, which comes in incidentally, and hence all the more convincingly. On the other hand, for the person who first made the identification of the four beasts in Revelation with the four gospels (or evangelists), the order was all that mattered, since the nature of the figures does not suggest—and is certainly not suggested by—any particular qualities in the gospels.

Or take the archaeological evidence from the Ravenna mosaics, which are old Roman, pre-Byzantine, pre-Justinian. In the tomb of Galla Placidia, outside the church of S. Vitale, the four evangelists are portrayed, and there is also a low ancient bookcase with sloping shelves on which the four gospels are lying, in the following order:

[MARCVS]	LVCAS
MATTEVS	IOANNES

"Mark, Luke, Matthew, John." (Marcus is in brackets, here, to show that the word has been added in the modern restoration of the inscription.) The mosaic dates from ca. A.D. 440, little more than a century after the Council of Nicaea, and some time before Augustine's literary conjecture became widely known and—supported by his theological prestige—widely accepted. It cannot be positively affirmed that a definite tradition underlies the order portrayed in the Ravenna mosaic, but neither can it be positively denied. And it is not at all unlikely that some artist or scholar of the early church, still living outside the growing circle of Augustine's influence, either preserved an old tradition, perhaps related to the one underlying Irenaeus' interpretation of Rev. 4:7, or else correctly guessed the true order of the gospels. It is to be noted that the same order is found in the medallion reliefs on the ceiling of the Sala della Presentazione in the Accademia at nearby Venice. Finally, the simplest explanation of the present order of the gospels is to assume that the original order (Mark, Luke, Matthew, John) was altered simply by shifting Matthew to first place, after it came to be thought that this gospel was the very first—following the Papian-Augustinian hypothesis of an original writing "in the Hebrew dialect."

But the theory that Matthew came first and was abridged by Mark is impossible for several reasons. One must study not only the relations between Matthew and Mark but also those between Mark and Luke—and between Matthew and Luke. Mark's relation to Luke is as close as its relation to Matthew; but it is inconceivable that an author should abridge two works and show equal dependence upon both. The greater probability is that the two other Synoptic Gospels used Mark, quite independently of each other. A glance at the chart on p. 39 will make this relation clear. The area a + d + f is that of the overlapping of Matthew and Luke. Much of it belongs also to Mark; the remainder, ex hypothesi, to Q. Mark we still possess, Q we do not; but it is probable that the Matthean-Lucan agreements in the use of Q are just as close as in the use of Mark. That is, their agreements in Marcan contexts, where we can compare our existing Mark, suggest the same kind of agreement in their use of Q. Moreover, just as there are passages of Mark (g) used by Luke but not by Matthew, and also passages of Mark (h) used by Matthew but not by Luke, so there probably are passages of Q used by one but not the other (b in Luke, c in Matthew). Further, it is possible that just as there is in Mark a small amount of material (i) not used by either Luke or Matthew, so there may have been some material in Q not used by either Luke or Matthew (= e, on our chart). Finally, it is possible, in fact probable (in view of the doublets in both Luke and Matthew) that Mark and Q overlapped, either as a result of their use of identical traditions or of Q's use of Mark or of Mark's use of Q (= d, on the chart). In fact, a close study of this material leads one to assume that here Mark is at least "echoing" the Q collection, whether as a document or—what amounts to the same thing—a body of fixed or stereotyped oral teaching.

But could not Luke have used Matthew, or Matthew have used Luke? And would not such a hypothesis be far simpler than the one just outlined? In answer to the first question, (a) it is far from probable that Luke can have removed—or could have wished to remove—the sayings of Jesus and other discourse material from their close-fitting arrangement in subject groupings as they are found in Matthew, and then have rearranged them in the more historical or anecdotal sequence which he follows, in some cases with a totally different tone and implication. Further, (b) it is not probable that Matthew would fill up the long lacuna in Luke (9:51–18:14), where he completely dismisses Mark, with discourse material (Q and L) which Luke has used, and fit it into his revision of the Marcan scheme with so little modification and with such apparent verisimilitude. The gospels are works of art—not a mere scissors-and-paste rearrangement of loose materials, like a child's scrapbook. These subtle interrelations do not lie on the surface, and cannot all be made out in a six months' study of the Greek text: they begin to stand out only after twenty or thirty years of close study, i.e., of microscopic analysis of the style and diction, the thought and feeling of the evangelists.

In brief, *Luke cannot have used Matthew* for the following reasons: (1) How could he separate the sayings of Jesus from their Matthean complex and locate them in a historical setting or background with such complete verisimilitude? (2) How could he escape every trace of Matthew's major doctrines, e.g., the reinterpretation of the Law and the permanent validity of the Law? Luke 16:17 is a problem, not a support: see v. 16. (3) How could he have ignored the great features in Matthew's picture of Christ, e.g., his compassion (8:17) or his gentleness (12:18–21), which were traits which especially appealed to Luke?

And *Matthew cannot have used Luke* for the following reasons: (1) The sayings in Luke 9:51–18:14 are selected out and grouped by Matthew without taking along any L passages, which are distinguished by their own peculiar style and diction. (2) The L material has its own peculiar theology or at least a peculiar religious point of view (Jesus is a prophet), distinct from that of Q. It is also reflected in the first half of Acts, especially in the speeches of Peter. But Matthew does not betray a trace of contact with this point of view. There are other reasons, but these are outstanding and ought to be conclusive.

In either form the theory of dependence (of Matthew upon Luke or of Luke upon Matthew) faces insuperable difficulties when applied to the detailed text of the gospels or when examined in the light of their theology (especially Christology) or religious teaching. If these later gospels were thus mutually dependent, or dependent one upon the other, why was the use so slight and the influence of one upon the other so infinitesimal? Later on, of course, their manuscript texts exercised a mutual influence—especially the text of Matthew upon that of Luke (and also upon Mark and John) and similarly the influence of John upon some manuscripts of Luke; but this was long after the composition of the gospels. It is comparable to the slight mutual influence of the planets as they move in their courses about the sun—Matthew being, so to speak, the Jupiter of them all. The genealogies in Matthew and Luke, the Beatitudes, the Sermon on the Mount (or Plain), the parables and their interpretation, the Passion Narrative—how could one gospel fail to influence the other in such passages, if there was any dependence at all? It is far more probable that, except for the use of Mark by Luke and Matthew, but not by John, the gospels were entirely independent of one another. The most probable view is that each gospel was meant to be used as the gospel in the locality that gave it birth, Matthew in Antioch or the neighborhood, Mark in Rome, Luke in Achaia (?), John in Ephesus or Alexandria. The only exception is Luke, which, as the first part of Luke-Acts, was an apologia for Christianity, not a purely intraecclesiastical book. It is merely modern fancy that sees in them successive revisions, expansions, supplements, or corrections of some basic Urmarcus, Urlucas, or Urmatthaeus.

The theory of Aramaic originals of the gospels, to which considerable attention has been given during the past thirty years, overlooks the real purpose of the gospels as a group, their "place in life," and the purpose or use for which they were compiled. It is not a question merely of explaining philologically the Greek of the evangelists—i.e., of translating it into Aramaic and thus discovering some preferred meaning or hypothetical error made by the original "translator" of the gospel out of Aramaic into Greek;

what is basically involved is the question, What were the gospels, and what were they for? And this question is one to which only the Greek-speaking, early gentile Christian church can provide the answer.

As we have seen, much of the supposed evidence in support of the Aramaic theory is purely hypothetical, e.g., the meaning of the term *gilyōnim* in tractate *Yadaim* in the Mishnah and Tosephta; it is probably not "gospels" at all, but perhaps "margins of manuscripts" (i.e., what is written there, as in many Jewish commentaries on scripture), for the question is whether or not they are inspired, and thus make the hands "unclean" or in need of ceremonial cleansing after handling or reading; at best, the experts are divided upon the question of the meaning of the term. Even assuming that *gilyōn* meant *euaggelion*, the latter term, as a designation of individual gospel writings, is no earlier than the second century. (Irenaeus, in his treatise *Against Heresies*, III. 1, 10 f., still refers to "the gospel" not as a book but as the message of salvation preached by the apostles and later written down.) But even had Irenaeus referred to "gospels," this is far too late a date to support the Aramaic theory. So is the reference in Justin Martyr's *First Apology*, § 66, and that in II Clement 8:5; cf. Ignatius, *Philad.* 8:2, *Smyrnaeans* 7:2. Further, the Greek term *euaggelion* would scarcely be the word for an Aramaic gospel; on the face of it, the term designates something Greek—and what would the rabbis be doing with Greek gospels? The term *gilyōn* is found in the Old Testament, e.g., in Isa. 8:1, where it means a blank tablet, not yet inscribed. Its later use, in the Mishnah (*Yadaim* 3:4), Tosephta (*Yadaim* 2:13), and Talmud (*Menachoth* 30a, *Sabbath* 116a), is an obvious development of the idea— the blank spaces at the top and bottom of the columns in a scroll. In *Sabbath* 116a the meaning is unquestionably "the margins of a Pentateuch roll." (See Jacob Levy, *Wörterbuch über die Talmud und Midraschim*, 2d ed., 1924, Vol. I, p. 334. See also Gerhard Lisowsky, Commentary on *Yadaim* in the new Giessen *Mischna*, VI. 11, 1956, which does not so much as mention the theory that *gilyōn* means "gospel"!) The later term *awōn-gilyōn* (lit. *awēn-gilyōn* or *even-gilyōn: awōn* = evil, *even* = stone), based upon this older meaning but reflecting the controversies of a later time (Pal. *Sabbath* 16:15c, Tos. *Sabbath* 14; it is also found in Syriac) is entirely different, and is a "cacophemism" for *euaggelion* (= gospel; see Levy, p. 41). It is contrary to all probability to assume that this abusive term goes back to the first century. Just what any-one, scholar or layman, whether ancient or modern, can make of

Yadaim 3:4 on the theory that *gilyōn* means "gospel" is a little hard to understand: "The *gilyōn* in a scroll [i.e., of the sacred scriptures], both above and below, at the beginning and at the end, renders the hands unclean." It is quite obviously the blank spaces of a manuscript that are being considered, not "gospels"!

Furthermore, the Aramaic experts are not agreed among themselves as to what are examples of "mistranslation": Wellhausen's examples are rejected by Torrey, Torrey's by Burney, Burney's by Black. There is no agreed and acceptable Aramaic version of the gospels, and we doubt if one could be made. At the same time, the main thesis, viz., that the traditional sources of the gospels at one time circulated orally in Aramaic is far more probable, and what little evidence we possess points in this direction; the surviving "tags" in Mark (*talitha kumi, elōi*, and other words) are found in words of Jesus, at the heart of the old tradition, not in the narrative "frames" which would be found in finished gospels.

The final objection to the theory of Aramaic originals of the gospels is the difficulty—indeed, the impossibility—of finding any place for Aramaic gospels in the history of early Christianity (unless it be in the second and following centuries, as translations into Aramaic of gospels originally written in Greek). This is also the objection to other bizarre theories, advanced by those who have no concern for a total view of the rise of Christianity and the Christian church. Such theories were advanced when the Dead Sea Scrolls were first published; many persons, unfamiliar with the details of early Christian history, drew inferences which were quite impossible in view of the assured historical facts about primitive Christianity. Fresh discoveries often lead, at first, to rash conclusions. For example, when the Orphic gold plates were found in southern Italy, some years ago, certain enthusiasts immediately concluded that now at last we knew where Plato and Pindar got their religious ideas! The relations between Jesus and John the Baptist, between the earliest Palestinian Christianity and the Jewish sect known as the Essenes, and between the later church and the "Nazōraeans" or "Nasaraioi"—these questions are further illustrated and much complicated, rather than answered, by the newly found scrolls. But the use of a few common terms, out of the rich religious vocabulary of either orthodox or sectarian Judaism between, say, 200 B.C. and A.D. 100, does not require us to assume dependence in either direction, i.e., either of the gospels upon the scrolls or of the scrolls upon the gospels.

CHAPTER VII

The Earliest Gospel: Mark

*T*he New Testament is the church's book—this is the viewpoint not only of traditional orthodoxy but also of present-day research. The New Testament is the classical, normative, and authoritative collection of the doctrinal-historical documents for the church's earliest period. True, there are other documents for this period; the existence of other documents is presupposed by the church's very choice of these to be the recognized "canon of truth." Not only the more or less heretical Gospels, Acts, and Apocalypses—these were for the most part of later origin; there were other writings, excluded from the canon, now roughly classified (since the seventeenth century) under the title "Apostolic Fathers," whose main period of composition was roughly parallel to the second half of the century A.D. 50–150. But these writings were secondary to the New Testament, not only in date but also in interest, authority, and doctrinal or ethical content. Nevertheless, it is easy to drift into the historically quite unreal assumption that the literary activity of the early church either ceased for the two generations between John and Irenaeus, and was confined to three or four faint luminaries who appeared in the darkness of this period, or that at least the church found its interests in an entirely different group of subjects—with the result that the New Testament literature remains in as great apparent isolation as before. Such a view will, of course, not stand the test of real knowledge of the facts, though that does not prevent its widespread and more or less unconscious acceptance. The New Testament is in no danger of losing its uniqueness and its recognized spiritual authority; but it needs to be set in relation to the other literary products of early Christianity, to the literary forms, tendencies, and interests—some of which it did much to create, and which long survived the first and even the second century.

There is something to be said for approaching the New Testament by way of Eusebius, as I have already suggested: that is, for viewing the earliest literature of the church as the earliest documents of the great religious-historical evolution which led from Peter to Constantine, from Jerusalem to Nicaea, from Paul to Eusebius himself. It would be interesting to take Eusebius as a starting point and work backward through early church history and literature to the origins of Christianity and its primary documents in the New Testament, tracing in reverse order the course of historical, institutional, doctrinal, and literary evolution. Eusebius' dates and traditions, inferences and interpretations are often enough at fault; but he does give us a picture of the rise and expansion of early Christianity which is not only, for lack of a better, indispensable, but which in its wholeness and continuity (for all the lacunae) is impressive and satisfying. Even his legends—e.g., King Abgar and the church in Edessa (*Church History*, I. 13), the martyrdom of James the Just at Jerusalem (II. 23), the arrest of the grandnephews of our Lord (III. 20)—have something to teach: they convey the atmosphere, if nothing more, of the times from which the stories come. And his quotations from earlier writers are among the most precious treasures that his narrative contains. For our present purpose, his most important quotation is the account which Papias of Hierapolis gave of the origin of the earliest gospel, in his *Exposition of the Divine Oracles* (III. 39. 15).

Papias' statement of the tradition handed down from "the presbyter" is still the starting point for a satisfactory historical and literary analysis of the Gospel of Mark, brief and anecdotal as the statement is.

This also the presbyter used to say: "*Mark, indeed, who had been the interpreter of Peter, wrote accurately, as far as he remembered them, the things said or done by the Lord, but not however in order.*" *For he had neither heard the Lord nor been his personal follower, but at a later stage, as I [Papias] said, he had followed Peter, who used to adapt the teachings to the needs, but not as though he were drawing up a connected account of the oracles of the Lord: so that Mark committed no error in writing down some of them just as he remembered them. For he had only one object in view, viz., to omit none of the things which he had heard, and to falsify none of them.*

Frequently as this statement has been quoted or alluded to in

discussions of the origin of Mark, it still carries with it an un-
exhausted freshness of suggestion—in strong contrast, for example,
to the impossible inference of Augustine that Mark was only "one
who followed Matthew and abridged his Gospel," or the curious
late "tradition" which made Mark the evangelist of Alexandria
and its first bishop. It is the generally held view, today, that the
presbyter's testimony, which Papias was quoting, does not extend
beyond the first sentence of the fragment; the rest is Papias' commentary upon it. Whence the presbyter derived his information,
supposing he was "the presbyter John in Asia," it is impossible to
ascertain. Not unlikely, however, the tradition had been current
in the province of Asia about the turn of the century, when, if not
earlier, the Gospel of Mark may have been fairly well known
there. When the Gospel of Mark was brought to Asia, it came,
no doubt, from Rome; and it bore with it the tradition of its
origin in the remembered discourses of Peter written down by
Mark. Now, there may be more of inference than of tradition in
Papias' supplement to the words of the presbyter. He is on the
defensive. Mark's order has been attacked. Compared with Luke's
claim to write "in order" (*kathexēs*, 1:3), or with Matthew's
rigidly methodical arrangement, or with John's grouping of his
material about a limited number of great "signs" or divine manifestations, Mark's order of events must have seemed highly questionable in Asiatic Christian circles. By the time of Papias (ca.
A.D. 135) there had been ample opportunity for such questionings
and suspicions to crystallize in definite objections to the Gospel
of Mark. In reply, Papias concedes that the book lacks proper
order; but then, he adds, that is just what we should expect—
Mark wrote, not *kathexēs*, i.e., in strict sequence, nor as though he
were drawing up a connected narrative (as Luke had undertaken
to do), but just as he remembered Peter's occasional discourses.
And he certainly made no mistake in doing so, for his aim was
not chronological exactitude nor even artistic, theological, or
edifying arrangement, but comprehensiveness and accuracy in
reporting. "For he had only one object in view [or two, as we
might say], to omit nothing of what he had heard, and to mis-
represent or falsify nothing."

As an expansion of the statement of "the presbyter," Papias'
words are admirable; and as a defense of the Gospel of Mark, they
are surely on the right line. With them tallies the oft-quoted
statement of Irenaeus:

After the deaths [of Peter and Paul in the persecution at Rome
under Nero], *Mark, the disciple and interpreter of Peter, himself*

also handed down to us in writing the things which Peter had proclaimed" (Against Heresies, III. 1. 1; cf. Eusebius, Church History, V. 8. 3). The main content of this statement is no more, perhaps, than an echo of Papias; but the phrase "after the deaths of Peter and Paul" adds something which is probably derived from the local Roman tradition, since Irenaeus had been in Rome. This tradition tallies well with the statement of the presbyter, contained in the first part of the quotation from Papias, and likewise with the expansion and apologetic application of the statement made in Papias' own words that follow. We may assume, then, that both Papias' quotation from the testimony of "the elder," and Irenaeus' testimony, go back to a common tradition—one form of it having come from Rome to Asia with the gospel, the other learned in Rome itself by Irenaeus—though crosscurrents are not to be reckoned impossible, especially in view of Irenaeus' Asiatic antecedents and his obvious familiarity with Papias.

What we are concerned with at the present moment is not the provenance, date, or authorship of Mark, but, first of all, with the form and structure of the gospel. It is significant, I believe, that the earliest known tradition of the origin of Mark throws real light upon this particular problem. Involved in the problem of the structure or order of the gospel is also the problem of its sources. What Papias has to say—or, rather, the presbyter, whom he quotes —has a bearing upon both. Of course Papias' statement is not exhaustive, nor final; for there are sections in Mark by no means derived from Peter. But as a suggestion for present-day research it is sound and illuminating.

Although the Gospel of Mark is appropriately designated "the earliest gospel," i.e., the first complete "gospel" in the literary sense of that word, it was by no means the first collection or compilation of source material on the life of our Lord. Luke uses it, among the writings of the "many" who had "taken it in hand to compile a narrative concerning the things which have been fulfilled among us, just as they were delivered to us by those who from the beginning were eyewitnesses and ministers of the word"— i.e., the things which he later defined, in the preface to Acts, as "all that Jesus began to do and to teach, until the day when he was taken up"—i.e., ascended. These sources cannot all have been gospels, like Mark; among them were the documents we now designate noncommittally by the letters Q and L; no doubt there were other sources, some written, some still oral, when Luke wrote. Mark lies about midway in the process of development from collections of Jesus' sayings and deeds to the finished gospels of Luke and Matthew and that "according to the Hebrews" (of which only fragments now remain). Of course Mark lies closer to Luke and Matthew than to L and Q; but it is in unbroken contact with earlier tradition and emerges just above the level of these somewhat less continuous and less fully organized collections. As we have seen, Q and L both seem to follow a certain order; the tradition has already been arranged in "blocks," for there were "sources" behind even Q and L. Parallel with Mark, and belonging to the same level of literary development, is Proto-Luke, if Canon Streeter and Vincent Taylor's hypothesis of the existence of that first form of the Lucan Gospel is accepted. And it was doubtless in contrast with the arrangement of the later gospels that Mark appeared to be lacking in order, to Papias' contemporaries: hence his appeal to the explanation offered by the presbyter.

Now, I do not doubt that the tradition handed down by Papias in the name of the elder is genuine tradition, not someone's fancy or guesswork, and that it contains a real historical nucleus. It was a most natural explanation of the way in which the Marcan Gospel arose—fragments, anecdotes, sayings, parables strung together with only a minimum of chronological consecutiveness. It was not a common or widespread tradition—at least not in Asia: otherwise Papias would not have been required to advance it against the detractors of Mark's Gospel, nor to labor the point as he does. Yet it fits very closely the phenomena of this gospel's arrangement, and explains the state of the material as the evangelist found it, or collected it—at least large parts of it—for his own purposes, in the first instance. But as a comprehensive and final explanation of our earliest gospel, the statement of the presbyter, and those of Papias and of Irenaeus, leave something to be desired. And it seems that they are both in error in combining two stages in the gospel's origin into one, viz., the author's collection of material (including the direct dependence of some of this upon Peter's preaching) and the actual writing of the gospel by its author. For there are certainly passages in Mark that can hardly go back to Peter, in addition to the fair number that most probably do—as we shall see. And it is certainly clear, upon a close examination of the gospel itself, that the presbyter's qualifying phrase, "not, however, in order," is scarcely the last word on the subject. Mark *does* have an "order" or arrangement, partly chronological, partly by subject, partly the result of incorporating older sources.

A still unsolved problem is the term used by Papias in referring to the contents of the Gospels of Mark and Matthew as *logia* kyriaka. It was also the title of his own work in five books, *Exegesis of the Logia Kyriaka* (Eusebius, *Church History*, III. 39. 1, 15, 16). The general reader does not realize how obscure this language is, nor does the theological reader who has assumed hitherto that *logia* means "gospels." As applied to the "proof-texts" from the Old Testament, such as we find scattered throughout the Gospel of Matthew, *logia* (which means divine "oracles," as we have seen) is a perfectly appropriate term. But how can the contents of Mark be so described? The most probable explanation is that already in the time of Papias, toward the middle of the second century, the term was beginning to be used of the *sayings* of Jesus, or to refer to his teaching as divinely inspired, and thus in a general way to his parables, interpretations of scripture, gnomic sayings or "proverbs," and even his "pronouncement sayings" (as Taylor calls them), and hence to the anecdotes told about him, including his miracles. So understood, as words of revelation, the term *logia* begins to approximate the total contents of the tradition of his life and teaching. These, according to Papias, it had been Peter's custom to quote and expound in the course of his teaching, without attempting, like Matthew, to arrange a *syntaxis* or compilation and orderly arrangement of them. For he only cited them "as need arose" in his teaching—or, he *taught* as need arose: *pros tas chreias.* This phrase—which has parallels in Acts 28:10; Maximus of Tyre, I. 3 *ad fin.*; Sirach 38:1; Sophocles, *Oedipus Rex*, 1174—probably means here simply "as needed." The whole point is not Peter's preaching or teaching, but Mark's lack of order: it was not his fault if he had before him only Peter's occasional citation of Jesus' sayings in the course of his teaching. Papias is trying to exonerate Mark, not Peter.

Most interpreters recognize two main divisions in the gospel: the first representing the early proclamation of the good news by Jesus, and leading up to a climax in Peter's confession and the Transfiguration in ch. 8 and 9, too naïvely rearranged by those who reverse their order; the second the long journey which led from Caesarea Philippi and the Mount of Transfiguration to Golgotha and the Empty Tomb. B. W. Bacon even went so far as to derive Mark's principle of arrangement from the two sacraments of the church, Baptism and the Supper of the Lord. Others have found in it a recollection of the initial success followed by the complete failure of the Galilean ministry. Both theories are too schematic. The division into two parts, i.e., the beginning of Jesus' ministry and the end, is so simple that nothing less could be expected of any writer of a narrative of Jesus' public activity.

Embedded in the second half is the Passion Narrative, surely the nucleus of any narrative of Jesus' life from the viewpoint of the early church. It would certainly be so in the Pauline churches —Paul himself refers to the tradition which he had received and handed on to his converts, and cites specifically the death, burial, resurrection, and appearances of the Lord (I Cor. 15:1-8). And we may infer from the traditions preserved in the early chapters of Acts that the same interest in the death of Christ was true of the presentation of the gospel to its first hearers in Palestine. Now the Passion Narrative was, ex hypothesi, an orderly and sequential statement of the final events in Jesus' life and ministry. As the form critics tell us, it was the earliest consecutive narrative of events in the life of Jesus to take fixed (or relatively fixed) form. The old pre-Marcan Passion Narrative, underlying ch. 14-15, contained a whole series of incidents (see below). Though Matthew and Luke do not hesitate to alter the arrangement of Marcan material in earlier chapters, they show greater respect for its order here. In brief, it was the normal account of the last scenes of Jesus' life, and though it might be abridged, expanded, or considerably supplemented (as by Luke), its general order was not altered. Sayings and incidents in the Galilean ministry might be rearranged and reset in different contexts; but the Passion Narrative was too firmly established in what must have been the approximate historic order for any serious changes to be introduced by the later evangelists. This general sequence is also confirmed independently by John: the dependence of John upon the synoptics (as we have seen) is not now as generally held as it was a generation ago. And this, we may believe, was the original nucleus of the Marcan Gospel. Interpretation was introduced by added touches here and there—interpretation of the kind that any writer using historical material inevitably introduces into his narrative, as it passes through his own mind on its way to formulation in writing. But the main substance and general order of the narrative was pretty well formulated before Mark wrote it down.

The basic pre-Marcan Passion Narrative has been reconstructed by a number of modern scholars, Martin Dibelius, Rudolf Bultmann, Hans Lietzmann, Erich Klostermann, R. H. Lightfoot, A. T. Olmstead, Maurice Goguel, Joseph Klausner, Vincent Taylor—see my *Earliest Gospel* (1943), ch. VIII. As usually reconstructed it contained the following verses: Mark 14:1, 2, 10, 11, 17, 18a,

21–27, 29–31, 43–53a, 15:1–15, 21, 22, 24a, 25–27, 29a, 32b–37, 39.
Perhaps we can see its outline better in tabular form:

The Pre-Marcan Passion Narrative
[Marcan additions are enclosed in square brackets]

14:1, 2	The conspiracy against Jesus.
[3–9	The anointing at Bethany.]
10, 11	The betrayal by Judas.
[12–16	The preparation for the Passover.]
17, 18a	Jesus foretells the betrayal.
[18b–20	The disciples' questioning.]
21	Jesus' woe pronounced upon the betrayer.
22–25	The Last Supper.
26, 27	Jesus foretells the disciples' desertion.
[28	Jesus foretells his resurrection and return to Galilee.]
29–31	Jesus foretells Peter's denials.
[32–42	Jesus in Gethsemane.]
43–53a	Jesus is seized and led before the high priest.
[53b	The council assembles—inferred from 15:1.]
[55–65	Jesus' trial before the Sanhedrin.]
[54, 66–72	Peter's denials.]
15:1–15	Jesus is tried by Pilate, and sentenced to death.
[16–20	The mocking by the soldiers.]
21, 22	Jesus is led to Golgotha.
[23	Jesus is offered wine and myrrh.]
24a	Jesus is crucified.
[24b	Jesus' garments are divided.]
25–27	The inscription; two robbers are crucified with him.
[28	A later interpolation from Luke 22:37 or Isa. 53:12.]
29a	The mocking by the people.
[29b–32a	Their words, and the mocking by the chief priests and scribes.]
32b	The robbers revile Jesus.
33–37	Jesus dies on the cross.
[38	The temple curtain is torn in two.]
39	The centurion's testimony: Jesus was a Son of God. This was the climax of the old pre-Marcan Passion Narrative—a very significant conclusion.
[40, 41	The women who witnessed the Crucifixion.]
[42–47	The burial of Jesus.]

When we turn from the Passion Narrative to survey the earlier

contents of the Gospel of Mark, we find a singularly clear arrangement of its materials—partly chronological, but only partly so;
much more definitely an arrangement by subject, what the Ger-
mans call *sachliche Anordnung*. And the subjects are those which
must have been of paramount interest in the church of Mark's
own time, that is, in the sixties or seventies of the first century.
Far from the traditional disorder attributed to Mark, ever since
the days of Papias, the earliest gospel displays a very specific arrangement, largely determined by its earlier sources and perhaps
influenced by the use of the teachings "as need arose" at various
times in the Christian-Jewish religious year.

THE STRUCTURE OF MARK

Title: 1:1.
   I. Introduction: Jesus and John the Baptizer, 1:2–13.
  II. Jesus in Galilee, 1:14–10:52.
     (a) About the Sea of Galilee, 1:14–5:43, including:
       the Day in Capernaum, 1:16–38;
       the Controversies, 2:1–3:6 (and 3:22–30);
       a collection of Parables, 4:1–34; and
       a collection of Great Miracle Stories, 4:35–5:43.
     (b) More distant journeys, one to the North, 6:1–9:50, the
       other to Jerusalem, 10:1–52, including:
       two more or less parallel accounts of the northern jour-
       ney in 6:30–7:37 and 8:1–26;
       four more Controversies, 7:1–23; 8:11,12; 9:11–13;
       10:2–12;
       "The Way of the Cross," 8:27–10:45,
       with groups of discipleship sayings in 8:34–38, 9:33–50,
       10:13–31, 35–45.
       These various groups of sayings and blocks of narrative
       material may well have been pre-Marcan collections.
 III. Jesus in Jerusalem, ch. 11–12, including:
       another collection of Controversies, 11:27–12:34, with
       12:35–40 as an editorial supplement.
 IV. The Apocalyptic Discourse, ch. 13, including:
       material from the Little Apocalypse (vv. 6–8, 14–20,
       24–27).
  V. The Passion Narrative, ch. 14–15 (also edited).
 VI. The Finding of the Empty Tomb, 16:1–8, followed by a
       later epilogue, 16:9–20, summarizing the Resurrection
       Appearances.

The "day in Capernaum" (1:16–38) seems to have its own
order, no doubt reflecting the Petrine reminiscences—which are

also reflected in the Passion Narrative and elsewhere in Mark. But it is the Controversies that arrest our attention at once. Here also is order, sequence, an artistic or logical arrangement. That is to say, a large number of the incidents and sayings recorded by Mark are grouped about a dozen or fifteen great controversies in which Jesus had engaged and in which the church, a generation later, was still engaged. They are, apparently, the following:

1. The controversy over healing, 2:1–12.
2. The controversy over eating with sinners, 2:13–17.
3. The controversy over fasting, 2:18–22.
4. The controversy over keeping the Sabbath, 2:23–3:6.
5. The controversy over the source of Jesus' "power," 3:22–30.
6. The controversy over the external requirements of the Law, the scribal traditions, and the food regulations, 7:1–23.
7. The controversy over "signs," 8:11, 12.
8. The controversy over Elijah's coming, 9:11–13.
9. The controversy over remarriage after divorce, 10:2–12.
10. The controversy over Jesus' authority, 11:27–33.
11. The controversy over civil obedience, and the payment of tribute, 12:13–17.
12. The controversy over the resurrection, 12:18–27.
13. The controversy over the interpretation of the Law, i.e., the chief commandment, 12:28–34.
[14. The controversy over the Messiah's descent from King David, 12:35–37.]
[15. The controversy over scribal ostentation and greed, 12:38–40.]

(A total of 117 vv. and parts of vv., or 17.7 per cent of the Gospel of Mark.)

It is evident that some of these are closely related—the controversies over eating with sinners (2), over Sabbath observance (4), over the externals of the Law (6), over divorce (9), and over "the greatest commandment" (13) are all questions of the interpretation of the Mosaic Law and concern its binding authority upon Jesus' followers and the Christian church—controversies that presumably were still alive in Mark's day, and even much later (as the Epistle to the Hebrews, the Gospel of Matthew, the Didache, the Epistle of Barnabas, and other and even later documents testify; see Matt. 5:17–20, Heb. 8–10, Barn. 1–17). Wherever Christians and orthodox Jews came in contact, there the old controversies were sure to burst in flame. The question of the source

of Jesus' power (5) and that of his authority (10) were "live issues" in the early gentile church, in its Graeco-Roman environment, even as in the days of his ministry among the Jews in
Galilee and Jerusalem. The controversy over the coming of Elijah
(8), though it may have possessed equal interest where followers
of John the Baptist were concerned, was no doubt another keenly
debated question at issue between Jews and early Christians, since
John was identified with "the prophet" whose return was to precede "the great and terrible day of the Lord," Mal. 4:5. The question of the tribute money (11) was a real question still—for Paul's
converts and for the readers of I Peter (Rom. 13:6, 7; I Pet. 2:13—
the question is now one of obedience to "every ordinance of man,"
not merely of the payment of taxes, though the major issue doubtless included the minor); certainly in its larger aspects of civil
obedience it was not without vital implications for Christians in
Rome in the days of Nero. "Signs" (7) were still as strongly de-
siderated among the populace of Graeco-Roman communities as
they were in Palestine; witness Acts, and the Apocalypse of John
—the demand continued down to the days of Cyprian (Acts 2:43,
4:30, 5:12, 8:13, 14:3, etc.; Rom. 15:19; II Cor. 12:12; Heb. 2:4;
Rev. 13:13, 15:1, etc.; see Harnack, *The Mission and Expansion
of Christianity in the First Three Centuries*, I. 203–213 = ch. v);
nor should we ignore Gregory the Great, and the whole host of
medieval "miracle-mongers." Fasting (3) was still a problem at the
date of the composition of the Didache, and later (Didache 8;
II Clement 16:4; Hermas, *Sim*. 5:1–3; Tertullian, *On Fasting*;
Clement of Alexandria, *Stromata*, VII. 12. 75). Eating with "sinners," i.e., nonobservant Jews (2), was a problem at Corinth in
Paul's day, as it had been at Antioch (Gal. 2:11–21)—though
now it took a somewhat different form—that is, a Hellenistic and
non-Jewish form, not the eating with Gentiles but the partaking
of the table of a god (i.e., for Jews and Christians, of a demon;
I Cor. 10:21), and the association of Christ (and of Christians)
with the unworthy was a charge still hurled at the church in the
time of Celsus (Origen, *Against Celsus*, III. 59, "Anyone who is
a sinner, or foolish, or simple-minded, in short, any unfortunate
will be accepted by the Kingdom of God"). Perhaps one more
anti-Jewish controversy should be noted—the one regarding the
Davidic descent of the Messiah (14)—which Jesus apparently
repudiates, perhaps because of its political connotations. This
certainly would be a crucial question at issue between Christians
and Jews; but Mark's interpretation had against it the growing
Christian alternative interpretation reflected not only in Paul's

statement (Rom. 1:3) but also in the later Gospels of Matthew and Luke, in the Pastorals (II Tim. 2:8), and in the letters of Ignatius of Antioch. The Fourth Gospel agrees with Mark in rejecting the Davidic messiahship (John 7:41, 42. See also the Epistle of Barnabas 12:10). As Easton pointed out (*Christ in the Gospels*, p. 39), Jesus does not claim to be David's son in the earliest Christian tradition. (Cf. Eduard Meyer, *Ursprung und Anfänge des Christentums*, II. 446. See also "Peter in Antioch," by Philip Carrington, in the *Anglican Theological Review*, XV. 1, January, 1933).

Still another controversy was the one occasioned by the cleansing of the temple—certainly related, at least in the minds of Mark's readers, to the attitude of Jesus toward the external requirements of the Law in ch. 7. Obviously much of Mark's material has a thoroughly intraecclesiastical interest and bearing. Indeed, it is not difficult to see that not only the Gospels of Luke and John, but even the much earlier writing of Mark, have a pronounced interest in apologetics—necessarily so, for Christianity was from the first as much on the defensive as on the offensive in the great competitive struggle of religious forces then taking place in the Graeco-Roman world. Though much in Mark is concerned with defense against Jewish attack, and with current controversy between Christians and Jews, it is not difficult to see that gentile Christian readers would also have a genuine and vital interest in the questions with which it dealt. It is amazing how large a place this controversial element holds in the Marcan tradition—and indeed in all the gospels.

The main structure of Mark was accordingly determined by the arrangement thus far observed, viz., the Passion Narrative prefaced by the mighty works of Jesus the Son of God and the controversies with the Jewish leaders which led to his death. This general arrangement provided the first answer to the perennial question, Why did Jesus die? For here was a question which must always have been asked, and always required an answer: If Jesus was the Messiah, the Son of God, why, then, did he die the shameful death upon the cross? How did it come about—historically, and as the end of what sequence of dire, unfortunate events? How did it come to pass—in the eternal counsels of God? To both forms of the question Mark undertakes to provide an answer: He died (a) because the Jewish leaders rejected him, and out of envy (15:10) delivered him up to Pilate—the reason for their envy is clear from the series of controversies which Mark gives. For he had worsted them in argument, and his following had continued in spite of all their efforts to oppose him. He died (b) because he willed to die, to lay down his life a ransom for many (10:45; 14: 24). He died (c) because it was the will of God, and so it had been written of him (8:31; 9:31; 10:33; 14:21, 36). The basic and fundamental structure of the gospel thus had a very clear and decisive motive. We may call it apologetic; but Mark simply had to answer the questions that were in the minds of his readers. Whether Jewish or gentile, every convert had to face them, and was probably asked them repeatedly.

But this was not all. There were controversies—or at least questions demanding answer—within the church itself. (a) Who were the true leaders of the church? (b) What prerogatives were Jesus' own family to enjoy in the church? (c) What was the relation of John the Baptizer to Jesus, and of his followers to the followers of Christ? (d) What were the marks of true discipleship—martyrdom, or something less? (e) What of the hope of the Kingdom? Was it still to come, and if so, when? What were to be the signs of the end of the present evil age? Must persecution continue indefinitely, or was the hand of the Lord still over the elect? These also were vital questions for Mark's readers, and to them likewise he undertook to give the answer.

(a) The true leaders of the church are "the Twelve"—a simple and definite enough answer (3:13–19), with a long train of consequences for his own and later ages laid up in it.

(b) The apostles appointed by Jesus, rather than the earthly family of the Lord, claiming prerogatives based upon Davidic ancestry (3:20, 21, 31–35; 12:35–37), were the divinely authorized leaders of the church. I cannot help thinking that the term "Jerusalem caliphate," used by some scholars, is much too strong, and yet there was certainly a tendency at work in the Palestinian church to exalt the family of Jesus to a position of authority—and we may well suppose this issue came to a head in the fifties; James, the Lord's brother, headed the Jerusalem community then and was martyred, presumably, in A.D. 62. (See Josephus, Antiquities, XX. 9. 1; Hegesippus in Eusebius, Church History, II. 23.) The "caliphate" came later—Hegesippus (quoted in Eusebius' Church History, III. 32. 6) says that the Lord's family was influential in the Palestinian church down to the time of Trajan: "They came, therefore, and ruled every church, as being martyrs and of the Lord's family; and, when profound peace was established in every church, they remained until [the time of] Trajan Caesar."

(c) The claims made for John the Baptizer by his followers—clearly repudiated in the first chapter of John (1:8, 15, 19–34) and

simply set aside by the author of Acts (1:4, 5; 19:1-7)—were of
sufficient importance when Mark wrote to require attention. According to Mark, John was simply identified with the returning
Elijah predicted by Malachi, the national "converter" whose coming was to precede "the great and terrible Day of the Lord" (Mal.
4:5, 6). John was thus definitely made the precursor and forerunner of the Messiah—in no sense his rival; John's followers
accordingly should turn and become followers of Christ, i.e.,
Christians. Here again a long train of inferences and interpretations was set in motion, leading to the representation of John in
the later synoptics, in the Fourth Gospel, in the Apocryphal Gospels and in later legend, in the Mandaean writings, and in Christian biblical theology.

(d) On the test of discipleship, Mark is very clear that *if*
martyrdom is required, the demand must be met: "he that loveth
his life shall lose it; he that loseth his life, shall find it [in the age
to come]" (cf. 8:34-37). As Bishop Rawlinson said (*Commentary*
on Mark, pp. 108-111): "The Marcan narrative . . . becomes at
this point virtually an impressive sermon addressed to the reader.
It enshrines . . . the kernel of a religious ethic appropriate to the
martyr and missionary church of Nero's time." And yet the Lord
will not fail to "shorten the days" of persecution (13:20), lest "all
flesh" perish—a hope apparently not shared by the author of the
Apocalypse of John, who looks forward to the prospect of the utter
annihilation of the faithful upon earth (Rev. 7:11). In passage
after passage Mark pictures the qualities of discipleship which
Jesus loved and commended—the greatest disciple is the humblest;
the cup of water shall not be forgotten; stones of stumbling must
not be laid for one another; riches are a hindrance; the spirit of
childlikeness is the spirit Christ expects of his "little ones"; their
share in Messiah's glory is to be won through lowly acts of service
—such was the spirit Mark looked for, in the light of Jesus' teachings, in the martyr-church of his day, a sacrifice "salted with fire"
and laid upon the altar of complete self-renunciation for Christ's
sake and the gospel's (9:49).

(e) The "Little Apocalypse," supplemented by sayings from
other sources, provided Mark with answers to the questions regarding the Parousia, its date, its preceding "signs of the end," the
relation of the fiery trial of persecution to the impending return
of Christ in glory. The motive underlying Mark's incorporation of
this material in his thirteenth chapter is patent to everyone familiar with the thought and aspiration, the hopes and fears of the
early Christian church. The explanation of the delay of Christ's

return, in v. 10, "The gospel must first be preached to all nations," was the profoundest one in all early Christian eschatology—probably in all Christian theology.

So much for the general arrangement and the motives that led to it. The specific arrangement of Mark's material may result, as some now hold, from conformation to the seasons in the very early, i.e., Christian-Jewish, observance of the church year. The evidence is variously interpreted, and some of it is more convincing than the rest. The probability of the use of gospel materials in Christian public worship, from the outset, is unquestionable, as is also the use of the Old Testament lections to which they may have been correlated in some kind of annual sequence.

It is evident that, although Mark probably found his material in scattered form, or at most in small "blocks" of related sayings or incidents—this would naturally be its form as derived from early Christian preaching and teaching—he by no means left it in this shape. Papias and the presbyter are wrong on this point. Mark *did* write "in order"; only, his order was hid from the eyes of his second-century reader. The order which Mark followed was never meant to be chronological, except in a broad general way. His principle of arrangement was by subject, not by order of time— and it may of course have been in some degree "liturgical," as many now hold. Probably he was no better off, as far as chronological order is concerned, than any modern "biographer" of our Lord. He had only the anecdotes and sayings derived from Christian preaching or teaching, the current *kērygma* of the gospel; and he had them in the order—or disorder—which Papias and the presbyter describe. It is really Irenaeus who gives the term "preaching" to the tradition; Papias, with more probability, had referred to "teaching" (Irenaeus, III. 1. 1; Eusebius, *Church History*, III. 39. 15). But instead of trying to recover the chronological sequence —a hopeless task, thirty years and more after the event, and one not laid upon him by his readers anyway—he arranged his materials in the order that best suited his purposes and the needs of the church in his day, viz., that which we now have in this gospel. If only this simple fact had been observed, the long reign of the "Marcan hypothesis" in modern New Testament study would have been impossible, and gospel research would have been much further advanced.

CHAPTER VIII

The Structure and Contents of Mark

e are now in a position to understand the form and structure of this gospel, in the light of the motives which Mark had in mind, and with a clearer view of the materials at his disposal when he set about his task.

The book opens, apparently, with a title: "[The] beginning of the gospel of Jesus Christ, [the] Son of God." This divine title reflects Mark's Christology (as I have tried to show in the Introduction to Mark, in *The Interpreter's Bible*, Vol. VII; see also the Introduction to *Mark*, in Harper's Annotated Bible Series), and it is echoed in the great climax of the old Roman Passion Narrative (15:39). It could easily have been omitted by the oversight of some copyist, since the sentence contained a continuous series of *nomina sacra*, often abbreviated by copyists, in this case a whole line containing several similar abbreviations: IOUXOUUIOUƟOU. Here omission is more probable than insertion. Nor is v. 1 a mere *protasis*: "The beginning . . . was John the Baptizer . . ." for the protasis to v. 4 is vv. 2a, 3 (2b is a later insertion from another prophet, Malachi, probably under the influence of Matt. 11:10, Luke 7:27). Hence v. 1 is probably to be taken as Mark's title, though not, of course, a title in the modern sense, but something more like a medieval *incipit evangelium Jesu Christi*.

The introductory section (1:2–15) was perhaps based largely on Q, which document (or at least cycle of tradition) presumably opened with an account of John's preaching and of Jesus' temptation. Naturally, there was no other place for these narratives than at the beginning. No principle of structural arrangement need be invoked to account for their location at this point, or for the location here of the Marcan account of Jesus' baptism and messianic vocation. The apostolic church invariably viewed the Christian movement as "beginning from the baptism of John" (Acts 1:22, 10:37). It may perhaps be possible to argue that Jesus' temptation came late in his ministry, and to connect it with the Transfiguration or with Peter's confession rather than with the Baptism (see 8:35–37; could "a man" have been "the Man," i.e., the Son of Man?); it may even be possible to argue with Renan that his baptism came later than the beginning of his ministry, viz., at a time when Jesus, hitherto an independent teacher in Galilee, accepted John's teaching and baptism and associated himself with the whole messianic movement initiated by John; but such arguments must necessarily make considerable use of hypothetical and subjective considerations, since historical criticism can hardly get back of the primary documents now accessible to us.

After the introductory section derived from Q—or echoing the contents of its underlying oral tradition—into which he has inserted his account of Jesus' baptism and call (1:9–11) and the formal statement of the beginning of his preaching (vv. 14, 15), Mark begins his narrative with the dramatic story of the day in Capernaum. This may possibly come from Peter; many writers have pointed out the traces of Peter's reminiscences which it contains, and they are doubtless patent to every careful reader. But to it Mark has added the account of the healing of a leper (1:40–45), which may come from almost any period of our Lord's activity—though there are indications that it belongs much later than the beginning; he then adds the narrative of the healing of the man "sick with the palsy" (2:1–12). The reason for this arrangement is clear: the day in Capernaum had been a day of healings, apparently at the very beginning of Jesus' ministry, and the whole section (1:16–2:12) reaches a climax in the controversy over this very activity of healing and the accompanying forgiveness of sins. It doubtless served Mark's purpose to represent Jesus as beginning his messianic career as a healer and forgiver of sins, as well as a teacher; though it is, of course, a question if, historically, Jesus came into collision with the scribes this early in his ministry. As J. Weiss pointed out, Mark aimed to represent Jesus as already Messiah, even during his life upon earth and preceding his resurrection and glorification as the Son of God. The first narrative block in the gospel thus has for its motive the representation of Jesus as a healer of sickness and disease, engaging in successful controversy with the scribes upon this very subject—i.e., the implied and demonstrated authority to forgive sins which his successful activity as a healer carried with it. If there was a special controversy "source," as we believe, this material was probably derived from it.

The next section, on the call of Levi and eating with sinners (2:13–17), introduces the controversy occasioned by his association with "publicans and sinners"—not necessarily outcasts, but those who disregarded the Pharisaic rules governing contact with persons who neglected the food regulations. This was a subject of keen dispute both within and without the church long after the date of Paul's Epistles to the Galatians, Romans, and Corinthians and the Apostolic Council in Jerusalem! In Paul's letters and in Acts 15 the basic problem is that of eating food offered to idols and of association with those who neglected the Jewish food regulations. The problem was thus not precisely the same as that presupposed in the gospels, but the general similarity is apparent. Mark gives the most closely relevant material to be found in the evangelic tradition (see also 7:1–23).

The third controversy follows in the next section (2:18–22), on the subject of fasting. Jesus' answer might have been understood, originally, almost as a rabbinic pleasantry and in the spirit of mild rebuke, like the clever retorts which the later rabbis loved to indulge in and to repeat; but it has been elaborated by Mark (or by the tradition) into a tragic prediction of impending doom, the words about the bridegroom and his companions; while the saying about wine and wineskins seems scarcely relevant to the incident related, but concerns the still highly controversial subject which Mark has in mind at this point. It was added here in order to set forth a principle which applied to all such problems. The new way of life could not be accommodated to the strait jacket of the old rules.

The next section (2:23–3:5) has to do entirely with Sabbath observance—and introduces what one might easily suppose was the fourth major subject of controversy between Jews and Christians, certainly in the period preceding the Fall of Jerusalem, though we find it also in Heb. 3:1–4:13 (toward the close of the century). At any rate, it certainly was not chronological considerations but controversial exigencies that led to the insertion of this section—and of those that precede—so early in the story. One may assume, perhaps, that a similar motive accounts for the preservation and formulation of the narratives in the tradition upon which Mark has drawn, and also their preservation as a collection of controversies, i.e., of Jesus' pronouncements upon these still-controverted questions. That Mark consciously held this motive is clear from the verse that follows (3:6), stating the antagonism of the Pharisees and Herodians and their determination to destroy Jesus. Nevertheless, Mark is not writing a handbook of polemics,

but a history—as his title, his introductory section, his general
framework, and his inclusion of the Passion Narrative all show.
He therefore next inserts a summary of Jesus' public ministry of
exorcism (3:7–12), not drawn from any of his sources but written
in his own hand—the first of several summaries and transitions
that serve to give continuity and movement to his book. Similar
summaries are to be seen in Mark 1:39, 45: 4:33 f.; 6:7–13 (based
on Q); 9:30; 10:1, etc. One notes also that in the earlier sections of
the gospel Mark has so completely rewritten his materials that it
is often difficult to make out the distinction between his sources
and his own additions (compare his treatment of Q in 1:2–13),
and to distinguish traditional elements from editorial. But, as all
writers know, fatigue sometimes overcomes ambition, and from
now on the signs of rewriting are less common. This would be the
more natural in a writer as nonliterary as Mark, and especially
since from now on his materials are somewhat fuller than for the
earlier sections.

The appointment of the Twelve comes next (3:13–19)—an
incident that Mark doubtless thinks of as coming early in Jesus'
ministry, as the foundation of his messianic community; moreover, as we have suggested, it may have had a bearing on the question of true leadership in the church. This view is strengthened by
the narrative that follows, the concern of Jesus' friends for his
health and safety (3:20 f.), and the definition of membership in
Jesus' true family (3:31–35). The Davidic claims of Jesus' family
may not have been extinct even as late as the time of Domitian,
and while James, the Lord's brother, headed the church in Jerusalem they may have been somewhat vigorously advocated. That
is to say, the question was probably a real one when the Gospel
of Mark was written.

The section on the scribes' charge that Jesus' cures were wrought
by collusion with Beelzebul (3:22–30) introduces the controversy
over the source of Jesus' "power" to heal, i.e., both the power and
the authority—the power evidencing the authority, and the authority explaining the power. It is inserted after the passage on
Jesus' friends in order to show the character of his activity, which
apparently suggested some kind of superhuman "possession" or
investiture with the Spirit—diabolical, said the scribes; divine, said
Jesus' followers and disciples and the church in Mark's day and
—most important of all—so Jesus himself had said. Unfortunately,
Mark omitted the great Q-verse which summarizes Jesus' whole
attitude toward his healing ministry and exorcisms (Luke 11:20,

Matt. 12:28), "If it is by the finger of God that I cast out demons, then the Kingdom of God has come upon you."

But controversy alone was not enough to give substance to the book Mark had in mind. Jesus was a teacher as well as a healer. Hence there follows the long section (4:1–34) giving a collection of Jesus' parables—somewhat as the later synoptists give an extended example of Jesus' preaching in their two great Sermons (Luke 6:20–49, Matt. 5–7). This collection of parables affords an excellent example of editorial interweaving of material, and may be analyzed in such a way as to discover how the chapter grew in the author's revision. From a purely literary, form-critical point of view, i.e., proceeding to analyze the literary form, it appears that (a) the basic material is contained in 4:2, 3–8, 26–29, 30–32, 33a; and that (b) into this have been inserted various interpretative and correlative passages, not wholly agreeing with the basic material, especially a traditional homiletical interpretation which represents the disciples as dull (a frequent motif in early Roman Christian books: see the Epistle to the Hebrews and the Shepherd of Hermas!), and also (c) a series of Marcan additions which assume that the teaching was a mystery, i.e., intentionally obscure, in order to withhold the teaching from "those on the outside."

Thus v. 10 is surely editorial: the question relates to "parables" (plural; cf. v. 2), though the explanation in 13–20 refers to "this parable." To this is attached the Q theory of parables, in vv. 21, 22, i.e., parables are meant to enlighten, and the quatrain, in Wisdom style, contained in 24a, c, 25,

> Take heed what you hear,
> And still more will be given you;
> For to him who has [viz., understanding], will more be given,
> And from him who has not, even what he has
> will be taken away!

[V. 24b is a textual gloss, of the kind found in several places in Mark; cf. Matt. 7:2b.] Verse 33b also belongs, presumably, to this secondary level of tradition; it is correlative with vv. 10, 13, but not 11, 12. Finally, into this combination of basic material and its homiletical expansion Mark has inserted, editorially, his own very different interpretation—though it may of course be based upon still another series of traditional sayings: v. 1 is editorial, and so also is the Listen! in v. 3 (which adapts the collection to a discourse setting); vv. 9, 11, 12 set forth the Marcan theory of parables (which Matt. 13:13 deftly altered from "so that" to "because"); v. 23, like v. 9, reflects the frequent admonition to attention heard on the lips of teachers of hidden wisdom or mystery-lore; v. 34 is Mark's editorial conclusion, written from the point of view of his own theory of the purpose of Jesus' parabolical teaching, not from that of the original compilation (v. 33a) or the great Q parable in 21 f. or the Wisdom quatrain in 24 f. Summing up the analysis in a formula, it runs:

4:[1], 2, 3–8, [9],
(10, [11–12], 13–20, 21–22, [23], 24a, c, [24b, a gloss], 25),
26–29, 30–32, 33a, (33b [34]).

The next block (4:35–5:43) illustrates and proves Jesus' divine power, the very thing called in question by the scribes. It extends to physical nature (the rebuking of the storm), to the demons (the Gerasene demoniac), to long-continued illness (the woman who touched Jesus' garment) and it is superior even to death itself (Jairus' daughter—the climax of the section). These miracle stories may possibly be derived from Peter's preaching; but one thinks rather of the general Christian tradition as their source, though some scholars think of local Galilean legend. The whole "block" is more or less homogeneous in character—the stories belong among the "great wonder tales," as Dibelius called them.

The next group shows the results of Jesus' preaching (and of John's)—i.e., the general situation about the middle of Jesus' ministry. It is noteworthy how one incident suggests another, in the kind of subject sequence already noted: the visit to Nazareth, and his rejection there (6:1–6), suggests the mission of the Twelve (6:7–13); this creates a setting for Herod's opinion of Jesus (6: 14–16), and this in turn suggests the story of John's death at Herod's hands (6:17–29); while the section closes with the statement of Jesus' withdrawal into retirement (6:30–34).

Another group of "great wonder tales" now follows, illustrating Jesus' power: the feeding of the five thousand (6:35–44), the walking on the sea (6:45–52), and the gathering of the multitude for healing (6:53–56)—the last passage sums up once more the general impression as in 3:7 ff.

With the beginning of ch. 7 we are introduced to still another controversy: the question of the washing of hands before eating and the statement of Jesus' rejection of the externals of the Law —a fundamental issue, taken in its broadest bearings, not only for the life of Jesus but for primitive Christianity as a whole. We may assume that it had not wholly disappeared at Rome in Mark's time, though the crisis had arisen long before—in Galatia, in Antioch, in Jerusalem itself—in the great days when the glorious apostles Peter and Paul were at the height of their power (cf. Rom. 14:1–15:6; Gal. 2:11–21; Acts 5:1–35).

Once more we can observe the editorial process by which Mark weaves together his materials in order to form a continuous discourse. There are three main sections:

(1) In 7:1, 2 [3, 4 is an explanatory gloss, possibly even later than the original manuscript of Mark], 5, 6–8, Jesus rejects the scribal tradition which required hand-washing before meals, and justifies his stand by appeal to the prophet Isaiah.

(2) In vv. 9–13, Jesus attacks the tradition (in this case the "corban" rule) as contrary to the Law of God (cf. the similar attack in 10:1–12).

(3) In vv. 14, 15 Jesus rejects the theory presupposed by the food laws, viz., the classification of certain foods as "unclean"; this theory was older than the scribal interpretation, and was set forth in the Torah itself.

V. 16 is presumably a gloss: cf. those in 4:9, 23.

Vv. 17–23 set forth a later explanation of the saying in v. 15; compare the similar pedestrian and purely homiletical explanation of the parable in 4:13–20. The style and outlook are certainly Mark's—note, e.g., v. 18a, the characteristic stress on the disciples' failure to understand.

V. 19c is a still later gloss—a statement impossible at the time, or in the old tradition, and like certain other glosses in the gospels, post-Pauline in outlook.

Summing up the analysis in a formula, once more, it appears that Mark has combined three or four bits of old tradition, as follows:

7:1–2, [3–4], 5, 6–8, 9–13, 14–15, [16],
(17–19ab, [19c], 20–23).

Next follows what might perhaps be designated as Mark's "great insertion" (7:24–8:26), taking over the term from the critical analysis of the Gospel of Luke. Although the existence of this section (which Luke omits) has been viewed as evidence of two editions of Mark, one used by Luke and the other by Matthew, there can be little doubt that the style and diction are Mark's own. The most probable explanation is that Luke recognized that 8:1–26 is more or less parallel to 6:30–7:37 and, since he was intent upon saving space (for his great Q and L insertion), omitted the material in ch. 8. The material appropriately follows 7:1–23. Jesus rejects the external Law, and turns to the Gentiles of Tyre and Sidon and the Decapolis—much as Paul did repeatedly, preaching "to the Jews first, then to the Gentiles" (cf. Acts 13:46, 17:2, 10, etc.; Rom. 1:16, 2:9 f.). Nevertheless, though this may have been Mark's motive, his material was extremely intractable; the very first incident, that of the Syro-Phoenician woman, seems to represent Jesus as unwilling to minister to Gentiles—the healing has to be wrung from his unwilling hands by the force of imploring love and faith. And it is to be observed that even in the midst of the section, i.e., outside Palestine proper, the Pharisees reappear (!) and demand a "sign" (8:11, 12). Why here, one wonders, in this section? Evidently, "the Pharisees" were a conventional editorial addition, introduced simply to make possible the insertion of the question and answer (from Q). This introduces the seventh controversy—one that no doubt continued through several decades after the close of Jesus' ministry: one thinks of the "signs of an apostle" demanded of Paul, and of the "lying signs and wonders" rejected by the Apocalypse of John, of the "signs" of the end in all the apocalypses, and the "signs" (in another sense) with which the Johannine Christ vindicates his divine nature and mission. The question was a vital one throughout the early church; Jesus' refusal to give signs was a fundamental problem—handled with uncertainty by Matthew, e.g., who adds, "except the sign of Jonah," and solved finally by the Fourth Evangelist only by a complete reversal of the tradition and the substitution of the seven great theophanic "signs" or manifestations of Jesus' glory.

Peter's confession (8:27–30) marks the turning point in the gospel. In spite of scribal and Pharisean antagonism, in spite of "the leaven of the Pharisees and of Herod" (8:13–21), Jesus is recognized as Messiah upon earth: "Thou art the Christ." But this position is gained only to introduce the prospect of rejection and apparent defeat, and even the death of Jesus, "the Son of Man," at the hands of his enemies. It is as when a lofty mountain height has been attained, after wearisome effort, only to discover that beyond lies a dark and rugged valley of shadows with other peaks beyond. Between the Mount of Transfiguration and the hill of Calvary lies a dark, mysterious, and dangerous passage. The first Passion Announcement (8:31–33) is followed at once by Jesus' words on self-denial (8:34–37), on confession of the Son of Man before men (8:38), and on the immediacy of the Kingdom (9:1) —a grouping undoubtedly due to Mark himself and full of significance to the martyr-church for which he wrote. The Transfiguration, the narrative of which follows at once (9:2–8), was probably viewed by Mark—as it was by the one who gave us our modern chapter divisions—(the ancient ones began with 9:2) as the fulfillment (or at least as one fulfillment) of the prediction of the immediacy of the Kingdom in v. 1. Essentially it is an anticipation of "the glory which was to be revealed" when the Messiah returned in triumph at the end of the age and the Kingdom came "with power"—some scholars take it to be the story of a resurrection appearance which has been shifted back into the earthly ministry of Jesus. The command of silence which follows is a characteristic Marcan addition (9:9, 10); while the discussion of the future coming of Elijah, which Elijah's appearance at the Transfiguration has suggested, serves a double purpose: it answers the question of unbelieving Jews, How can Jesus be the Messiah if Elijah has not yet appeared, since Scripture made it clear that his coming was to precede the end? (Perhaps it also answered the questions of some Christians as to the real nature of the strange prophet of the wilderness.) And it also introduces once more the theme of the Messiah's impending fate. I assume that the question of the disciples, "How is it that the scribes say that Elijah must first come?" was answered in the affirmative, John the Baptist being identified with the coming Elijah. The words (12b), "And how is it written of the Son of Man, that he should suffer many things and be set at naught?" should either be inserted between vv. 10 and 11 or moved down to follow v. 13, as in Matthew. The healing of the dumb child at the foot of the mountain (9:14–29) serves to illustrate once more Jesus' power, and to set off at an appropriate distance the second Passion Announcement which follows (9:30–32).

Just as in Q and in L we find material on the duties of disciples, so Mark also gives a series of sections—indeed, three series of sections (9:33–50; 10:15–31; 35–45)—on the same subject; and the principle is likewise followed by the two later synoptists. Two of the incorporated sayings, at least, are derived from Q (9:37; 10:15), though in somewhat modified form. We shall not pause to examine them in detail, but it is obvious that they continue the presentation of Jesus' teaching. It is extraordinary how much of that teaching, as Mark gives it (and likewise Matthew, following Mark), has to do with the high privileges and stern duties of discipleship; one has little difficulty in imagining how welcome and how inspiring it was to the harassed church in Rome in Mark's days.

The historical note, Jesus' journey to Judea (10:1), is Mark's own, and at once we are back in the midst of controversy with the statement of the law of marriage (10:2–9), the prohibition of divorce (10:10, 11), and Mark's editorial addition (10:12) applying the principle still further to Roman and non-Jewish conditions. The blessing of the children (10:13, 14, 16) introduces the second section on discipleship (10:15–31), and this in turn sets off the third Passion Announcement (10:32–34), followed at once by the continuation of the teaching on discipleship: the request of James and John (10:35–40) and Jesus' words on the glory of service (10:41–45).

It is not at all impossible that the incident in 10:35–45, leading up to the saying, "For even the Son of Man came not to be ministered unto but to minister, and to lay down his life as a ransom for many," had some relation to the controversy over the true leaders of the church, noted above. It would have an added significance, if such was the case, in view of the martyrdom which the leaders of the Roman church might be (i.e., already had been) called upon to face: the spirit of the church's true leaders was to be seen in Jesus' saying, not in the request of James and John— they too must be ready to lay down their lives "a ransom for many." (Was there an implicit contrast here to the family of Jesus?) That the "cup" and the "baptism" of v. 39 imply that James and John are already martyred seems obvious, quite apart from the evidence of the DeBoor fragment of Papias, the Syriac Martyrology, etc. The contrast was all the sharper if, as the early tradition represents, Peter and Paul had *recently* been martyred in Rome, where Mark was written.

Looking back, we may see in the section 8:27–10:45 ("The Way of the Cross," as Bacon and others have called it), another example of the author's interweaving of discourse material.

(a) The basic narrative is found in 8:27–29, 9:2 f., 7 f., 14–27, 30a, 33–35, 10:2–9, 35–37, 41–44, the last three fragments being especially closely related.

(b) Into this, Mark has inserted material from what may have been a homily on renunciation, addressed not to the disciples but to the multitude, in 8:34 f., [36 f.?,] 38, [9:1 is from some other source,] 10:17–31 (which attaches closely to 8:34–36), in four sections, 17–22, 23–27, 28–30, 31.

(c) In addition, Mark has inserted a large amount of editorial material, sayings from other sources than those already used under (a) and (b), and various connecting links:

8:30, editorial: the messianic secret once more;

8:31, the first Passion Announcement;

8:32 f., Peter's protest and Jesus' rebuke;

9:4–6, further Petrine dialogue;

9:9, 10, the messianic secret again;

9:11-13, Elijah = John; the Son of Man also will suffer;

9:28 f., the failure of the disciples' exorcism explained;

9:30b, Jesus' journey kept secret;

9:31, the second Passion Announcement;

9:32, editorial (cf. v. 10);

9:36 f., another saying—surely no illustration of the saying in v. 35 and no answer to the disciples' question—cf. 10:15, which quite possibly might have been more appropriate here;

9:38-40, another independent saying, having no connection with what precedes—not even if the strange exorcist is identified with the believer in v. 42;

9:41, a related saying, but not relevant here—cf. Matt. 10:42;

9:42, really connected with v. 37, and in turn related in some way to 10:42, where the theme is similar;

9:43-48, illustrations of the terrible responsibility of causing other persons to sin;

9:49, 50, a catena of sayings related only mnemonically: fire suggests salt (and see the marginal reading, D itala, etc., based on Lev. 2:13), salt suggests the saying about "savorless salt" and also the exhortation to peace which rounds off the pericope but would go better with vv. 33-37, or 10:41-44;

10:1, editorial;

10:10-12, editorial, setting forth the corollary rule (which was possible only under Roman law, not Jewish, since Roman wives could divorce their husbands, but Jewish could not);

10:13-16, probably an independent pericope, attracted here by the teaching in such sayings as 9:36 f., 42, rather than by the teaching on marriage in 10:2-12;

10:32-34, the third Passion Announcement, introduced editorially (v. 32); in this way Mark heightens the dramatic tension of the story;

10:38-40, a *vaticinium ex eventu*, as v. 41 shows—since it refers to 37, not 38-40;

10:45, the example of the Son of Man, a saying which forms the climax not only of vv. 42-44 but of the whole central section of Mark, "The Way of the Cross." That it formed the climax is clear from Luke 22:24-27; for, although Luke shifts the whole pericope to the Last Supper and also entirely rewrites v. 45, it remains the crowning rebuke of the disciples' ambition.

Again, the analysis of the literary structure of the sequence may be set forth in a formula. Once more three strands—at least three —have been woven together. For clarity, the second is enclosed in parentheses, the third (and others) in square brackets.

8:27–29 [30, 31, 32f.] (34f.) [36f.] (38)
9: [1] 2f. [4–6] 7f. [9f., 11–13] 14–27 [28f.] 30a [30b, 31, 32]
    33–35 [36f., 38–40, 41, 42, 43–48, 49, 50]
10: [1] 2–9 [10–12, 13–16] (17–22, 23–27, 28–30, 31) [32–34]
    35–37 [38–40] 41–44 [45]

A series of historical narratives now follows: Bartimaeus (10:
46–52), the Triumphal Entry (11:1–10), the entry into the temple (11:11), the cursing of the fig tree on the following day (11:
12–14), the cleansing of the temple (11:15–18)—surely another
occasion of controversy, as Matthew clearly recognizes, though
Mark notes only the final determination of the chief priests and
scribes to destroy Jesus. The following verse (11:19), clearly Mark's
own addition, notes that Jesus and his disciples spent the night
outside the city, and their return in the morning provides the
setting for the lesson from the withered fig tree (11:20–22), in-
troducing in turn a tiny group of three sayings on the power of
faith (11:23), on the power of prayer (11:24), and on forgiveness
in prayer (11:25).

The real sequel to the cleansing of the temple is the controversy
over Jesus' authority (11:27–33), which introduces the series of
major controversies leading up to the Passion Narrative. The parable of the vineyard, or of the wicked husbandmen (12:1–12), fits
rather unevenly into the context; and, though it seems here and
there to reflect Jesus' own style and manner in telling a parable, it
has become, in its present form, almost an allegory. It is not impossible that Jesus should utter a parable like this—at the very end
of his life, and face to face with the death which he recognized
and accepted. But the parable before us has been at least retouched
in transmission, from the early Christian point of view. The parable seems to interrupt the sequence of the controversies with the
authorities in Jerusalem; and, if authentic, it was certainly addressed to the disciples, not to the scribes. I imagine that it was
handed down in the early Palestinian church, and has been edited
for inclusion here in the series of controversies. However, a similar
parable (or allegory) in Hermas, Sim., V. 2.1 ff., must not be
overlooked. Some such parable might well have been a commonplace of Christian preaching, teaching, or polemics in the early
Roman church. The economic and industrial background it presupposes suits better the Italian management of latifundia than
the simple peasant land tenure of Palestine. True, the description
of the vineyard is based on the LXX of Isa. 5:1 ff., but the geōrgoi
act more like a company of rascally operators of a distant holding

than workers on a Palestinian homestead. For example, they assume that the owner is dead, and that if they kill the heir the vineyard will be theirs—unless here, as elsewhere in the context, the requirements of the allegory are determinative. But there is no accounting for the perverted logic of criminals. The parable was one which was perhaps frequently used in controversy with non-Christian Jews.

The controversy over Jesus' authority was probably followed at once in Mark's souce (viz., the Controversies) by the question about the tribute money (12:13–17); this by the controversy over marriage and the resurrection (12:18–25), followed immediately by the anti-Sadducean proof of the resurrection (12:26, 27); and this in turn by another controversy over the interpretation of the Law—this time the question of the chief commandment (12:28–34). So closely do these controversies follow one another, just as in ch. 2–3, that the suggestion lies close at hand that Mark is making use either of a written document or of a catena of oral tradition already fairly fixed in form and sequence, and, like 12:1–12, frequently used in controversy with non-Christian Jews. At least, it is fairly probable that these three questions were commonplaces of Jewish-Christian controversy in Palestine between A.D. 30 and 60 and perhaps also in Rome from the time of the first Christian mission in that city to the date of Mark's writing—and later, in both Palestine and Rome and wherever Jews and Christians came in vigorous contact. There can be little doubt that the ultimate source of Mark's tradition is mainly Palestinian—as is true of the synoptic tradition generally. This consensus does not rest in the least upon the possibility of translating Mark or his sources, or those of Matthew or Luke, back into Palestinian Aramaic. It is important to note, however, that the tradition behind Mark had been circulated in Greek for some time prior to the author's use of it; and that Q and L also are Greek documents. Easton even went so far as to maintain that "Greek-speaking Christianity is practically as old as Christianity itself" (Christ in the Gospels, p. 37).

There is no reason why these pericopes should not also have been commonplaces in Jesus' controversy with the religious teachers in his day. Their form has been touched up and amplified; their substance goes back, through the oral tradition in which they were preserved, to Jesus himself. However, the suggestion of a written document (or stereotyped sequence of oral tradition) is strengthened by the inclusion of the passage immediately following (12:35–37) in which Jesus repudiates the scribal identification of the Messiah with the Son of David (and likewise, no doubt, the whole associated complex of mundane and political eschatology, connected with the expectation of the Son of David Messiah). This was as much a problem within the church as it was a subject of controversy with orthodox Jews. And I venture to believe that Jesus' repudiation of it was much more emphatic than the present form of the tradition would lead us to think. Here it is presented in the form of an enigmatic question—reminding one of the style and manner of Jesus' references to John the Baptist and Elijah "who is to come." Perhaps this was all that survived the strong countercurrent, equally operative in the pre-Marcan tradition, of identification of Jesus with the Son of David—a terminology and a set of ideas that reached a climax in the Matthean and Lucan Gospels; i.e., it had triumphed probably by A.D. 80–85, certainly by the end of the century, at least in Palestine and Syria, and Matthew and Luke simply record the fact and incorporate the legends—variant as they are—that had grown up about the identification. The remarkable thing is that any protest whatsoever survived, even one voiced by the Lord himself, or at least attributed to him.

Now, if we are not mistaken about the source used by Mark here (either a written source or one in stereotyped oral form), the warning against the scribes (12:38–40) may readily be viewed as the summary and conclusion of that document (or oral sequence) of controversial commonplaces. The notion that there existed primitive Christian handbooks of apologetics, collections of scripture proof-texts, of anti-Jewish polemics, or of ethical counsels to disciples (e.g., the "Two Ways") is not only probable but seems to be supported by such evidence as has survived. The facts of Marcan order and arrangement speak for themselves; and some hypothesis of this nature seems to be all but inevitable.

The conclusion of the series, with the appended anecdote of the widow's mite (12:41–44), suggested no doubt for inclusion here by the mention of "widows' houses" in v. 40 (from Q?), forms the transition to and the setting for Mark's famous eschatological chapter (13), on the approaching end of the age and its preceding events viewed as "signs." Here we are almost certainly dealing with a pre-Marcan document, the "Little Apocalypse" (vv. 6–8; 14–20; 24–27), presumably from the time of Caligula (A.D. 41), who undertook to erect his own statue in the temple at Jerusalem—another "abomination that desolates" like the pagan altar in 168 B.C. (See Josephus, War, II. 10. 1–5; also the commentaries on Mark 13). This Little Apocalypse was pieced out by

Mark with sayings (some of them perhaps derived from Q) which for the most part undoubtedly go back to our Lord. But the setting (in 13:1, 2) is certainly Mark's own; it was suggested by the conclusion of the controversy sequence, and involved merely Jesus' withdrawal from the temple to the Mount of Olives, v. 3.

With ch. 14 begins the Passion Narrative, which, we may assume, was probably in more or less fixed and final form long before Mark wrote; its general order and contents were a commonplace of current Christian tradition. Mark's Passion Narrative contains more than one insertion, interpretation, and emphasis—definite additions may be seen in many places (compare the reconstructed pre-Marcan narrative, on p. 79, with the present text of Mark). For these additions from other sources, the author himself was no doubt responsible. Back of both Mark's Passion Narrative (in ch. 14–15) and the old pre-Marcan narrative that underlies it, is the divergent form found in John, and the old tradition which it presupposes—probably Judean, perhaps Syrian or Egyptian. But the general order, the arrangement, and the main contents were clearly well fixed long before the gospels or their sources were written. Some of the features in Mark's Passion Narrative may perhaps go back to Peter—especially the account of Peter's denials; though the distinction is not easy to draw between Peter's own reminiscences and the details of the growing Petrine legend—at whose basis no doubt lay his own recollections, in one form or another. Such a legend grew swiftly, following his martyrdom—note how swiftly, a century later, the Polycarp legend arose; and many another instance might be adduced from the literature of martyrdom in the early church—some even from the book of Acts and elsewhere in the New Testament.

It may seem that too much space has been given to this detailed examination of the structure and contents of Mark; but there is no other way to study the structure of the gospel than by a detailed analysis of its contents. As for results, certainly one or two facts are clear. First, Papias' statement of the disorder of Mark gives us a clue—but no more than a clue—to the ultimate derivation of Mark's material. It was not from Peter's preaching alone (Irenaeus says "preaching," but Papias had said "teaching"—see p. 86), though there are doubtless elements derived from Peter, but from the early Christian preaching or teaching in general that Mark has drawn a large amount of his material. In particular, he has drawn much from some collection of early Christian anti-Jewish polemics, whose order and sequence provide the order for long sections of the gospel. If this was the substance of a considerable amount of early Christian preaching and teaching, we need not be surprised—not all early Christian preachers were Pauls. Nor need it surprise us as a sample, in particular, of the preaching to which the early Roman church was accustomed: one thinks of Clement, Hermas, and Justin as a singularly uninspired succession of preachers and leaders and representatives of that nevertheless enormously influential church.

What especially impresses us is the relative absence of the tradition of *Jesus' teaching* (contrast Matthew and Luke!), and the curious interpretation placed upon such teaching as Mark gives (e.g., the parables in ch. 4, or the antiscribal tradition in ch. 7, or the eschatological teaching in ch. 13). The early church in Rome was a church of martyrs; but how cold and unimaginative must many of those early Roman Christians have been, and how stern, even severe, was their faith! By contrast with Luke, and his great document L; by contrast with Q, of which Mark makes such slight use, though he quotes sayings from it again and again, perhaps from memory; by contrast with John, with his warm enthusiasm and deep feeling for spiritual realities; by contrast, above all, with the letters of Paul, little as they give us of the life and teaching of Jesus, but much of his influence, his character or "mind" (Phil. 2:5)—by these contrasts, Mark seems decidedly narrow and severe in his conception and representation of Christ. What stuff those Roman Christians were made of, to be inspired to heroic testimony to their faith, steadfast even unto death, by a religious life so largely controversial! And yet there is little doubt that the spirit of that age and locality is accurately reflected in this earliest gospel, i.e., in Mark's selection from the current evangelic tradition. We may look back upon those ancient controversies, thankful that they are now among the "old, unhappy, far-off things"; and at the same time recognize that the very sternness of this creed had much to do with its survival in a heroic time and amid a people whose religion had for countless generations been nourished upon the sternest and most austere practices and ideas.

The ethical and religious outlook of Mark is almost entirely overcast by the thought of martyrdom; it lacks the ascetic element found in Matthew and the sweeping ethic of renunciation found in Luke, and also the full note of hope and of glorious assurance that went with the transcendent eschatology of Q—heightened as it no doubt also was by the experience of persecution; it lacks also the sunny "humanism"—if the word may be ventured—which we detect in L, with its table talk, its note of friendliness, its parables of human kindness and goodness. It is an austere gospel. Its Christ reminds us of the pensive, indeed severe, faces that look down from the old Roman frescoes of the apostles, with their typically Roman seriousness, *gravitas*, so different from the usual Italian insouciance and levity of spirit; not sad, yet unsmiling; not grim, yet fully aware of the desperate issues confronting the faithful in a hard and cruel world which viewed their faith as only a novel kind of folly; not cast down in defeat, yet firm in a conviction that even death itself may have to be endured, and that on the farther side of death, somehow in part through their own endurance of the struggle and as sharers in his sufferings, Christ's final victory is assured. It is the Christ who inspired such determined faith and hope as this who is the Christ of the Marcan Gospel. Its ethic is the ethic of Jesus of Nazareth viewed from the vantage point of a martyr faith. It is this fact of its general character and purpose that must help to account for the meager emphasis upon Jesus' teaching upon other subjects which we find in Mark, quite as much as the fact (for it is a fact) that its author knew and presupposed his readers' acquaintance with some oral or written collection of Jesus' words.

As Johannes Weiss said, in his penetrating chapter on Mark in the posthumous volume of his *Urchristentum* (p. 544 == Vol. II, p. 697 of the English translation, *History of Primitive Christianity*), "The ecclesiastical-historical significance of the oldest Gospel consists chiefly in this, that it produced, once and for all, a picture of the earthly Jesus, with those vivid features which became the model of later writers and made so deep and ineradicable an impression upon the church. One may see in St. Mark the meaning the historical Jesus possessed for the Christian Mission. We have already observed that the missionary preaching could not forego a certain measure of detailed information about the life of Jesus— even St. Paul could not do without it altogether. Faith in the heavenly Lord always implied that it was he who had lived upon earth and had been crucified as Jesus of Nazareth. The Gospel of Mark now teaches us that the demand for a vital and clearly defined view of Jesus was much greater than has ordinarily been assumed. The newly converted were eager to learn more about him, of whom it was said that he was the Son of God; the churches required a vivid presentation, for purposes of worship and personal faith, of him who for their sakes had laid down his life. Moreover there was certainly not lacking a genuine historical interest—especially as the eyewitnesses of the life of Jesus died, one by one, the need became apparent for conserving the tradition they represented. The oldest gospel is the literary crystallization of this oral tradition—and also of certain pre-literary written sketches or outlines of the first generation of missionaries. Hence it is correctly understood and appraised only when, on the one hand, it is read as expressing the views and convictions of the evangelist, and on the other as a collection of older traditions which in part at least emerge out of an entirely different set of attitudes. Stated in terms of doctrinal history: it is dominated by the Christology of the Pauline and post-Pauline generation, but it contains material reflecting the conception of Jesus of the earliest Christian community. The Jesus of Mark is the Son of God, equipped with divine knowledge and might; but he is also the one-time Jewish teacher and prophet, with human feelings and limited knowledge and power—deity and humanity interpenetrate each other in an inseparable unity in this picture. In effecting this, Mark set the tone, for all time to come, both for the popular view and for the theological conception of the earthly Jesus."

[On the Son of God and Son of Man Christologies in Mark, see the Introduction to Mark in *The Interpreter's Bible*, Vol. VII, or the Introduction to *Mark* in Harper's Annotated Bible Series. The alleged "Paulinism" of Mark has undoubtedly been greatly exaggerated, and rests on very weak grounds. As Professor Martin Werner shows in his book, *Der Einfluss paulinischer Theologie im Markusevangelium* (Giessen, 1923), the agreements of Mark with Paul do not go beyond the views common to primitive Christianity; moreover, the specifically "Pauline" views and doctrines are either ignored by Mark or else quite divergent ones are presented (*op. cit.*, p. 209; see also my *Earliest Gospel*, ch. IX). And he quotes with approval the words of Professor Wernle (*Die Synoptische Frage*, p. 200): "To understand Mark, one must forget all about 'Paulinism.'"]

Weiss goes on to prove the statement that for Mark our Lord is specifically and unconditionally the Son of God—no longer in the adoptionist sense, viz., that he "became" Son of God at his exaltation, nor in the sense of the old "Western" reading of Luke 3:22 ("This day have I begotten thee"), since a symbolic or theocratic-political interpretation of the title lies far outside his horizon: "Son of God" is more than "Messiah," as Weiss puts it. The sense in which Mark understands the title is the one meant by the centurion at the cross (15:39), a wholly popular conception, of a being by nature related to God. This title the early gentile church, probably even before the time of Paul's great letters, had adopted, reinterpreted, and filled with fresh Christian meaning, as the best available term in the Greek language for the conception of the exalted Christ which lay at the heart of the church's message. Popular also is the characteristic trait, that Mark does not reflect upon the way in which deity came to appear in human form. It is impossible to say whether he thinks of a divine pre-existence, of a descent from heaven, of an incarnation or divine birth—and the very fact that we cannot answer the question is most significant of all; the evangelist feels no conscious need for doctrinal or philosophical definition on this point. He is entirely satisfied to show that Jesus is proclaimed divine by the activity and the knowledge he displays and by the voices around him, divine, supernatural, and human. "His point of view is not even that of St. Paul, viz. that the Incarnate One foregoes the exercise of the divine power and the display of the divine glory [his self-abnegation or kenōsis]; he stands much closer to St. John, who conceives the divine doxa as manifested even during Jesus' earthly life (John 1:14; 2:12)—of course not publicly, but to those whose eyes were opened—the disciples. Already, as in John, they compose the believing church" (p. 545).

The Jesus of Mark is the Jesus of the gentile Christian mission; and the traits, human and divine, of Mark's Jesus are those that interested the Christians of his time. It is interesting to note the features that are omitted—taking the normal round of modern biographical "interests" as our standard. In spite of the emphasis Mark laid upon the human features in his "portrait" of Christ, there is nothing here in the way of a sketch of his "personality"— either his physical characteristics or his manners, moods, and habits of life; nothing of his early years, education, environment, calling, his first efforts as a teacher or prophet, his spiritual experiences and development. None of these things interested him, apparently —and none were recorded in the tradition he made use of. Our only knowledge of Jesus' inner life is derived indirectly, by inference from his words and acts. Of course this holds true of the gospels generally; but it is especially noteworthy in Mark. The later writers, especially Luke, try to repair the lack—but not very successfully. Above all, the absence of a chronological scheme (save of the simplest kind) marks off the earliest gospel as decidedly lacking in biographical interest. The reason for this absence of a chronological sequence we have already considered, viz., Mark's arrangement of his material by subject and the anecdotal absence of order in the available tradition. Yet how powerful must have been the impression created upon the minds of his readers— the "submerged" and persecuted Roman Christians, and gentile

Christians generally throughout the empire—as they read this story or heard it from the lips of "teachers" or "evangelists" or listened to the reading of it at the services of worship! Jesus, the friend of publicans and sinners—since the sick have need of a physician, not the well (2:17); Jesus, the forgiver of men's sins (2:15)—must not the heavenly Christ, soon to come as men's Judge, be the same as the earthly Jesus, mild, loving, ready to help? (for the stories proved not only his power but also his willingness to heal); Jesus, hated and despised, betrayed by his friend, deserted by his followers, and led out to death at the hands of his enemies, draining to its last bitter dregs the cup of suffering—yes, even abandoned, apparently, by God (15:34)—what must all this have meant to the persecuted Christians in Rome, hung up as living torches in Nero's gardens, or flung to the famishing wild beasts in the arena?—or to Christians who, escaping martyrdom, were nevertheless persecuted in many another way, and bowed down with the burden of life as it was forced upon the slaves and dispossessed lower classes in that ancient world, especially in the city of Rome? One can readily see how precious a document it was, and how inevitably it set the standard for the later evangelists.

This point of view, elaborated with great clarity by Professor Weiss in this and in other writings on the gospel from his pen (notably in his *Aelteste Evangelium*, 1903, and in *Die Schriften des Neuen Testaments*, Vol. I, 2d ed., 1907), is one which has commended itself increasingly to modern New Testament scholars. Our Gospel According to Matthew is fundamentally a new edition of Mark, enlarged by the incorporation of other material, chiefly from Q; while Luke wholly revamped Mark, incorporating material from Q and other sources, chiefly L. (On the Proto-Luke theory, see ch. X.) Although Luke and Matthew each in his own way undertook to supply information omitted by Mark, neither of them wholly abandoned the standard set by this earliest gospel; while its *normative* influence, in theological outlook (elementary as this was), in historical perspective, in the interpretation of Jesus' teaching (e.g., the parables, where Mark is clearly wrong in his view of Jesus' purpose), in the significance attached to his "mighty works," in the assignment of motives that led to his condemnation—in all these respects its normative influence is so far-reaching as to be practically dominant. Thus Mark created the synoptic type. If we ask, as in fact we have already asked, why we have gospels, the answers must inevitably center about this one writing, this earliest of the group which set the tempo and gave the tone to a whole series of compositions. Every historical or literary consideration of the later gospels must therefore begin with Mark. Though its influence was exerted in a different way upon each of the two later synoptists, there is no question that it was profound and determinative. Only John seems to have escaped its influence. As a creative achievement, therefore, in the history of literature and in the history of the Christian church, it is impossible to rate too highly this severely limited and incomplete and far from perfect writing of some Roman Christian, put together in the strenuous days of the later sixties—while Nero still sat on his bloodstained throne, and Antichrist was looked for far and near.

CHAPTER IX

The Sources of Mark

*T*here is much in the Gospel of Mark that cannot possibly come from the Apostle Peter; the very form and structure of the work betray alike its author's motives and his use of various sources. Turner's view that many of Mark's narratives can be shifted from the third person singular or plural to the first person—not "he went" or "they went" but "I went" or "we went," meaning Peter and the other disciples—is suggestive but untenable. Papias' statement—or the elder's—accordingly does not go far enough, though a valuable clue has been retained in this saying. As far as we can now make out, the following are the major sources or strands in Mark's Gospel (i.e., in addition to the underlying Passion Narrative, the Little Apocalypse embedded in ch. 13, the Great Miracle Stories, and the Controversy sections, which we have already discussed), naming them in the order in which they may be isolated in a critical analysis of the gospel:

(1) Most easily recognizable are the sections or single verses derived from Q—for the "doublets" in Matthew and Luke are very clear signs of the presence of Q in Mark, and aid us in distinguishing the following passages:

1:2–8	John's appearance and preaching.
1:12, 13	Jesus' temptation.
3:22–27	The charge of collusion with Beelzebul.
3:28–30	Blasphemy against the Holy Spirit.
4:21, 22	Light.
4:24a, c, 25	"In the same measure . . ."
4:30–32	Parable of the mustard seed.
6:7–13	Mission of the twelve disciples.
8:12	A sign refused.
[8:15	The leaven of the Pharisees.]
8:34, 35	Renunciation.

8:38	Confessing the Son of Man.
9:35	"He that would be first . . ."
[9:37	Receiving a child.]
9:42	Causes of stumbling.
9:50	Salt.
10:11	Divorce.
11:23	Faith.
13:33–37	Parable of the watchful servants.

(70 verses, out of a total of 661 [Nestle's text], or just over 10.5 per cent of the gospel.)

Some sections, like the first two (1:2–8, 12, 13), are implied by the Matthean-Lucan contacts in their parallel sections, rather than by the existence of doublets. That is, the best explanation of the situation is to suppose that Mark is here echoing, if not abridging, the source Q which Matthew and Luke give at greater length.

Many of these passages are quoted in an abridged and even a garbled form—as if from memory, and that a rather poor one. On the other hand, they are marked by a style of their own, fairly distinct: e.g., the solemn *Amēn, legō humin,* "Truly, I say to you," found in Mark *only in these sections taken from Q,* or in passages close at hand (3:28; 8:12; 9:1, 41; 10:15, 29; 11:23; 12:43; 13:30), and in the Passion Narrative (thirteen times in all). This solemn formula of affirmation meets us again in Matthew (thirty-two times), where it is doubtless derived from Q as well as from Mark, and in the Gospel of John (twenty-six times), where it has the peculiar form of the doubled *Amēn*—"Truly, truly, I say to you." Luke has the phrase only six times (three of these derived from Mark).

(2) Having isolated the Q sections, we may without much difficulty proceed to isolate the *editorial* introductions, transitions, reflections, inferences, and summaries which Mark has added, and also the sections which he has rewritten entirely in his own style. Though by no means exhausting the editorial material in the gospel, the most obvious of these are:

1:1, 9–11, 14, 15, 21, 22, 27, 28, 32–34.
2:1, 2, 10–12, 13, 14, 19b, 20.
3:6, 7–12, 20, 21, 31.
4:1, 2, 10–20, 33, 34.
6:1, 14–16, 30–34, 53–56.
7:1–4, 14–23.
8:11, 13, 14, 16–21, 31.
9:1 (?), 9–13 (?), 30–32, 33, 34, 36, 49.

10:1, 10, 12, 32–34.
11:11, 19, 20–22.
13:3–5.
14:1, 2, 10, 11, 21, 26, 51, 52.
(119 verses, or nearly 18 per cent of the gospel.)

Most of these passages are clearly recognizable at once as editorial additions or compositions. Their style is that noted by Hawkins in *Horae Synopticae* (pp. 10 ff.) and by other investigators.

(3) The next step is to examine the residuum—473 verses, or 71 per cent of the gospel. Of this, a fair number of sections may be attributed with some certainty to *the Petrine element:* perhaps not to Peter's reminiscences, or to Peter's teaching, but to the Petrine "element," a term which covers not only reminiscences but also material gathered together in the swiftly growing Petrine legend, following the martyr's death in A.D. 62 or 64. There seems to be no other process for detecting and isolating the "Petrine element" in Mark than simply to take the passages that remain, after we have isolated the Q element and the editorial matter, and then inquire which of them contain references to Peter, or read like possible "reminiscences" (or anecdotes told by Peter), or appear to fit the Petrine "legend"—i.e., to be stories or incidents told of Peter after (or even before) his death: incidents, that is to say, in which Peter figures. It is noticeable that Peter does not figure in the Controversies (save the first, which arose out of Jesus' ministry of healing); and it is certainly unlikely that these were due to Peter's preaching in Rome—they bear the marks of a longer usage by the church than would thus be possible. More likely they represent the polemical teaching of the *didaskaloi* in the early Roman church. That there was such a tradition of controversy with Jews in Rome is evident from Romans, Acts, even from Justin Martyr, ca. A.D. 150.

Within the "Petrine element" it may be possible to distinguish material going back to Peter *himself*—e.g., the denials; as Rawlinson points out (*Commentary*, p. xxix), "When this Gospel was written, the character of St. Peter had been transfigured by martyrdom." Here the criteria seem to be: (1) Peter's own self-derogation; (2) extraordinary vividness; (3) separation from the context; (4) a distinct point of view—though this latter is rarely traceable.

In other words, we pass a strong magnet over the residuum of gospel materials, and certain passages appear to respond to the attraction. There is no finality or absolute certainty about the process or its results. But we can scarcely escape the conviction that at any rate some of these selected passages are of Petrine origin, and justify the tradition of Mark's dependence upon Peter for at least a part of his material. One may, of course, easily dismiss this method as "subjective," or point out that most writers on the Gospel of Mark are in disagreement when it comes to the specific identification of Petrine passages. Nevertheless, the conviction persists that some of these passages go back to Peter.

The term "legend" has a highly technical meaning in literary and historical criticism and does not prejudge the truth or untruth of the data which form its nucleus. Many a chapter in both sacred and secular history could never be written if "legend" were to be equated with "fable" or "myth." The stages in the development of the Petrine legend are easily traceable, the earlier of them lying within the period of the New Testament: (1) Marcan material derived from Peter; (2) other Petrine material found in Mark, some of it apocryphal, but certainly early; (3) the position assigned to Peter by the author of Acts, reflecting a tradition of Peter's leadership in the early Jerusalem and Palestinian church (confirmed in general by the Pauline epistles: Galatians, I Corinthians, etc.), though the speeches ascribed to him are composed "in character" by the author (note the absence of this material in Luke!); (4) the more fully developed Petrine legends in Matthew (especially in Matthew's special material); (5) the story of Peter's deliverance from prison by the angel (Acts 12); (6) the Commission to Peter in the Appendix to John (ch. 21); (7) the Epistles of Peter—II Peter dating from ca. A.D. 150; (8) the Gospel of Peter, Apocalypse of Peter, Preaching of Peter, etc., in the New Testament Apocrypha; (9) the Clementina, containing second- and third-century material; (10) the fully developed Petrine claims and "traditions" of the later papacy.

Among the sections containing at least a nucleus of Petrine material may be listed the following, chiefly from the earlier half of the gospel:

1:16–20	The call of four disciples.
23–26	In the synagogue at Capernaum.
29–31	Peter's wife's mother is healed.
35–39	Jesus' departure at dawn.
2:3–9	Healing the palsied.
4:35–41	Rebuking the storm (?).
5:21–43	The daughter of Jairus, and the woman who touched Jesus' garment (?).
8:27–30	Peter's confession of faith in Jesus' messiahship.
32, 33	Jesus rebukes Peter.

9:2–8   The Transfiguration.
  14–29   Healing the dumb child.
14:27–31   Prediction of the disciples' dispersal.
  43–50   Judas' betrayal and the arrest (?).
  66–72   Peter's denials.
16:1–8   The women at the tomb (?).

(This is a total of only 111 verses out of the 473 still to be accounted for—barely 23.6 per cent; and only 16.7 per cent of the whole gospel.) I do not presume to say that these figures are final, or that the identification of "Petrine" passages is beyond dispute. It is a minimum rather than a maximum assignment and includes passages that should be among the first to be examined as to their Petrine origin. There may be other Petrine sections—possibly 3:1–5, for example, or 10:17–22, or 14:12–16, 17–20. But it certainly appears that the Petrine element in Mark is far less extensive than is commonly assumed, and much less than the words of Papias and the elder would lead us to assume.

(4) Having isolated these fairly certain sources, we are left with a final residuum of material which seems quite unlikely to have come from any one source, but was probably supplied by the *common Christian tradition*, by local and personal tradition, and by legend.

As we have already observed, a large proportion—two whole chapters (14–15), minus the Petrine, Q, and editorial passages noted above—comes from the Passion Narrative, which was no doubt as well known in the Roman church in the sixties as anywhere else in the Mediterranean world. To this has been added the account of the empty tomb (16:1–8), which is as close an approximation to a resurrection narrative as Mark provides (unless the Transfiguration, 9:2–8, was originally a resurrection appearance: see p. 95).

The Little Apocalypse (13:6–8, 14–20, 24–27) accounts for three more sections—fourteen verses in all. This material was perhaps non-Christian Jewish in its ultimate origin.

The remainder contains material of most diverse character—and probably of diverse origin: some of it plainly legendary, as we have already observed, e.g., the healing of the leper (1:40–45), the Gerasene demoniac (5:1–20), the death of John the Baptizer (6:17–29), the feeding of the five thousand (6:35–44), the walking on the sea (6:45–52), and the cursing of the fig tree (11:12–14). Some sections represent variant accounts of the same event—e.g., the block from 7:24 to 8:10, containing the stories of the

Syro-Phoenician woman, the deaf man in Decapolis, and the feeding of the four thousand. On the other hand, some of the remain-
ing sections are much less legendary in character (in the popular
sense of "legendary")—e.g., the blessing of the children (10:13–16),
and the incident of the rich young man (10:17–22) that immediately follows it—both are incorporated in the section on discipleship.

Among questions that still remain to be asked are these: Have
we any evidence of an *Urmarcus*—i.e., a "Proto-Mark," a primitive
form of the gospel different from the one we now have? Are there
any traces of a growth of this gospel through successive revisions?
Granted that the Passion Narrative came first, can we trace the
next stage—and if so, which material was added next, the Petrine
element or the Controversies? To all such questions the answer
must be in the negative. Wendling's famous theory of a growth
of Mark through three successive stages has not commended itself
to modern scholars generally; though the brief additions noted by
J. Weiss and others, amounting to a verse or two and a few phrases
here and there, may suffice, in the estimation of some scholars, to
justify the term "second edition." Even so, the majority of these
"additions" appear to be in Mark's own style, not that of a later
hand.
It is not the single Gospel of Mark which has grown by successive stages, but only its separate strands of material—as we have
noted in analyzing the discourses. What we have learned from
Mark and the other evangelists, and from the New Testament as
a whole, is that the growth of the gospel tradition and of the
gospels as a group took place in three stages: (1) the oral period
—this is the level with which form criticism specially concerns
itself; (2) the period of the sources (Q, L, etc.)—this is the subject of source criticism or source analysis; (3) the stage of the
final gospel writings—and this is the subject of the whole range of
literary, textual, grammatical, lexical, exegetical, theological, and
historical study of the gospels as it is conducted by modern scholars. True, historical and literary criticism are also concerned with
the underlying sources of the gospels, and likewise with the oral
traditions which underlay the gospel sources; but these we do not
possess in documentary form—only in hypothetical reconstruc-
tions.
One inclines to think, perhaps, that the designation "new editions" only reflects the ease with which modern works are repro-
duced. Instead of a growth of the book itself through successive

stages—an assumption contradicted by the obvious unity of the work—it appears more probable that the development took place in the sources prior to Mark's use of them. After incorporation in the gospel they underwent no further elaboration or modification. Up to the date of the actual writing of the book, then, there was ample room for modification and development; and, if conjecture may be admitted where certainty is impossible, the largest amount of development will probably be assigned to the Great Miracle Stories and the Little Apocalypse; the least, to the Controversies and the Passion Narrative. (a) Such traditions as the legends of the death of John the Baptist and the Gerasene demoniac have passed through a course of oral repetition and development, i.e., of modification, which may have been long or short, but which it is now impossible to trace. (b) What lies back of the Little Apocalypse also is hard to make out, with our present knowledge; though we may of course someday come upon further survivals of Jewish apocalyptic literature which will throw real light upon its origin, date, and external circumstances. The theory of its origin in the last year or two of Caligula's reign, i.e., ca. A.D. 41, seems at present most probable. (c) The Controversies seem to be so clearly arranged that it is only a step to assume that they already existed in stereotyped form when Mark took them over. That they existed in written form seems impossible of proof—the Marcan style is as clear in these sections as anywhere else in the book—though their orderly arrangement points in this direction. But as stereotyped oral material it is not an unreasonable guess that they represented commonplaces of Christian-Jewish controversy and were derived either from the preaching (kērygma) of the early Roman church or from its teaching (didascalia or didachē) addressed to converts and designed to strengthen them in their new faith, answer their questions, and solve some of their difficulties. (d) The Passion Narrative was already firmly fixed in the liturgical usage of the Roman church, as its very form suggests and its references to intervals of time, "morning," the "third" hour, "the sixth," "evening" (15:1, 25, 33, 42)—the ancient Roman "watches" of the day which marked the vigiliae of the early Christians.

To sum up the hypothesis briefly, then, the order of the growth of the Gospel of Mark in its author's own mind was perhaps as follows:

1. First came the Passion Narrative—its basis derived from the common Christian tradition of Jesus' last days in Jerusalem, available to Mark in its Roman form.

2. To this were prefaced the Controversies with the Jewish

authorities, leading up to the Passion Narrative, and explaining how Jesus came to be rejected by the Jewish religious leaders. These controversies were divided into two main sections, corresponding to the Galilean and Judean periods of Jesus' ministry.

3. The Petrine element was introduced into this combination, chiefly at the beginning—adding much of the vividness for which Mark is famous.

4. In order to give examples of Jesus' teaching, certain passages from Q—presumably from the common oral tradition of Jesus' sayings designated by that symbol—were added, chiefly sayings relating to discipleship, a subject of central importance in Q. They were added, apparently, from memory rather than by citation of a document.

5. The collection of parables in ch. 4 was added as a further example of Jesus' teaching.

6. The Great Miracle Stories, in 4:35–5:43, illustrated Jesus' "power," i.e., both his ability and his authority. So vivid and impressive are these that some students have described the whole Gospel of Mark as "the good news of the mighty works of God done through Christ."

7. The Little Apocalypse was added and amplified for a similar reason; it satisfied in some degree the urgent demand for Jesus' own answer to the question of the date of the Parousia and the "signs of the end." It was of course assumed by Mark to contain authentic teaching of Jesus.

8. Finally, the mass of current oral tradition (not so extensive in Rome, probably, as in Palestine and Syria) was drawn upon for additional material upon numerous points as the narrative proceeded.

9. Hence the whole work took shape in a more or less predetermined form, considering the probability that the Passion Narrative, the Controversies, and the Little Apocalypse were already in fixed oral if not documentary form. Perhaps more or less in the order followed by the lections at public worship in the early Christian-Jewish calendar—i.e., in relation to the great religious festivals—or perhaps only in the "order" (which Papias and the elder failed to recognize) of the author's own view of the course of events—at any rate, the book took shape in the author's own mind in something like the order just sketched, and in the actual writing of it the author supplied the introductions, summaries, transitions, and moralizing applications so characteristic of his work.

Thus grew the Marcan Gospel, not, I think, by successive stages but in its author's own conception before he sat down and wrote it out at length, laboriously and painstakingly. Its growth is the growth of its materials and sources, as they already existed in the tradition current in one particular church, that of Rome—not as a result of repeated redaction either by the author himself or by a succession of later "hands." No writing in the New Testament bears more clearly the marks of unity of authorship, from its brief title and swiftly moving first sentences to its abrupt and perhaps fragmentary close.

Such is the light which a study of the form and structure of the Gospel of Mark throws upon its purposes, its method of composition, its materials, and its sources. If it no longer betrays "the freshness and vividness of original composition," except in a very few sections or pericopes, it at least bears the marks of the hard age in which it arose, reflects the circumscribed outlook of its author and first readers, and reveals most clearly the paucity of the materials at the author's disposal, especially for a presentation of Jesus' teaching—unless Mark presupposes the use of Q (or of some of its contents) by the contemporary teachers of the church. We are a whole generation and more removed from the events described in its pages, and many leagues removed geographically. Its author lives in another world than the Palestine of Jesus' days —one can scarcely believe that he ever saw Palestine or knew Judaism and its sacred scriptures intimately and sympathetically. He may, of course, have known John Mark, as well as Peter; he may, indeed, have been John Mark—i.e., our John Mark, known from the book of Acts, though Papias definitely stated that Mark had *not* been either a hearer or a personal follower of Jesus. But it would probably be far safer to describe him as a Roman Christian —Marcus was certainly one of the commonest of Roman names— who reflected at an early day the somewhat cold and unimaginative outlook characteristic of that ancient church. Yet such as it is— and the more certainly so, the more clearly we recognize just what the book is—it remains the most priceless document of primitive Western Christianity; though it by no means provides us with all we wish to know about the life and teaching of our Lord or about the life and teaching, activities, and beliefs, of the early church.

CHAPTER X

Luke the Historian

*J*t is obvious, from even a casual reading of the first three gospels, that they are somehow interrelated and share a more or less common view. Hence the name given them, "synoptic" gospels, for they invite comparison, they are to be seen and studied "side by side." Upon a closer examination of the Greek text, it becomes clear that hundreds of words and phrases, and even many whole sentences, are identical in two of the three, sometimes in all three gospels. Ninety per cent of the contents of Mark is found in Matthew, fifty-one per cent in Luke, most of Mark's actual words appearing in one or the other. Only thirty-one of Mark's 661 verses are omitted by *both* Luke and Matthew. Furthermore, the order is much the same, as may be seen at a glance if one consults the table of contents of the R.S.V. *Gospel Parallels*, Huck's *Synopsis*, or any other good modern "Harmony," or the excellent chart prepared by Allan Barr. Whenever one gospel has an order independent of the other two, or either omits or adds material of its own, not in the others, *the other two always include Mark*. The key to the "synoptic problem" is accordingly the centrality, and therefore the priority, of Mark. Luke and Matthew have edited, revised, abridged, and amplified Mark, chiefly no doubt in the interest of adding much more material containing the teaching of Jesus, which Mark often mentions but rarely gives in detail. (See the "sequences" in Mark noted above: his arrangement of the sayings of Jesus in discourses was not very logical or consistent.)

The most widely held view at present is that Mark came first (ca. A.D. 68) and was later incorporated by Matthew and Luke in their gospels. In Matthew, this earlier writing was made the basis of the narrative, being divided into five main sections, each now supplemented by a teaching discourse (see the Outline of Matthew,

p. 193). In Luke, it is a question whether Mark was the basis of the narrative or was not, instead, abridged and inserted, in seven main sections, into a collection of teaching material which had already been formed into a primitive kind of "gospel" or, rather, a small *vademecum* used either by teachers in the early Palestinian church or by Luke himself. This is the theory of "Proto-Luke," i.e., of an earlier stage in the composition or compilation of the Gospel of Luke, made prior to the author's discovery and inclusion of Mark's narrative among his sources. Luke omits the long section of Mark, 6:45–8:26, but he more than offsets it by his great central section, 9:51–18:14. Some of the omitted material seems to duplicate what is included elsewhere (e.g., the feeding of the multitude), and hence one account could be omitted without too great loss. The motive for the omission, like that which led to Matthew's frequent abridgment of Mark, was no doubt the desire to save space for the teaching material, while the long interpolation (9:51–18:14) represents a large body of teaching material for which Luke had found no suitable locations in the earlier narrative sections taken over from Mark. It is therefore left in the form of incidents on the southward journey of Jesus from Galilee to Jerusalem, though when the journey approaches its end Jesus is no nearer Jerusalem than when he left Galilee at the beginning. The device is purely literary.

The common material in Luke and Matthew *not* found in Mark (= Q) amounts, as we have seen (p. 59), to about 242 verses. In Matthew this material is arranged by subject, and is distributed throughout the five great discourses in that gospel. But in Luke the original order is retained, and reflects a subject arrangement of its own. The material peculiar to Luke (= L; see p. 61) amounts to 264 verses, and is distinguished by both its style and subject matter, and even by its primitive "theology," from both the Marcan and the Q material found in Luke. Since in Luke it is already closely associated with Q, the other main teaching source, it naturally follows the order of that source. Nevertheless, when detached and studied by itself, it appears to have an order somewhat independent of Q (see p. 56, and Int. to Luke in *Harper's Annotated Bible*).

It is the theory of those who advocate a Proto-Luke that Q and L were first combined to form an embryonic gospel, beginning with Luke 3:1, 2, "a capital beginning for a gospel," as Streeter remarked. Into this combination, Mark was inserted in seven sections (= Luke 4:31–44, 5:12–6:19, 8:4–9:50, 18:15–43, 19:28–36, 19:45–21:33, 21:37–22:13), the Infancy Narrative being added later, and also the special Lucan Passion and Resurrection Narratives. Thus "grew" the Lucan Gospel, the first volume in Luke's historical defense of the Christian faith against the view which made it a dangerous subversive movement—the first great *apologia* for early Christianity. Just where Proto-Luke ended is not certain, i.e., whether or not it really contained a passion narrative, and whether or not it merely anticipated the tragic outcome of Jesus' journey to Jerusalem. (A more fully detailed presentation of the theory may be seen in the chart on p. 130.) The main opposition has come from such scholars as the late J. M. Creed, who insisted that the Marcan narrative was basic, and may not only be found intruded into Q and L sections (e.g., 4:16–30, 5:1–11) but is fundamental for the whole Passion and Resurrection Narrative. Perhaps, as we have suggested, the most probable view is that L represents "the contents of Luke's notebook," and that he had already amplified his "copy" of Q (whether document or fixed tradition) by the addition of this L material before he began combining Q and Mark to form his first volume, his account of "all that Jesus began to do and teach until the day when he was taken up." In the modern view, the gospels grew out of the oral tradition, first forming oral, then written, sources (Q, L, Mark, etc.), and finally the completed gospels which we now possess.

Though both Matthew and Luke deal very freely with Mark (more freely as a rule than with the sayings of Jesus, though there are notable exceptions), it is evident that Luke deals with Mark much more freely than Matthew does. For Matthew, and for the church in his time, Mark was already scripture. Luke, writing somewhat earlier, did not hesitate to alter Mark's *meaning* (note, e.g., how he revised Mark 10:45 in 22:27 and Mark 16:7 in 24: 6 f.). Hence the rule of thumb followed by many synoptic students in reconstructing Q: "Follow Luke's order but Matthew's wording"—a rule that will not bear the fullest scrutiny. Each saying has to be studied in its full variety of attestation, text, form, and context.

When Luke is described as a Hellenistic historian, it must be remembered that in the first and second century history was still a branch of rhetoric, as Quintilian said (*Institute*, IX. 4. 129; X. 1. 31). Rhetoric was the art of the *rhētōr*, the public speaker, the orator, the advocate. Herodotus, we recall, recited his "histories" at the festivals in Athens and in connection with the quadrennial games. In the days of the younger Pliny, under the early empire, historians still gave "readings" from their works at late-afternoon receptions. It was expected that the historian, as a creator of good literature, would write interestingly, persuasively, even movingly, and usually with a lesson. The classification under oratory indicated, at least during the first and second centuries, that the author would also be expected to prove a case—e.g., that Alexander was a great general, that the Athenian fleet outnumbered the Persian, that the wheat crop compared with that of Mesopotamia, and so on. The great objective historians—Thucydides, Polybius, Tacitus—were different, and took their task much more seriously, though each had a fine and distinctive style of his own. They were the patriarchal ancestors of the modern scientific historian, and they would have rejoiced over the tools which the modern historian has at hand, accurate statistics, government reports and official documents, contemporary journals, not to mention indices and catalogues, surveys and reviews of outlying works. At the opposite extreme were the entertainers, the writers of endless compilations drawn from the voluminous works of earlier compilers and narrators—men like Diodorus Siculus—who wrote only to interest and amuse their readers or hearers. Somewhere between these two extremes was the historian with a purpose, not to amuse, not to settle school debates, not to discuss literary topics, but to persuade his readers—first of all the reader to whom the work was dedicated —of the truth or falsity of the views held about certain persons, a people, a group, a movement. Thus Josephus' *History of the Jewish War* in seven books was designed to persuade the "up-country" (i.e., Mesopotamian) Jews not to revolt against Rome, and to point out to the Romans which of the Jews had been really guilty of starting the revolt—i.e., the Zealots, whose revolutionary movement was of long standing and did not suddenly originate in A.D. 66. So also his vast *Antiquities of the Jews* in twenty books, followed by his own *apologia pro vita sua*, his autobiography (as Bk. XXI), was designed to explain the peculiarities and distinctive advantages of the Jewish law, religion, national history, and national character. Its apologetic purpose is obvious from beginning to end. And the same is true of Luke's two books, the Gospel and the Acts: he writes, not to entertain or to provide "good reading" for intelligent and interested readers of current Greek literature, but to "show the certainty" of the things which Theophilus and others had heard about the Christian movement, from the very beginning.

The preface to Luke-Acts is our best clue (it is not a preface to the gospel only but to the whole work): *In view of the fact that many persons have undertaken to put together an account of the things which have taken place among us* [Christians], *in accordance with what was handed down to us by those who from the*

beginning were eyewitnesses and "ministers of the word" [i.e.,
Christian preachers, evangelists, prophets], *it seemed good to me
also, having traced everything accurately from the outset, to write
out for you, Most Excellent Theophilus, an orderly narrative* [of
the Christian movement], *so that you may know the whole truth
about the things concerning which you have been informed.* We
are not told who Theophilus was: presumably he may have been a
Roman official, perhaps in some provincial city—not necessarily in
Rome or even in Italy. Presumably he had been informed about
the Christians, perhaps in a way similar to the various ways described in Acts, where charges were brought against them in local
courts; the old translation, which implied that Theophilus was
himself a Christian, a catechumen in process of instruction, is
impossible. (The Greek, as now understood in the light of *koinē*
usage, does not bear this meaning; and the first century is probably far too early for the Christian catechumenate; worst of all,
Luke would scarcely call in question the truth of the instruction,
even to the extent of undertaking to defend it.) Nor are we told
who were the "many" who had taken in hand to draw up similar
narratives: the usual view that Luke is only indicating his sources
seems improbable—these were parallel, possibly rival, narratives.
(Perhaps Luke had to answer libels, somewhat as Josephus did in
both his *Vita* and his *Contra Apionem.*) As for the sources, they
seem to be clearly distinguishable, partly with the help of Mark
(which fortunately survives), partly with the help of Matthew,
who also used Q, partly on stylistic considerations (his Infancy
Narrative, for example, perhaps once circulated in Hebrew, not
Aramaic or Greek, as its phraseology slips back with the greatest
ease into the classic language of the Old Testament). His sym-
pathetic understanding of Judaism is evident on every page, and
nowhere more clearly than in this Infancy Narrative. The other
sources, both in the Gospel and the book of Acts, can be made
out with fair probability, for like other Hellenistic historians, he
preserved them more or less intact, even when he revised them;
i.e., he introduced them *en bloc*, so that the expert reader can
sense the transition from one to another. Burton Easton once said
that he believed he could tell the points at which Luke grew tired
in his laborious undertaking. Henry St. John Thackeray, I understand, had a similar feeling about Josephus. Certainly Luke had
far more sympathy with Judaism than Mark or John possessed; his
sympathy was virtually the same as that of Matthew, though it
was popular Judaism, not scribism or exegesis, that interested him.
The Preface aims to interest and attract cultivated readers; it is

far more literary in style than the rest of the work. It also resembles the prefaces of the great Hellenistic historians, e.g., Arrian, Polybius, Josephus, who dedicate their works to eminent or well-known readers, sum up their reasons for writing, stress the importance and value of their sources, and state what they hope to accomplish—or trust they have accomplished—by their efforts.

In Luke-Acts the Christian church is fortunate to possess a work which is not only the sole surviving history of the earliest period in its long career, but one which was written with extraordinary skill and from a point of view which grappled seriously with living issues at the time. If Mark shows us the church face to face with martyrdom and threatened with extinction by irresponsible mob rule and tyranny, Luke presents us with a no less serious situation at a later date, when the Roman government was steadily moving toward a policy of suppression and ostracism. In both these earliest gospels the inevitable conflict between the cross and the sword has already been joined. The outlook is very different in Matthew, where only local misrepresentation, persecution, or antagonism is anticipated, and in John, where the conflict is mainly ideological, and persecution takes place partly within the church (i.e., from schismatics, especially Gnostic sectaries) and partly in the steady rivalry and conflict between the church and the synagogue—the "unbelieving" Jews who rejected Jesus and now hate his followers.

Luke's purpose, we have said, was to prove, by a careful presentation of the historical evidence—i.e., by telling the whole story—that the Christian movement was not subversive and revolutionary. Neither Jesus himself nor his apostles had been rebels or insurgents. The charges against him (Luke 23:2-5) had been false, a libel circulated by his enemies. Pilate, the Roman governor, made a strong effort to release him but was borne down by the mob, egged on by the Jerusalem high priests and their satellites. Neither Pontius Pilate nor Herod Antipas had found any fault in him (23:6-16). In fact, the insurrectionist, Barabbas, was released at the insistence of the mob, and Jesus was crucified, altogether against the better judgment of Pilate (23:18-26)—a scene which every educated and honest Roman would know, even without reading Cicero or Tacitus, had been repeated innumerable times in provincial courts all over the empire. Similar unfounded charges had been brought against Jesus' disciples—now the apostles of the Christian church. They had been "everywhere spoken against" (Acts 28:22) and accused of trying to "turn the world upside down" (17:6) and of "acting against the decrees of Caesar, saying that there is another king, Jesus" (v. 7). But one has only to read the story to discover how unfounded these charges had been. At the very end of Acts, Paul, a prisoner awaiting trial before the emperor (this was his right as a Roman citizen) and always under guard (28:16), nevertheless lived in his own rented dwelling (vv. 23, 30) almost in the shadow of the palace—either the one on the Palatine or Nero's new Golden House east of the Forum. There he continued to preach to all comers "for two whole years," welcoming all who came to him and "preaching the Kingdom of God and teaching about the Lord Jesus Christ quite openly and unhindered" (v. 31)—not merely without anyone's forbidding him, as in the older versions, but *akōlutōs*, absolutely without interference! That final word of Luke-Acts is like the crashing finale of a triumphant symphony: one note, with all the trumpets and drums!

Luke was not only a historian; he was also a poet—and as Ernst Haenchen has said (*Die Apostelgeschichte*, 1956, p. 118), one must be something of a poet in order to understand him. There is of course a large amount of poetry in the old evangelic tradition—for Jesus also was a poet, like many ancient religious teachers, especially in the East; and there is a vast amount of poetry in the Old Testament, i.e., in the Bible as a whole. This poetry is nonmetrical, alliterative, parallelistic, and relies upon stress or accent for its rhythm. Its parallelism is like that of the Old Testament (e.g., the Psalms), and is either synonymous, antithetic, or synthetic—as Bishop Robert Lowth recognized and named the types in 1753. The freedom exercised by the evangelists in quoting the poetic passages in the tradition (e.g., in Q) results from a recognition that the words are translated. One would scarcely quote Greek poetry, in a Greek writing, this freely. And yet there are plenty of Hellenistic writers who quoted Greek poetry from memory, with considerable freedom—and there were also Greek scribes or copyists who were careless in transcribing poetic passages! A fair number of passages even in Mark are poetic (see the edition in Harper's Annotated Bible Series). An examination of the use made of these passages by Luke and Matthew discloses that the later evangelists (a) carefully preserved the structure and wording of passages from the Old Testament (this was scripture), (b) were a little less careful in retaining the exact wording of sayings of Jesus, and (c) did not hesitate to alter the lines attributed to others, e.g., to John the Baptist (Mark 1:8) or the Passover pilgrims at the Triumphal Entry (11:9 f.). Further, (d) Matthew often turns Mark's version of Jesus' sayings into balanced poetic prose, while (e) Luke often paraphrases and thus turns the poetry of Mark and Q into prose—he did not do this with his quotations from Greek poets in Acts or his quotations from the Old Testament in the gospel. Finally, (f) Mark also often turns poetry into prose.

In Luke's Infancy Narrative—the "Lucan idyll"—there is a large amount of poetry, as there is also in the older historical narratives of the Old Testament, especially in Genesis, Judges, Samuel, and Kings. (See Luke 1:13–17, 28, 30–33, 35, 38, 42, 45, 46–55, 68–79, 2:14, 29–32, 34 f.) As the oracle at Delphi gave answers in hexameter verse, so in the Bible the angels usually speak in poetry; in Luke 1–2, Gabriel does so repeatedly. The hymns in these chapters are modeled on Old Testament poetry, so admirably that a famous critic of art and literature once attributed the Magnificat (Luke 1:46–55) to "the psalmist"—a perfect tribute to poetic genius. Luke, we may be sure, would have viewed it as high praise.

When we turn to the second book, later separated from the gospel and named the Acts of the Apostles, we find the same method of composition, the same style, diction, use of sources, arrangement by "blocks," outlook, "theology" (of a simple and early variety), and purpose as are reflected in the first volume. The church advances steadily in its swift expansion from Jerusalem to Rome—the stages are marked by Luke's frequent summaries of the progress of the gospel: 6:7, Jerusalem; 9:31, Judea, Galilee, and Samaria (including the coastal plain); 12:24, Antioch; 16:5, central Asia Minor; 19:20, Macedonia, Achaia, Asia; 28:31, Rome. The author maintains that Christianity is a sect or "way" within Judaism and therefore is entitled to the same rights and privileges as the older religion—not official recognition, but only toleration, by a kind of "gentlemen's agreement" among magistrates not to interfere with the religious practices of its adherents. Although Tertullian used the term *religio licita* (see his *Apology*, 21), it does not seem to have been a common term; it does not occur in the Roman legal codes. But the idea seems to have existed, and perhaps the term was commoner than the surviving evidence would indicate. Tertullian was probably a lawyer, and the phrase sounds like a lawyer's summary phrase. In any event, what Luke was endeavoring to do was to show that Christianity was entitled to the same rights, however named, described, or defined, as those enjoyed by Jews—who ever since Herod the Great, if not since Maccabaean times, had enjoyed favorable relations with the Roman government. Thus the Christian headquarters, like the Jewish, were located at Jerusalem (1:8; cf. ch. 15), and their official leaders were the "apostles and elders" living there, an official group comparable to the Jewish "chief priests, scribes, and elders" (Luke 20:1). Questions were referred to them, even as the Jews referred their difficult cases to the great council, or Sanhedrin, of seventy (or seventy-one) members in Jerusalem. This apostolic college exercised authority over distant churches, indeed over whole territories, even outside Palestine (Acts 15:23). The members were also interpreters of the ancient Law, the Torah, applying it to new conditions—in ch. 15 the question of whether gentile Christians must keep the law of Moses, be circumcised, pay tithes, observe the Sabbath and the food laws, was decided by applying to them the ancient regulations governing resident aliens, metics or gērim (Lev. 17–18). They were to abstain from fornication and idolatry and from improper food, i.e., meat from animals that had been strangled and therefore still contained the blood, or from sacrifices offered to idols (15:20, 29; the "Western" text, which includes the Golden Rule and interprets "blood" as murder, is clearly later and comes from the second or third century). Other arguments for a favorable consideration of the Christian plea are the fact that all the earliest Christians, including the Twelve Apostles, were Jews; that their exclusion from the synagogue was involuntary, that the gospel had always been presented to the Jews first, then to the Gentiles, and that many Jews had become Christians, including even priests and Pharisees, while such a famous jurist as Gamaliel had counseled moderation in dealing with the new movement (5:33–40). But, above all, it was the personal experience of conversion and the succeeding career of the well-known Jewish leader, Saul, or Paul, of Tarsus, the one-time persecutor of the Christians who had become their great apostle, which was most impressive. The story of his conversion is told three times (in ch. 9, 22, 26), and in the end the Jewish king Agrippa II says to Paul, "A little more, and you would make me a Christian!" while the Roman governor Festus agrees (as Pilate had said of Jesus), "This man is doing nothing to deserve death or imprisonment. . . . He might have been set free if he had not made his appeal to Caesar" (26:28–32).

Whether or not the plea was successful, we do not know. Apparently Paul's appeal to Caesar failed, in the end, but we are not surprised, for madness darkened the mind of the tyrant Nero in his later years. And apparently Luke's argument failed likewise, for the Jewish opposition to Christianity only increased with the years, and Romans saw through the weak defense; the later apologists found other and firmer grounds upon which to prove their faith the true one.

It is often argued that the sources underlying the first half of Acts can be assigned to Jerusalem, Caesarea, and Antioch. Acts

1:12–5:52, 9:31–11:18, 12:1–23 is mainly Petrine and probably goes back to early Jerusalem or Judean tradition. Chapters 6:1–8:1a is very different in tone and vocabulary—Stephen is the central figure, and his speech in ch. 7, or what remains of it, may be part of some early polemical tract against orthodox Judaism: some scholars attribute this source to early Jerusalem tradition of the Hellenistic type, i.e., tradition preserved there among the "Hellenists" or Greek-speaking Jews. Chapter 8:1b–40 is possibly Caesarean; Philip is the subject, and his mission to Samaria, the neighborhood of Gaza, Azotus, and Caesarea. Chapter 11:19–30, 12:24–14:28, 15:1–16:5 is presumably Antiochene tradition, concerned with "Barnabas and Saul," distinct from the Pauline tradition, which names Paul first and centers in his missionary activities. (Barnabas was already mentioned in 4:36 f., a passage which may belong with this Antiochene tradition.) Finally, ch. 9:1–30, some of 12:24–14:28, some of 15:1–16:5, and all of 16:6–28:31 is Pauline material, much of it firsthand. It includes the so-called "we-sections," where the author suddenly shifts from third person to first ("we sailed," etc.), 16:10–18, 20:4–21:18, 27:1–28:16.

This striking phenomenon has been variously interpreted, as the author's use of some contemporary diary or letters or as a careless lapse into his own recollections. Perhaps the latter explanation is the better. It has parallels in later literature, e.g., in the *History of Montreal, 1640–72*, by Dollier de Casson (tr. by Ralph Flenley, 1928). Father Casson was a Sulpician, superior of the order in Montreal and a seigneur in the island. Although he wrote of his own doings, especially among the Indians, leading up to the important Peace of Montreal which ended the Indian wars and established a treaty with the thirty-one tribes (in 1701), he wrote with entire objectivity—save on one page of his manuscript, where he referred to "the journey Galinée and I made" to Lake Erie. Other examples have also been found—authors are not always at pains to disguise their identity!

It has also been urged that the legendary material included in this source (e.g., 16:25–31, 20:18–35) or the extraneous and non-Pauline address in 17:22–32 proves that it cannot be early or firsthand. But the use of apologetic or polemical speeches (as also in ch. 7) is not impossible—or unwarranted—in ancient historical composition; and the growth of legend has no time schedule! As George Foot Moore remarked in his work on *Judaism* (I, 208), "In a favorable environment the growth of legend may begin with the earliest reports of what happened." Even in the New Testament we are treading Catholic soil, and there is no sudden break when we enter the second or the third century. The later *Lives of the Saints* are continuous with, in fact modeled upon, the miracle stories of the New Testament.

Whether the traditions used in Acts were already in written form, or still oral, or partly written and partly oral, we cannot determine—though we may feel strongly about some of them. As a recent commentator on the book, Alfred Wikenhauser in the "Regensburg New Testament" (1951), points out, it is scarcely possible to deny that written traditions underlie the first twelve chapters, especially the speech of Stephen in ch. 7. But the difficulty of isolating and reconstructing these sources is so great that many scholars (like Dibelius, Haenchen, and Bauernfeind) have given up the attempt (made by Harnack, J. Weiss, Schwartz, and others a generation ago) and think only in terms of oral tradition, which they proceed to investigate with the help of style criticism. At the least, one can say that here, as in the gospel, Luke has so completely woven together his sources and has so thoroughly rewritten some of them that without the aid of parallel accounts (such as we find, for the gospel, in Matthew and Mark) it is impossible clearly to distinguish and identify them. That the material in the early chapters of Acts is old and authentic, no one will question. Such archaic terms as "Servant of God," "Prince and Saviour," a man "anointed with holy spirit and power"—these belong to the earliest stratum of Christology, not to that of Luke's own time.

The Lucan writing is of course the largest single work in the New Testament. It totals 78 + 71 = 149 pages in the Revised Standard Version, out of a total of 552 pages in the whole New Testament. Thus Luke-Acts forms approximately 27 per cent of the whole New Testament. Taking the fullest measure of the Pauline letters and including the disputed three, they total only 121 pages, which is considerably less than Luke's total. The quantity of Luke's material is a fitting symbol of its importance for our knowledge of the life of Jesus and the beginnings of the Christian church.

Though we are dealing with probabilities, not certainties, it is not impossible that the author of Luke gathered his material in Palestine or Syria early in the decade 70–80, if not before; then (on the Proto-Luke hypothesis) combined with it the major portion of Mark sometime in the seventies, and issued his gospel about 80 or 85 (his reference to the Fall of Jerusalem is still vivid). Later, perhaps five years later, he supplemented the original writing with a second treatise, which we know as Acts, designed to answer the

questions of educated and perhaps highly placed Roman officials
like Theophilus, and issued the whole work about 95. As for a
third volume, designed to continue the narrative broken off at the
end of Acts, there is no hint of this in either the Gospel or Acts.
Nor on a just view of the purpose of Luke-Acts is there any need
for such a hypothesis. The arrival of Paul in Rome, his quiet residence there for two years "in his own hired house"—whatever the
later course of events—sufficiently proved that the Christian
movement was not inimical to law and order and the public de-
corum which Romans valued so highly, even in the degenerate
days of the emperor Nero. Luke's purposes were achieved—historical, apologetic, religious—viz., to "trace the course of all things
accurately from the first"; to confirm the faith of new converts
and to encourage inquirers, and to provide a "demonstration of
the gospel"; to set Christianity in the right light relative to the
Roman government; and to bring to men still further knowledge
of Christ. It is significant that these purposes are perceptible even
in Proto-Luke—if that hypothesis is adopted. Luke 3:1 would interest Theophilus—or readers of his class—at once; "In the fifteenth
year of the hegemony—i.e., principate or *imperium*—of Tiberius
Caesar, Pontius Pilate having charge of affairs in Judea, Herod
being tetrarch of Galilee and his brother Philip tetrarch of Ituraea
and the region of Trachonitis, and Lysanias tetrarch of Abilene,
under the high priesthood of Annas and Caiaphas, a word of God
[an inspired message] came to John the son of Zacharias . . ." An
examination of the Q and L material in Luke will show how this
interest on the part of his readers would be sustained by the contents of Proto-Luke as a whole. (See 3:1, 18; 4:5–8, 26; 7:2–10;
8:3; 13:32; 14:31, etc.) Or, abandoning the Proto-Luke theory, the
same holds true of the finished gospel. (Of course, Proto-Luke may
be only Luke's amplification of Q from other sources, chiefly L.)

Whether or not the author of Luke-Acts as we have the work
today was the Luke "whose praise is in the gospel," the companion
and fellow traveler of Paul, is a question not admitting of a ready
answer. The data are too scanty for a precise solution of the problem. Loisy thinks the work has been revised by a later editor; but
he dates this redactor in the second century and takes insufficient
cognizance of the probable use of early sources. It may be thought
that our Luke compiled the material of L, and combined it with
Q to form Proto-Luke—a task which could easily have been accomplished by a companion of Paul; later on, Mark was added to
Proto-Luke, and the book of Acts appended to the gospel, by some
later hand. But the major and really insuperable difficulty in the
way of this hypothesis is the stylistic identity of the author of

Luke (especially if we disregard the Marcan sections) with the author of Acts—see Hawkins, *Horae Synopticae*, 2d ed., pp. 15–25; and it would be easier, if the distinction were necessary, to assume that the author of Luke-Acts used material gathered at an earlier date by someone else. Even so, a large part of the difficulty would still remain: for the style of Proto-Luke is the style of Luke-Acts as a whole. It is, of course, not impossible that the same person accompanied Paul in the fifties; gathered his materials for the gospel in the late fifties, in the sixties and seventies; wrote the gospel before 80 or 85; gathered the materials for Acts before 90, and "published" the whole before 95. Suppose he was thirty years old or thereabouts in the year 55; by 95 he would have been a septuagenarian, at the ripe peak of literary activity for a man who had used notebook and pen all his life. This may be no more than a possibility, but at least it is that.

Whether or not we accept the Proto-Luke theory, it appears to be an assured result of recent study of the Gospel of Luke that it is not merely a new edition of Mark, but an independent work, based upon earlier sources, with which has been incorporated the substance of the Gospel of Mark, and that in its process of growth it passed through the following stages:

(1) The beginning was the basic document "Q," already recognized as underlying the Gospels of Matthew and Luke. In its Lucan form it preserves its original order practically unaltered—for it was Luke's method to use his materials in "blocks" or groups of sections, rather than weave them together and reorganize the whole under different subject divisions.

(2) With this document has been combined the material drawn from L—whether this was another document or only a cycle of oral traditions emanating from a particular locality or group may be questioned; the evidence appears to point toward either a document or a firmly fixed body of tradition. The fact that the bulk of Luke's Q and L material is found in the central section (9:51–18:14) suggests that the combination took place independently of Luke's use of Mark—a view which has been held by several American scholars, e.g., E. D. Burton and E. W. Parsons. A recent suggestion that this Q and L material was correlated with the book of Deuteronomy, either for purposes of instruction or for use in public worship, deserves careful consideration (see C. F. Evans, "The Central Section of St. Luke's Gospel," in D. E. Nineham, ed., *Studies in the Gospels*, 1955).

(3) Next came the task of incorporating the substance of Mark —or, it would be safer to say, of combining Mark with Q + L.

THE PROTO-LUKE THEORY

Q	Proto-Luke L	Marcan Inserts
Luke 3:[2b], 3a, 7b–9		[3:1, 2a is editorial] [3:3b, 4 (= Mark 1:2a, 3, 4) [3:5, 6 is editorial]
	3:10–14	
3:16, 17 [18–20 is editorial]		
		3:21, 22 (= Mark 1:9–11)
4:1b–12	[4:17–22a, (25–30?)] 5:1–11	4:31–44 (= Mark 1:21–39) 5:12–6:19 (= Mark 1:40–3:19)
6:20–49	7:11–16	
7:2, 6b–10	7:36–50	
7:18b, 19, 22–28, 31–35	[8:1–3]	8:4–9:50 (= Mark 4:1–9:41, omitting 3:20–30, 4:26–34, 6:1–6, 17–29, 6:45–8:26, 9:9–13, 42–50; some of this material is used elsewhere in Luke)
9:57b–62	9:51–56	
10:2–16, [17b–20], 21b–24	10:29b–37, 38–42 11:27, 28	10:25–28 (= Mark 12:28–31)
11:2–4, [5–8], 9–26		
11:29b–36, 39b, 42, 43, [44], 46–52		
12:2–12	12:13–21	

12:22-31	12:32, 33a, [35-38], 47, 48
12:33b, 34, 39, 40, 42-46, 49-53, [54-56], 57-59	
13:18-21, 24-29, 34, 35	13:1-17, [31-33]
14:11 (= 18:14)	14:1-10
14:16-23, 26, 27	14:12-14
14:34, 35	14:28-32, [33]
15:4-7, [8-10]	15:11-32
	16:1-12
16:13, [16-18]	16:19-31
17:1-4, 6	17:7-10, 12-19, 20, 21
17:23, 24, 26-30, 34, 35, 37b	18:1-14
19:12, 13, 15b-26	19:2-10
19:40, 42-44	
[22:28-30]	22:31, 32, [35-38]
23:27-31	

17:31, 33 (= Mark 13:15f., 8:35)
18:15-43 (= Mark 10:13-52, omitting 9:42-10:12, 35-45)
19:28-36, 38 (= Mark 11:1-10)
19:45-48 (= Mark 11:11-19, omitting 12-14)
20:1-19, 21-26, 27-47 (= Mark 11:27-12:40, omitting 11:20-26)
21:1-33, 37 (= Mark 12:41-13:32, omitting 21-23)
[21:34-36] (= Mark 13:33-37, wholly rewritten)
22:1-13 (= Mark 14:1-16, omitting 3-9)
22:14-20, 21-23, 24-27 (= Mark 14:17-25 + 10:42-45)
22:34, 39, 41-47, 50-71 (= Mark 14:32-72, much rewritten)
23:3, 18-26, 33, 35, 38 (= Mark 15:2, 11-21, omitting 16-20, 22-32)
23:44-47, 48b, 50-56 (= Mark 15:33-47)
24:1-9 (= Mark 16:1-8, rewritten)

That neither was entirely rewritten and that both sources were used *en bloc* is clear from the analysis of the gospel; it was a method very different from Matthew's distribution of Q material over the Marcan framework.

(4) Finally, the Nativity and Resurrection Narratives were added, though some scholars have argued that these narratives already belonged to L. But among the reasons for thinking them to be derived from still other sources there are the following: (*a*) This would explain the discordance between the account of the Annunciation and the question of the neighbors at Nazareth (Luke 4:22—contrast the form of the question in Mark, where the difficulty is avoided). Vincent Taylor has suggested that the Virgin Birth Narrative was a last-minute addition to the gospel (see *The Historical Evidence for the Virgin Birth*, 1920, ch. IV); but if Luke 1–2 is a final addition to the gospel, the situation is still more easily comprehensible. (*b*) The formal statement in 3:1, 2 reads like the beginning of a treatise, rather than a new chapter—as Streeter pointed out. (*c*) The *content* of Luke 1–2, with its strongly marked Jewish atmosphere, its equally strong Christian Jewish messianism of the "Son of David" type, reads more like a body of tradition preserved locally and outside the current Palestinian church tradition of Q and L; indeed, it reminds us of other features in the tradition of Jesus' family preserved in the gospels and elsewhere, in particular of the later emphasis upon their Davidic descent and blood relationship to the Lord. Martin Dibelius found three strands of tradition here: the story of Mary, that of the Shepherds, and that of Simeon. (*d*) In *form*, as a long, consecutive, finely wrought, artistic narrative (compare the Lucan Resurrection Narrative, especially the Journey to Emmaus, 24:13–35), it is sharply distinguished from the brief anecdotes and incidents preserved in L. Even the Passion Narrative is less consecutive, for it is made up of a series of brief sections. All this is compatible with the general identity in language and coloring of L and the Nativity Narratives, sufficiently at least to satisfy the requirements of Hawkins' and Easton's tabulations of the linguistic data.

So much for the stages of growth through which our Gospel of Luke has passed. In its final form, it not only justifies the verdict of Renan, "the most beautiful book in the world"—which every critic quotes!—but it is also the most interesting, from a historical viewpoint, and the most valuable of our four. If we had to choose between them—God forbid!—there is little question which of the gospels many would prefer to keep, and let the others pass into oblivion. The personality of its author is very real, as real to us as the authors of Mark and Matthew and far more real than John— whether or not we can still identify him with the "Luke" named elsewhere in the New Testament and in early church tradition. He was obviously a gentile, and a gentile of warm feeling, wide interests, genuine historical taste and ability, and deep faith. But it is not the personality of the author that makes his work supremely interesting and valuable. It is his intelligent use of good and reliable sources, and the authentic note of reality which characterizes his picture of Jesus and his account of the Master's life and teaching; it is his defense of the early church and its faith and his explanation of its Jewish antecedents and origin—this is what makes Luke-Acts the most valuable writing in the New Testament. If a final personal estimate may be hazarded, it is Luke who brings us closest, of all the gospel writers, to the Jesus of history who is also the Lord of the church's faith.

CHAPTER XI

The Ecclesiastical Gospel: Matthew

hristian tradition for centuries has recognized in Matthew "the Jewish Gospel," i.e., a gospel addressed to Jews, replete with Old Testament quotation and allusion, emphasizing Jesus' messiahship and his fulfillment of the Law and Prophets, and designed to prove that "this is very Christ." The modern approach to Matthew is equally clear in this recognition, but it enjoys a greater wealth of information regarding the type of Judaism presupposed, the Christianized Judaism expressed, and the Christian Jewish character of its sources. The great collection of rabbinic material in the *Kommentar zum Neuen Testament aus Talmud und Midrasch* (5 vols., 1922–28; Index vol., 1956) by the late Hermann L. Strack and Paul Billerbeck, and also the second edition of Claude G. Montefiore's *Synoptic Gospels* (1927) with the supplemental volume, *Rabbinic Literature and Gospel Teachings* (1930), and especially Israel Abrahams' *Pharisaism and the Gospels* (1917, 1924), all serve to make this approach more clear. Even more important for the Judaism of the period is George Foot Moore's monumental work, *Judaism in the First Centuries of the Christian Era, the Age of the Tannaim* (2 vols., 1927; Vol. III, Notes, 1930). There is also the revised edition of Bousset's *Religion des Judentums* from the pen of the late Professor Hugo Gressmann (1926), and Gressmann's own work on *Der Messias* (1929), and the new edition of Paul Volz's *Eschatologie der jüdischen Gemeinde im Neutestamentlichen Zeitalter* (1934). There is also, in French, the great work of Père J. Bonsirven, *Le Judaïsme palestinien*, 2 vols., 1934 (abridged edition in one vol., 1950). Readers of English who are unfamiliar with Hebrew have access to the *Mishnah* in Canon Herbert Danby's excellent translation (1933), to the *Mekilta* in Jacob Z. Lauterbach's text and translation (3 vols., 1933–35), and to the great Soncino translation of the *Babylonian Talmud* (1938–52).

The proper point of departure for the study of Matthew is a consideration of Judaism, and especially of the Jewish Christian church, during the period between the Fall of Jerusalem in the year 70 and the even more disastrous and ruinous second revolt, in the time of Hadrian, A.D. 132–135.

The Fall of Jerusalem was an overwhelming blow not only to the Jewish apocalyptists (as we may see from passages in the nearly contemporary IV Ezra and II Baruch), but also to the ordinary faithful observer of the Law, for whom the land of his fathers was sacred, and the covenant between God and Israel in a real sense a guarantee of the continued holiness and inviolability of the temple and of Jerusalem itself, "The city of the Great King" (5:35). But now Jerusalem "lay in heaps," as the prophet had foretold, and the temple was no more. What was to be done to save Judaism from complete annihilation must be undertaken by leaders equally energetic but less fanatical than those whose violence and foolhardiness had plunged all Palestine into war and brought red ruin upon the Holy City and the sacred House. It was a time for retrenchment, for readjustment, for strengthening the religious institutions that remained unshaken and had survived the struggle, for concentration upon the study of the divine Torah—even without the temple this could continue; it was inevitably, therefore, a period of growing conservatism. Sects were discouraged, and either faded away before triumphant Pharisaic scribism (like the Essenes and the curious group which produced the so-called *Zadokite Fragments* and the more recently discovered *Dead Sea Scrolls*), or suffered increasing ostracism (like the Christians, the record of whose strained relations with their neighbors is to be found even in the early sources Q and L, not to mention other New Testament documents, and possibly also in the malediction upon the *minim* introduced into the daily prayer, the *Shemoneh Esreh* or *Eighteen Benedictions*). The Sadducean hierarchy disappeared—Sadduceeism never recovering from the destruction of the temple and the cessation of its cult. From now on, Judaism was to be dominated by the scribal-Pharisaic type of religion, theology, liturgy, and observance of the Law.

Even before the fall of the city, according to the later legend, while the siege was still in progress, Rabbi Jochanan ben Zakkai escaped and obtained permission from the Romans to establish his school at Jamnia. Here Judaism continued to flourish vigorously, even without the temple worship. Here the questions were debated and decided which were of fundamental import for the religion of the Law, such as the yearly calendar of fasts and festivals, the regulations concerning things "clean" and "unclean," the elaborate minutiae of the application of the sacred code to the life of the people. Thenceforth the Jewish religion was to be a religion of school and synagogue, the temple with its sacrificial worship being no more. But that the Pharisaic leaders had not abandoned all hope of a future restoration of the temple, and that they viewed it as their main responsibility to preserve and safeguard the religious inheritance intact until a brighter day should dawn, is clear from the careful preservation in the Mishnah (i.e., in tractate *Middoth*) of the precise measurements of the temple—the day would surely come when the house of the Lord could be rebuilt in all its former glory!

Along with the renewed study of the Law and the exclusion of Sadducean and other sectarian errors went a careful definition of the canon of holy scripture, the exact stereotyping of its text, and the minute elaboration of the rules governing its interpretation. The motto of this period was quite obviously *Strengthen the things that remain*. If Judaism was to survive in its very homeland, in Palestine itself, strong efforts were needed to unify, co-ordinate, and harmonize its most sacred elements. It is to this period—perhaps stretching it to include the years immediately following the insurrection under Hadrian—that we must assign the virtual suppression of the apocalyptic movement and its exclusion from the main line of development which Moore called "the rise of normative Judaism," i.e., the Judaism which was now steadily moving in the direction of the classical type known to history from the second and third centuries to the present. There was a marked contrast between the free and widely variegated religious ideology of the period prior to A.D. 70, which had been the golden age of apocalyptic, and the strict legalism of the second century, leading up to the codification of the oral law by Rabbi Judah ha Nasi at its close. The late R. H. Charles and others have accounted for this contrast by the hypothesis that the apocalyptists (who were for them the representatives of the "higher," more "spiritual" Judaism of their time) must have been attracted into the Christian church, and thus left the legalists in possession of orthodox Judaism. But a simpler hypothesis surely lies close at hand: the successive disasters of the Fall of Jerusalem and the crushing defeat of Bar-Kochba two generations later, followed by the bitterly repressive measures adopted by the Romans, demonstrated clearly both the dangers of apocalyptic messianism (as championed by

Akiba) and the falsity of its presuppositions. Only fools would continue to foster a movement which had encouraged, if not incited, the excesses of the two rebellions; and which was undeniably in large measure responsible for the destruction of temple and city, for the endless bloodshed, famine, and desolation, and all the overwhelming woes that had accompanied and followed defeat. This situation, as S. G. F. Brandon, W. D. Davies, and others have shown, is important for the background it supplies to certain phases of early Christianity; but it is surely going too far to credit the Christian movement with the disappearance of Jewish apocalyptic. Instead, it belongs with the whole tendency of postwar Judaism in the direction of consolidation, unification, conservatism, and exclusiveness. Even out in the Diaspora, far beyond the borders of Palestine, the effects of this movement were soon felt. The world-mission of Judaism was brought to a halt. Syncretistic efforts like those of Philo and his predecessors in Alexandria, aiming to combine orthodox Judaism with Greek philosophy, came to a fruitless end. Even the Septuagint, the classic Greek translation of the Old Testament, was abandoned to the Christians, along with much of the Apocrypha and most of the Apocalypses—all of them, in fact, save the Book of Daniel, which had already been included in the Hebrew Canon. In place of the Septuagint new and more accurate—i.e., painfully literal—translations of the Hebrew Scriptures came into use among Greek-speaking Jews.

Professor Moore has pointed out the importance of our Gospel of Matthew as a source for Tannaite Judaism—the most important, in this regard, of the three synoptics, "not only for its contents but for its attitude; it is at once the most conservatively Jewish of the gospels and the most violently anti-Pharisaic. For the prominence of both these features it may be surmised that the history of the Nazarenes in their relations to Gentile Christianity on the one side and to the Jewish authorities on the other was decisive" (*Judaism*, I. 186). Indeed, *this double attitude helps to date the book*—especially its attitude toward Judaism.

(a) Not only is Matthew the most thoroughly "apocalyptic-eschatological" of the gospels in its general outlook—a fact which suggests a milieu and a time when apocalyptic messianism was in the ascendant; but the references contained in the most eschatological of its sections, the Matthean version of the Little Apocalypse, indicate fairly well its time and place. (Of course the date must not be brought down too late—the *terminus ad quem* is obviously the earliest indubitable citation or reference to Matthew

or its contents in the second century; the parallels in Ignatius are
not absolutely certain, though *Smyrn.* 1 seems to rest either upon
Matt. 3:15 or upon its equivalent in the tradition of the church
of Antioch.) The warning in ch. 24:23 f.—"Then if any one says
to you, Lo, here is the Christ! or There! believe it not. For false
Christs and false prophets will arise, and will show great signs and
wonders, so as to lead astray, if possible, even the elect"—is taken
directly from Mark 13:21, 22. But the addition of the word
"Christ" in v. 5 and of "the sign of the Son of Man in heaven"
in v. 30 may be viewed as a heightening of the eschatological outlook. And when we turn to v. 15, where "the abomination of
desolation" is described as "standing in a holy place" (i.e., in the
holy land, as the context of Daniel itself suggested—cf. Dan. 11:
16, 41), contrasting clearly in explicitness with Mark's "standing
[or, set up] where it ought not to be" (Mark 13:14), and not at
all suggested by Luke's "Jerusalem surrounded by armies" (Luke
21:20)—it seems clear that the author of Matthew has made his
own fresh study of Daniel, and is in vital touch with a Christian-
Jewish apocalyptic tradition. No longer is it the Fall of Jerusalem,
or the Roman armies in Palestine—but *Antichrist*, standing in the
midst of the holy land! With this agrees the interpretation assumed
in the Didache (16:4)—another point of contact with that document.

   (*b*) Moreover, such a saying as that in 26:52, "All they that take
the sword shall perish by the sword," has added significance if derived from the tradition of a time when the temptation to resort
to violence was pressed upon the Christians by some at least of
their Jewish neighbors. Such a time was clearly that of the up-
rising under Bar-Kochba, when Christian Jews were tortured if
they refused to renounce Jesus as their Messiah and fight under
the banner of Akiba and Bar-Kochba against Rome (see Moore,
Judaism, I. 91; Justin, *Apology I*, 31:6). We do not hear of such
violent methods in the days of Josephus and the first revolt; nor
during the generation immediately following the Fall of Jerusalem
in A.D. 70. Obviously, this does not prove that our Matthew comes
from a time immediately preceding the second revolt; but the
gospel certainly suits such a background remarkably well—when
Bar-Kochba was hailed as Messiah not only by his followers but
also by no less a person than the saintly Akiba. "Many shall come
. . . saying, I am the Messiah . . . with great signs and wonders,
so as to deceive, if possible, the very elect."

   (*c*) Slight as they are, the added touches to the material taken
over from Mark seem to require a time when apocalyptism was

dominant, in at least one particular area, and when messianism was a personal issue between real leaders of men. The atmosphere is very different from that of the early Roman gospel, where we first meet with the Little Apocalypse and where the expectations it encouraged were vague and indefinite. No doubt the source was originally Palestinian—though Matthew takes it over from Mark and not independently, and hence adds his touches to Mark's own version, making concrete what had hitherto been indefinite and impersonal, and adding (as was his wont) material from other sources—chiefly Q, at first, then from his own peculiar source or sources—to fill out the discourse.

It may of course be thought that the background of Matthew is just as likely to have been the years A.D. 66 to 70 (the first Jewish war against Rome), or those just following that tragic, never to be forgotten fiasco, as the turn of the century and the events leading up to the second revolt two generations later; but it is not likely that political messianism had revived among the Jews to anything like the extent here presupposed, within a generation after the Fall of Jerusalem. (It is scarcely possible that a date prior to 66 is presupposed: the book is too obviously written after 70.) How sternly even suspects were dealt with by the Roman authorities may be seen from the story of Hegesippus regarding the two grandsons of Jude, the Lord's brother (Eusebius, *Church History,* III. 20—it was in the time of Domitian). Further, be it noted that IV Ezra and the Apocalypse of Baruch urge anything but a program of *practical* messianism! And we do know that the Bar-Kochba revolt was a messianic movement, bringing to a head a *revived* political messianism early in the second century. A date, then, sometime about the turn of the century, or a little later, seems required by the general situation out of which the specifically apocalyptic section of the book arose.

With all this agree the temper and outlook of the Gospel of Matthew as a whole—a heightened apocalyptic messianism, obviously contrasting with the political hopes of the author's countrymen, cherished within the Christian group as *their* solution of the darkening enigma of the nation's fate. "Because wickedness [= lawlessness, *anomia*] is multiplied, most men's love will grow cold" (24:12)—this could, indeed, refer to the state of affairs preceding the first revolt in 66–70 (Josephus makes clear the lawlessness of the times: see his *Antiquities,* Bk. XX, *Vita,* and *War,* Bk. II); but taken in connection with other passages in the gospel it seems more appropriate to a later period, when the second wave of misguided messianism was beginning to gather strength. It is not surprising therefore that a large number of modern scholars, e.g., B. W. Bacon, B. T. D. Smith, A. H. McNeile, S. E. Johnson, G. D. Kilpatrick, tend to date the gospel late rather than early, and to reject entirely the hypothesis that it was the earliest of the gospels.

The location, also, seems fairly certain—not Jerusalem or Judea (the "Judea" in 24:16 comes from Mark, i.e., from the Little Apocalypse), but northern Palestine where several scholars, including R. H. Charles, Ernst Lohmeyer, and others, have located the center from which apocalyptic writings emanated. Thus the writer of at least some sections of I Enoch undoubtedly lived there: he refers to Abilēnē, the "waters of Dan," and Enoch's *southward* journey to the holy land! It seems clear that the author lived in northern Palestine, and indeed on the very border, if not over the line in Syria. And it was also this region, apparently, with which the author of Matthew was specially familiar: see Matt. 4:12–16, "Galilee of the Gentiles," and 28:16, where the resurrection appearance of Jesus to his apostles (also the Ascension?) takes place on a mountain in Galilee, one which had been designated in advance by the risen Lord. Was it the Mount of Transfiguration (17:1) or—more likely—that of the Sermon (5:1)?—especially if "where he commanded them" is taken to mean "where he delivered the [New] Law to them" (so Bernhard Weiss understood it; see his *Meyer-kommentar*, 1910, p. 506).

A strong case has been made for Antioch as the home of the Matthean Gospel; to Antioch points the marked emphasis upon Peter, who was a great figure in the Antiochene church before Rome successfully laid claim to him. But it is difficult to localize the gospel thus definitely in a city. Equally suitable would be some place in the neighborhood, somewhere in northern Palestine or Syria; and perhaps somewhat more suitable, in view both of the contacts between Matthew and the Didache, which many scholars would locate in some Syrian village, and of the later tradition of the use of "Matthew's Gospel" by the Syrian "Nazoreans." (See Bacon, *Studies in Matthew*, Introd., ch. III–IV; Irenaeus, *Against Heresies*, I. 22=Harvey, I. 212; Eusebius, *Church History*, III. 27; Jerome, *Illustrious Men*, III; Epiphanius, *Panarion*, XXIX.) Further, northern Palestine was never a strong Christian center, as was Syria. Is a local interest reflected in 4:15 ("Zebulun and Naphtali")? It sounds like a direct quotation from the Old Testament; but note v. 24 ("all Syria"). Bacon's phrase, "somewhere in the hinterland of Antioch," is still good. At any rate, it must have been a community strongly Jewish in its thought and outlook, where (as in the Didache) the Christians were in daily contact with orthodox, conservative Jews.

The author of Matthew is no doubt a Jew. Unlike Mark, who does not understand "the Jews" and has little sympathy with them, and unlike Luke, who understands them well enough and recognizes the strength and beauty of their faith but whose own cultural background is the broad world of the Roman Empire and of eastern Hellenism, Matthew understands the Jews and sympathizes with their outlook as only a born Jew can do. Even his bitter tirades against the Pharisees and their "hypocrisy" do not obscure for him the fact that "not one jot or one tittle shall pass from the Law till all be fulfilled" (5:18). And when he sadly acknowledges that the woes which have fallen upon the nation are due to its rejection of Jesus as the Messiah ("his blood be on us and on our children," 27:25), he writes as a Jew—already touched, one may even say, with the pathos of that eternal Jew, the* immortal sufferer of later literature. His interests are Jewish: the Law, the messianic hope, the fulfillment of prophecy, the relation of (Christian) Jews to "heathen and publicans," the duties of worship, prayer, fasting, and almsgiving. He has no sympathy with the "emancipated" type of Christian, to whose attitudes and behavior Paul's gospel seems to have lent unfortunate encouragement. Though it is scarcely possible to see an allusion to Paul in the one who is "least in the Kingdom of Heaven," who has taught men to ignore the minute requirements of the Law (5:19), still it is clear that Paul the Hellenist and Matthew the Jewish evangelist faced in almost opposite directions in their view of Jesus' work and teaching. And yet the author of the gospel is a "universalist" in his interpretation of the destiny of the gospel: it is to be preached to all nations (24:14; 28:19) before the end can come. This note is clear in spite of the narrower outlook of one of his sources: "You will not have gone through all the towns of Israel, before the Son of Man comes" (10:23). Consciously or not, here he shares the view of Paul (Rom. 11:25 f.) as well as that of Mark (13:10). The Gentiles are to be evangelized, and then Israel will be saved along with them.

Moreover, he writes and thinks as a Jew. (a) It has often been pointed out that he gathers his material together into great subject sequences or discourses, five of them, in fact, each introduced by an appropriate narrative section based on Mark: (1) On discipleship, 5:1–7:29; (2) On apostleship, 9:35–10:42; (3) On the hidden revelation, 13:1–52; (4) On church administration, 17:24–18:35; (5) On the Judgment, 23:1–39 (against the scribes and

Pharisees) and 24:1–25:46 (the doctrine of the Parousia). It may
be thought that he arranges his material for purposes of study or
of memorization, i.e., *katēchēsis* (like the Mishnah, which is pre-
eminently a textbook, not a treatise), or possibly for reading at
public worship, like the *parashahs* chosen from the Law and the
haftarahs or lections from the Prophets, for use in the synagogue
services. The arrangement in groups of 3, 5, and 7 sayings (noted
in the commentary in Harper's Annotated Bible Series) also looks
like a device for memorization as well as interpretation. The arrangement of the teaching in five discourses has many parallels in
Jewish literature—*Pirqe Aboth*, the Book of Psalms, the five Megil-
loth, and so on.

(b) In addition to all this, Matthew certainly reflects the usages
and discipline of his church, and his work deserves the title "the
ecclesiastical gospel." And in this respect also he is not only a
Jew, he is also a Jewish churchman. The divine revelation which
came to Peter (16:17–19) is the foundation rock upon which the
church is to be built, viz., Jesus' messiahship: not Peter, or Peter's
faith, or the growing convictions of the multitude, but a divine
revelation, supplementing, completing, and bringing to a climax
the revelation in the Old Testament and in Jesus' own teaching.
Yet the Jewish scribes still sit in Moses' seat (23:2; "the Pharisees" may be a later textual addition, for they had no such authority)—their teaching is authoritative, though their example is
reprehensible. The church, accordingly, is the congregation of
Messiah's chosen ones—"the new Israel" within the larger body
of the elect nation, though it is destined to include Gentiles also
(there were many Jews who held a similar view of Judaism, in
the first century). The church's standards are high, its discipline
must be strict. Its members are expected to keep the Law *plus* the
new commandments of the Lord. And yet there are signs of a
relaxation of this requirement—as was inevitable when Jesus'
prophetic teaching of the ethics of the Kingdom became the
Canon Law of the church. An exception was allowed in the otherwise absolute prohibition of divorce—unless this is a mere logical
deduction, quite in scribal style, the "cause of fornication" presumably having taken place *before* marriage, and thus rendering
the marriage covenant void (5:32, 19:9; see notes in Harper's Annotated Bible Series).

(c) In brief, it is easy to recognize the author himself—or at
least men of his class or "school," as the term is now used—in
"the scribe who has become a disciple to the Kingdom of Heaven,
who is like a householder who brings out of his treasure things

new and old" (13:52). Not only his interpretation of the ancient Law but also his interpretation, codification, and application of the teaching of Jesus combines the new with the old—fresh interpretation in view of new situations combined with the affirmation of unchanging basic principles. It is also easy to recognize in the gospel some of the same interests and tendencies that characterized Judaism generally in the generations immediately following the destruction of Jerusalem—a growing rigidity, an increasing definiteness of view, a stronger emphasis upon a specific code of ethics (based naturally upon the Law; for Christians this included also the teaching of Jesus), a careful working out of the principles of interpretation and exegesis of the Old Testament, for the Christians an underscoring of the apocalyptic hope, for the rabbis an effort to play it down, and along with all this a free play of the religious fancy—strictly limited, however, within the moral area of the *haggadah*, and not ranging freely, as in the earlier apocalyptic, over all subjects in heaven and earth, astronomy, demonology, world history, and the nature of man. True, Matthew does not transform the gospel into a code of *halakoth*; but his tendency is clearly in that direction. And we must beware of assuming the exclusively legal interests of first-century scribism. The scribes were lawyers; but the stories from the Tannaite period indicate that rabbinic Judaism was a vital and not moribund religion, and that it was not solely concerned with the maximum requirements of the Law, or the proper method of guaranteeing its full observance.

(d) Both the Judaism and the Christianity reflected in Matthew belong to the period "between the wars," i.e., between A.D. 70 and 135, the dates of the two destructions of Jerusalem. The spirit of the gospel is not too remote from the first-century recension of the *Shemoneh Esreh*; the bitterness of the conflict between church and synagogue reflected in Matthew is also found in the imprecation against the apostates in the great Jewish prayer. The emphasis on apocalyptic in IV Ezra and II Baruch is also found in Matthew's final "book," on the Last Judgment. Much of the teaching in Matthew is good Pharisaism: it was the Pharisees' policy and attitude, not their doctrine, which the Matthean Christians opposed. Moreover, like all the Jewish literature of the time, Matthew is a thoroughly "traditional" book and uses much older material—often without revising it (as in 10:5, 6, 23).

(e) Some of Matthew's sources seem to have been quite formal collections. Thus "M," his special document or source, seems usually to be nothing more than a revision or recension of Q; but in certain places it reads like an organized body of teaching. As the late Alfred M. Perry demonstrated, in his important paper on "The Framework of the Sermon on the Mount" (*Journal of Biblical Literature*, LIV. 2, 1935, pp. 103–115), if we remove the Q material from the Sermon, what remains will show a definite structure: (1) Seven Beatitudes, in 5:3, 5–10; (2) three contrasts between the ancient Law and the new ethic, introduced by 5:17—20, viz., vv. 21–24, 27–30, 33–37 (and also 48?); (3) three contrasts between ostentation and the new piety, introduced by 6:1—viz., vv. 2–4, 5–8, 16–18, concluding with 7:6 (?). In 7:13–23 he saw a collection of "verses from other portions of the M document, or from other sources of tradition." (See p. 49.)

(f) Matthew had also a collection of "logia," which we may perhaps view as the explanation of the name of the gospel, in the light of Papias' statement that "Matthew gathered together the *logia* in the Hebrew dialect" (see p. 65), Professor C. H. Dodd has published a study of the use made of the Old Testament in the New Testament and in other early Christian literature (*According to the Scriptures*, 1952). He has listed the "testimonies" most commonly cited in the early Christian literature, in four groups of "primary sources," and also four groups of passages used in "subordinate and supplementary sources." In the first list are: (1) Joel 1–2, Zech. 9–14, Dan. 7; (2) Hosea, Isa. 6:1–9:7, 11:1–10, 28:14, 40:1–11, Jer. 31:31–34; (3) Isa. 42:1–44:5, 49:1–13, 50: 4–11, 52:13–53:12, 61, Ps. 69, 22, 31, 38, 88, 34, 118, 41, 42–43, 80; (4) Ps. 8, 110, 2, Gen. 12:3, 22:18, Deut. 18:15, 19. In the secondary sources: (1) Mal. 3:1–6, Dan. 12; (2) Isa. 29:9–14, Jer. 7:1–15, Hab. 1–2; (3) Isa. 58:6–10; (4) Ps. 32, 16, II Sam. 7:13, 14, Isa. 55:3, Amos 9:11, 12—quite a sizable anthology for an early Christian to carry about, whether in a "testimony book" or in his head! Now, it is an interesting task to take this list and check it with the list of Old Testament passages, quoted or echoed in the New, which we find at the back of Nestle's Greek New Testament (published at Stuttgart by the Württemberg Bible Society). Even a casual comparison of the lists will show what large use Matthew made of the Old Testament *testimonia*, the messianic prophecies, "Christ in the Old Testament" as interpreted by the early Christians.

In view of Matthew's use of earlier sources, all woven together with the deftest literary skill, the remarkable thing is that he should have taken over and made so much use of the Gospel of Mark, in spite of Mark's very different point of view (contrast Matt. 5:17–20 with Mark 7:1–23, which rejects both the scribal tradition and the corban rule, and also the food laws!). The fact speaks strongly for the recognition of the authenticity of Mark's materials—i.e., their agreement with the common tradition—though Matthew characteristically disregards Mark's order at many points, except in the Passion Narrative. It also speaks strongly for the early dissemination of Mark; for, unlike Luke, Matthew has had the Roman gospel in his hands for so long a time, and is so familiar with its contents, that he can use passages and phrases quite outside and far in advance of their immediate context. He seems to have memorized Mark—another scribal trait; his procedure is very different from that of Luke, who obviously has a copy of Mark before him as he writes. He was equally familiar with Q, which (perhaps in a revised form) was probably the teaching manual used in his church, i.e., Christian community, just as later on the Didache was probably thus used. Q contained the teaching of Jesus, the Didache, presumably, that of the Twelve Apostles, i.e., of the later church.

If we assume that Matthew was a teacher—or perhaps a "catechist," if we forget some of the later technical connotations of the word—this feature will be the more readily explained. For certainly he had no modern copy of Mark, with a multitude of cross references in the margin, or even a book made of bound-up sheets; an ancient roll of papyrus could not easily be thumbed through to find the passage he was looking for. Matthew's ability to quote a statement of Mark's at some distance from the passage immediately before him is evident from such passages as 7:28, 29; 9:34, 36; 10:17–22, 40; 23:11 (though Luke also has a few examples of such interweaving: e.g., 14:3, 35c; 16:13). His familiarity with Mark was important for his purpose, which was to reorganize the material of both Mark and Q and arrange it in a new subject-order. An excellent example of his method is to be seen in ch. 12, where verse after verse weaves Mark and Q together into an artistic whole. For perhaps twenty years or more he had been familiar with Mark—the contacts between Rome and Antioch (or Syria) were so close that Mark's gospel would be known in the East very soon after its appearance in the capital of the Roman Empire. And it is also significant that Matthew relies upon the general outline of Mark, even outside the Passion Narrative, for his account of Jesus' ministry. In a true sense, his gospel is a new edition of Mark. Now, if Q, as some scholars assume, was a continuous narrative (like Bacon's "S," for example), on a par, let us say, with Streeter and Taylor's "Proto-Luke," it is difficult to see how Matthew could have abandoned a Palestinian document of such extent in favor of the Roman document. Q can hardly have been a gospel, or even an outline of one.

Into this combination of Mark plus Q, Matthew weaves other material—derived we can scarcely say whence, but probably from the local tradition accessible to him in his own northern Palestinian or Syrian church. Some of this material is haggadic, some of it is drawn from early Christian teaching and exegesis, some of it is plainly apocryphal, some of it apocalyptic, some of it legal, i.e., Christian-Jewish interpretation of the Law, some of it is indubitably authentic recollection, on a par with the most reliable parts of Q and L; and some of it was plainly drawn directly from the Old Testament, and not by way of exegesis.

(1) As an example of *Christian Midrashic haggadah*, it is sufficient to mention the Nativity Narratives in Matt. 1–2; or the story of Peter walking on the water, 14:28–31; or the blessing of Peter and the promise of the keys, 16:17–19; or the stater in the fish's mouth, 17:24–27; or the end of Judas, 27:3–10.

(2) *Christian exegesis and homiletics* may be seen in the explanation of John's baptism of Jesus in 3:14, 15; or in such passages as 12:5–7; 13:36–43. For Matthew, as for Mark and Luke, the baptism of John already possesses the Christian or ecclesiastical significance. It is "valid," but incomplete, for it does not yet convey the Holy Spirit. The value of Jesus' example in his baptism "to fulfill all righteousness" (3:15) was probably very real in Matthew's circle. The problem it raised, however (3:14), depends largely on the conception of John's part in the baptism which resulted from this Christian interpretation—whereas historically John's "penitents" or "converts" had probably baptized themselves. The phrase "by John," which is found in all the sources, and means at his direction, by his authority, expresses the Christian view of the procedure (cf. Acts 19:1–6).

(3) Material approaching the formulation of a *Christian code* (cf. the Didache) is found in the Sermon on the Mount and in such passages as 10:41; 18:18; 19:10–12; 23:2, 3, 8–10—passages no doubt familiar to early Christians in the Greek-speaking Jewish community in which the gospel arose, and reflecting alike the interests and practices of that church.

(4) Even *early liturgical material* may be suspected of underlying such passages as 11:25–30, the Great Rejoicing and the Divine Invitation—which Martin Rist views as a baptismal hymn; or the final commission, 28:18–20; or the saying in 18:19, 20, "where two or three are gathered together in my name"—not to mention the

Matthean version of the Lord's Prayer, 6:7–13, which was doubt-less derived (like that in the Didache) from current church usage. These are all passages upon which the late Professor Bousset laid emphasis in his interpretation of early Christian worship, in his famous *Kyrios Christos*. We have begun to recognize liturgical passages in many of even the earliest New Testament documents, and certainly in a gospel as late as Matthew they are to be ex-pected.

(5) *Apocalyptic material* is found frequently, e.g., 13:24–30; 20: 1–16; 22:1–14; 25 *passim*. Most of the Matthean parables, i.e., those peculiar to Matthew, are emphatically apocalyptic-eschato-logical in outlook.

(6) *Apocryphal material* is found in the message of Pilate's wife, 27:19; the guilt of the Jews, 27:24, 25; the earthquake at the Crucifixion and the bodies of the saints appearing in the Holy City, 27:51b–53; the guard at the tomb, 27:62–66; the description of the angel of the Resurrection, 28:2–5; the origin of the current Jewish explanation of the Resurrection, 28:11–15. It is observable that these latter materials, found in the Passion Narrative, are usually not worked in carefully with the main narrative, but are easily separated, almost as if they were later interpolations; re-move them, and the narrative moves forward without interruption. And yet there is no textual warrant for pronouncing them inter-polations, as is the case with several additions to the Lucan Passion Narrative, the so-called "Western noninterpolations," as Hort named them. Either they belong to the original gospel or they were added at so early a date that no copies survive in which they are not found. Perhaps a second-century manuscript, if one were discovered, would show that they were early additions to the text—interpolations in fact. Yet the style is clearly that of Matthew. Similarly, the Trinitarian baptismal formula inserted into 28:19—Eusebius quoted the verse in a form which continued directly, and more naturally, from "make disciples" to "teaching." Many schol-ars believe that there were still manuscripts, in the fourth century, from which the baptismal reference and formula was absent. (But see p. 150. Eusebius may have quoted from memory, or the quota-tion, as it appears in Eusebius' text, may be truncated. The quota-tion is too unique to be impressive.)

(7) Another factor, present to some degree in all the early Christian accounts of the life of Jesus but especially prominent in Matthew, is the determinative, and even productive, *influence of the Old Testament*. It is apparent in the early sources underlying the first half of Acts, and also in the other gospels. (a) Not only is Old Testment prophecy adduced to explain this or that event or

teaching: "This came to pass that it might be fulfilled, which was written in the prophet, saying . . ." (see above on the *logia*); not only is the language of the Old Testament used, by preference, in describing various scenes, and even in giving the teaching of our Lord; but it can hardly be doubted that (b) the Old Testament has exercised a formative, even a creative influence upon the tradition—especially in the Nativity and Passion Narratives. Quite naturally, this tendency is especially observable in Matthew. The residence in Egypt (Matt. 2:15; Hos. 11:1) and the reference to Rachel's weeping (2:17; Jer. 31:15) come to mind at once. So does the reference to Nazareth (2:23), though the source of the text here quoted is now unknown. So also is the Wisdom passage in 11:25–30 (cf. Ecclus. 51:1, 23 f., 26, 24:19, etc.), and the Woe upon Jerusalem in 23:37–39, with its Old Testament echoes, especially from Jeremiah, and its direct quotation from Ps. 118:26. The number of the animals used at the entry into Jerusalem is doubled to suit the requirements of the Old Testament as understood by the evangelist, who ignored the prophet's parallelism (21:2, 7; Zech. 9:9).

In the Passion Narrative, again and again, the Old Testament seems to have suggested something more than the external form of the narrative, for example:

Mark 14:27, "smite the shepherd" (so Matthew);
15:24, the parting of Jesus' garments (so Luke, Matthew, John)
29, "wagging their heads" (so Matthew);
34, "Eli, Eli, lama . . ." (so Matthew);
36, vinegar (so Luke, Matthew, and John);
Luke 22:37, "numbered with the transgressors";
23:30, "to the hills, Fall on us";
35, the mockery by the people;
46, "Into thy hands";
49, the friends watching from afar;
Matthew 27:9 f., "thirty pieces of silver," and the potter's field;
43, "he trusted in God";
John 19:36, "a bone of him shall not be broken" (the Paschal lamb);
37, "they shall look on him."

Of these fifteen references, eight are found in Matthew.

It is scarcely possible to account for the stories of the children shouting in the temple (Matt. 21:14–16) and the disposition of the thirty pieces of silver (27:3–10) apart from the Old Testament quotation which crowns the narrative in each case.

Strange as such use of the Old Testament seems to us, nothing was more natural in the first or second century. The mind of the author of Matthew was steeped in the Old Testament and, indeed, in the Greek Version—as Paul Wernle rightly insisted sixty years ago in his *Synoptische Frage*, Matthew was "a Hellenist." And for Matthew, as for many another student of the Old Testament at that early time (before the New Testament writings had come into general use), the Old Testament was a book of divine revelation in which everything relating to Christ and his church had been either openly or secretly described in advance. Indeed, the Old Testament, had the question been asked, would have been reckoned among the valid sources for the life of our Lord. As a divine prediction and foreshadowing it was equally as reliable as the testimony of eyewitnesses. No rabbi—and likewise no Christian before the rise of modern biblical criticism—would have questioned such an attitude: the Holy One, blessed be He, knew in advance all that would ever transpire, and He had made known to His servants the prophets such future facts as were needful for teaching, or reproof, or correction, or training in righteousness (cf. II Tim. 3:16)—or for confirmation of the earlier revelation, the two now supporting each other. Hence, especially in the earliest formulated gospel tradition, the Passion Narrative, we find traces of a formative influence on the part of the Old Testament far exceeding mere literary style or allusion; not the form only but the inner core of the narrative has frequently been affected by the Old Testament. And, indeed, this is true precisely in those parts of the narrative where the testimony of eyewitnesses would be most uncertain or improcurable—the procedure at the Crucifixion (when all the disciples "forsook him and fled") and the words from the cross (which none of them were there to hear). Matthew was not primarily a historian or apologist, as Luke was; but he unquestionably assumed the accuracy of his material. Only, like most of his contemporaries, he was uncritical; he entirely lacked the critical bent of the modern scientific historian—which is of course nothing against him as an ancient religious writer.

And yet what precious sayings have been preserved in the Matthean special material—sayings which, regardless of their setting, bear upon their very face the imprimatur of their authenticity! Such sayings as the five beatitudes peculiar to Matthew (5:5, 7–10); or the words "Unless you turn and become like children, you will never enter the Kingdom of heaven" (18:3); or "See that you despise not one of these little ones" (v. 10); or "I will give to this last even as to you" (20:14); or the little parable of the two sons—"which of these two did the will of the father?" (21:31): the mere citation of such passages suffices to show that the "living and abiding voice" of tradition (Eusebius, *Church History*, III. 39. 4; cf. I Pet. 1:23) was not silent even at the end of the century, and that many a doubtless authentic saying of Jesus had failed to be incorporated in the compilations of Q, L, and the other discourse material of Mark and Luke.

It remains to discuss the theology of Matthew. He was a church-man, an ecclesiastic of an early type. The frequent references to prophecy and to false prophets, to the error of false teaching and the distinction to be drawn between the authority of the scribes and their practice, between the "righteousness" demanded by Jesus and that taught and exemplified by the scribes and Pharisees: such data suggest that the author was himself a teacher, if not a prophet, a Christian scribe—one might almost say a converted rabbi, whose mind traveled on in the same general direction it had hitherto pursued, but now with a new enthusiasm and under a new inspi-ration. The form and arrangement of his material is a further con-firmation of this hypothesis: he writes as well as thinks like a teacher. It is not surprising, therefore, that a definite theological stamp is to be seen upon his work—though with this proviso, that it is not the full-fledged theological development observable in Paul, John, the author of Hebrews, and the apologists, men who breathed deeply the atmosphere of popular philosophical and theological thought found in more thoroughly Hellenized areas. His theology is built on Jewish lines: its two foci are still the Law and the Community, a practical theology rather than speculative. Contacts with Jewish Gnosticism, of which there is some trace, are fewer than in Paul—far fewer than in John. Jewish Gnosticism was no doubt speculative, but it affords little clue to the interpre-tation of Matthew's point of view. He is obviously concerned with the practical interests and empirical problems of the actual com-munity in which he lived and taught—its worship, its discipline, its relations both with the orthodox Jewish authorities and with the heathen outside, its faith, its missionary efforts, above all with its exalted hopes of the coming end of the age. Even the baptismal formula found in his concluding paragraph (28:19) need not be —as a whole—a later liturgical interpolation; it sums up the ex-perience of the converts and combines their inherited Jewish faith in God ("baptizing them into the name of the Father"), their new faith in the Son [i.e., the Son of Man], and their experience of the Holy Spirit which had been "given" as the earnest and guarantee of the coming of the New Age. (Matthew used "Son of God" ten times; "Son of Man" twenty-nine times; "the Son," absolutely, in 11:27 and 17:5. But by his date "the Son" clearly meant Jesus Christ, without further definition.)

It is a theology born of apocalyptic eschatology, as the full context clearly shows; but like most biblical, i.e., ancient Jewish and early Christian, theology it is practical to the core, not speculative. And if it leaves us finally with a question—Was Jesus as Jewish as Matthew represents?—it also helps us with the answer. For, after all, Jesus rose even higher above the limitations of his time and place than this ardent but nevertheless rabbinically minded teacher was able to conceive. He was more, and he has meant far more to mankind, than the transcendent Messiah of an ancient Jewish Christian sect. There is no doubt that Jesus was quite as Jewish as Matthew represents; but it is another question if he was as thorough an apocalyptist as this gospel portrays him. A comparison of this gospel with the others makes it clear that Matthew has heightened the effect of many a saying, has added new editorial touches and new material which give the impression that Jesus' teaching was primarily and thoroughly apocalyptic-eschatological. The final result may be seen in the conclusions of Albert Schweitzer and other "thoroughgoing" eschatologists, with their uncritical overdependence on Matthew. Schweitzer even makes one verse, 10:23, the pivot about which the whole gospel story moves, the teaching of Jesus, his career, even his own self-consciousness! A careful source analysis would have made impossible this extremely one-sided and exaggerated interpretation.

But even in the first century there were forces tending in the direction of a different interpretation, lessening the emphasis upon apocalyptic messianism. The question is not to be answered simply by preferring one divergent interpretation to the other, and identifying Jesus' teaching and outlook with, say, the noneschatological or with the ultraeschatological. His real view probably lies back of both, at their point of divergence—a view I have tried to describe elsewhere, in *The Gospel of the Kingdom* (1940) and *An Introduction to New Testament Thought* (1950). As Johannes Weiss and Burton Easton maintained, there is a double Christology in the gospels; and either it goes back to Jesus (as Easton affirmed) or else it represents this divergent development at a point some distance (however slight) from the actual thinking of our Lord.

In brief, it seems undeniable that apocalyptic eschatology formed a real if minor factor in Jesus' thinking—though not on the scale reflected in Matthew. Indeed, Matthew holds a view about as extreme in this direction as it was possible to go and still maintain contact with the earlier sources. Even outside the apocalyptic chapters (24–25) there are passages that read almost as if they were drawn from some early Christian apocalyptic writing (e.g., 7:15 f., 22.) But it is impossible to believe that the teaching of Jesus was as thoroughly "apocalyptic-eschatological" as Matthew presupposes. Nor was the Judaism of his time identical with apocalyptic eschatology. In fact, (a) transcendental or apocalyptic messianism can be fairly severely delimited in its influence upon Judaism to the three centuries from the book of Daniel (165 B.C.) to the end of the second revolt (A.D. 135)—perhaps its flourishing period was narrower still, if we begin with I Enoch (at least with the "parables") rather than Daniel as the point of departure. (The fragmentary passage at the end of Mishnah *Sotah* is not found in the best manuscripts or editions.) Whatever its origin (many scholars think of Persia or Iran as the original home of these ideas), it never became entirely popular in Palestine, nor did it eventually characterize what Professor Moore called "normative" Judaism; and it was eventually rejected and wholeheartedly repudiated by the Jewish authorities. Its bizarre, visionary, dualistic, pessimistic scheme of ideas fitted very badly the noble ethical monotheism inherited from the prophets. The central line of development in Judaism, including the oral law and the deep and concentrated study of the Torah, was still in line with prophetism—not apocalyptic. As Julian Morgenstern has said, "The real founder of the Second Commonwealth was Jeremiah the prophet, rather than Ezra the scribe." Moreover, (b) it is not wholly accurate to describe apocalyptic as "the form which Jewish prophecy took in this age," i.e., under the Seleucids and the Romans—for its motives, aims, outlook, and presuppositions were quite different. And there can be no doubt that the presuppositions of Jesus' religious teaching are fundamentally prophetic, not apocalyptic. The relatively minor apocalyptic element has been added on to the prophetic. The *ideas* often enough are apocalyptic—especially as stated in Matthew—but the underlying religious *motives* (faith, love, repentance, humility, and obedience) are undeniably prophetic. And it was the motives, not the ideas, that molded the religion of Jesus.

Temporary as it was, and not affording a permanent clue to either the teaching or the personality of Jesus, apocalyptic messianism did provide, for a time, the terms in which a transcendent conception of Christ could be stated, and also a transcendent conception of the life to come; both sets of terms were of great value to the church in making the transition from its early Palestinian to its later Hellenistic-Roman environment. Eventually, of course, the "Son of Man dogma" was dropped—i.e., totally reinterpreted, and viewed as a description of Christ's human nature, not his divine; but during much of the early New Testament period it continued in use. The apocalyptic "Messiah" (i.e., The Son of Man) is not the exact equivalent of the Hellenistic "Kyrios" (= Lord), but it was as close an approximation as Jewish thought provided; and in the Gospel of Matthew the former term has undoubtedly already taken on some of the connotations of the latter. Christ is now the Lord of the church's cult, the head of the church, present at its services of worship, the heavenly possessor of all authority, the one to whom the church's authorities must look up, and from whom the right to "bind" and "loose" is derived—for he is the final Judge of all mankind. Quite obviously, apocalyptic messianism was an important stage in the development leading up to the very frontiers of the later Catholic doctrines of Christ and the church.

Throughout the centuries, the Gospel of Matthew has been the "ecclesiastical" gospel *par excellence*. It heads the list, in the New Testament, not only of the gospels but of all the early Christian writings. The original order (see ch. VI), which was that of composition, was probably Mark, Luke, Matthew, John; but when the theory gained ground that Matthew had been composed in Hebrew (or Aramaic), and hence was the oldest of the four, this gospel was shifted to first place, leading to the order we now have (Matthew, Mark, Luke, John). Moreover, it has been the most frequently quoted of the gospels, from the days of the church fathers to the present. It was the most popular gospel in the liturgies: the traditional Western "gospels" for Sundays and holy days are taken mainly from Matthew. In the *Book of Common Prayer*, forty-one of these passages are from Matthew, seven from Mark, thirty-six from Luke, thirty-three from John. Its liturgical use elsewhere is equally marked. The *Benedictus qui venit*, for example, is taken from the messianic salutation as reported by Matthew (21:9), not from one or other of the parallels in Mark, Luke, or John—even though one or two of the others would be entirely appropriate. This valuation set by the whole Christian church upon the Matthean Gospel is both natural and appropriate: no gospel maintains a higher doctrine of the church than this very "Jewish," very "ecclesiastical" compilation of the life and teaching of the Lord.

CHAPTER XII

The Gospel of the Hellenists: John

*T*he past fifty years have seen a great change in the approach to the Fourth Gospel. William Sanday's "Criticism of the Fourth Gospel" (1905) was almost the last work of the old school derived from Westcott and the conservatives. Alfred E. Garvie's *The Beloved Disciple* (1922) showed a weakening of the case for "Johannine" authorship, while later works definitely break away from the traditional approach. Even Sanday himself, before he died, acknowledged that he had been won over to the "non-Johannine" view by Friedrich von Hügel's article on the Fourth Gospel in the eleventh edition of the *Encyclopaedia Britannica* (Vol. XV, 1911, pp. 452–458). One of the books which probably had most influence in advancing this view was Ernest F. Scott's *The Fourth Gospel, Its Purpose and Theology* (1906). Written with great clarity and deep insight, it is still one of the best general introductions to the Gospel of John. Archbishop Bernard's commentary in two volumes was a much later book in date of publication (1929); but it was somewhat disappointing—it took almost no account of the newer problems in historical interpretation and might have been written, for the most part, before the First World War. On the other hand, the commentary by G. H. C. Macgregor (1928) in James Moffatt's series (designed for *Everyman* but renamed by the publishers *The Moffatt New Testament Commentary*) was a really outstanding and up-to-date work (1929). Mention may also be made of Lord Charnwood's *According to St. John* (1925), Canon Streeter's *The Four Gospels* (1924), with its long section (Part III) devoted to this subject, J. Estlin Carpenter's *Johannine Writings* (1927), Walter Bauer's commentary in the German *Handbuch zum Neuen Testament* (3d ed., 1933), and the chapter on the Johannine writings and their Christology (ch. 5) in the late Wilhelm Bousset's

Kyrios Christos (3d ed., 1926). Professor W. F. Howard's book, *The Fourth Gospel in Recent Criticism and Interpretation* (4th ed., revised by C. K. Barrett, 1955), contains an excellent survey of modern work in the field. It is supplemented by his smaller volume, *Christianity according to St. John* (1946). R. H. Strachan's *The Fourth Gospel* (1941) is well worth careful study, as is also E. C. Hoskyns and F. N. Davey's theological work, *The Fourth Gospel* (1948).

The little volume of P. Gardner-Smith, *St. John and the Synoptic Gospels* (1938), has had a very widespread influence in convincing scholars that John is independent of the synoptics (see above, ch. I). The great commentary by Rudolf Bultmann in the Meyer series (Göttingen, 1941) was a wartime product, not widely circulated at the time, but it has since appeared in new and revised editions. The new commentary by C. K. Barrett (1955) takes full account of Bultmann's views, and is a very important work of exegesis in its own right. The magnum opus of C. H. Dodd, *The Interpretation of the Fourth Gospel* (1953) is, of all the works published, not only since 1900 but in the whole history of New Testament interpretation, one of the most outstanding. It deals first with the background of the gospel in early Christianity, in Hellenism, and in Judaism, especially as represented by the Hermetica, Philo, rabbinic thought, Gnosticism and Mandaeism. Then the leading ideas are discussed, and the use of symbolism: eternal life, the knowledge of God, truth, faith, union with God, light, glory, judgment, Spirit, the Messiah, Son of Man, Son of God, the Logos. Finally, the whole structure of the work and its underlying argument are discussed in detail: the Prologue, the Book of Signs, the Book of the Passion with its Farewell Discourses on the special themes of Christ's departure and return and of Christ and his church, and the Passion Narrative itself. The work has about it the inevitability not of one man's conclusions, after a lifetime of research, but of long decades and generations of research, ever since the rise of modern biblical criticism. It marks the completion of the whole half century of change, which we have already noted. If a new period is now beginning, perhaps as a result of the new manuscript discoveries—chiefly the Coptic Gnostic and Manichaean documents in Egypt and the Dead Sea Scrolls, but also others—it will probably turn out that the achievements of past research will not need to be repudiated but only refined, elaborated, and carried further.

The change has come about, first of all, in the interpretation of the author's purpose in the Fourth Gospel. For a long time it had been held that John was fully aware of the existence of the three synoptics, and wrote only to supplement or—in one or two cases—to correct them. It was thought that the cleansing of the temple, for example, had purposely been placed by John at the beginning of Jesus' ministry—for then, as the aged John recalled, was when it had taken place. The date of the Crucifixion he similarly corrected, placing it on the eve of Passover—the day the Paschal lambs were slain. The synoptic record he supplemented by an account of the "Judean" ministry, all but ignored in Mark, Luke, and Matthew. Moreover, while the synoptists represent the growth of Jesus' popularity in Galilee but not its decline, John supplements this by showing the decline, and hints at a messianic crisis (of a political kind) as the cause leading to the conclusion of our Lord's work in the north. When "they would have taken him by force and made him king," following the feeding of the five thousand, he withdrew to the hills, sent his disciples away at evening, and himself departed later in the night (6:14–21). In brief, John shows why our Lord left Galilee and why "many of his disciples drew back" and deserted him (6:66). The short note in 7:1 may even suggest that for a time he was a fugitive—the basis of Oscar Holtzmann's famous theory of the "flight" of Jesus from the territory of Herod Antipas which he introduced into the Marcan scheme in order to account for the visit of Jesus to the north, the region of Tyre and Sidon, Mount Hermon and Caesarea Philippi.

Now, it may be true that John does undertake to supplement and correct what he knows of the earlier common tradition, oral or written—though the incident of the temple cleansing appears to have been moved forward for a symbolic purpose, as was also perhaps the date of the Crucifixion. But the question arises at once, Did John know the Synoptic Gospels? It used to be held, as by B. H. Streeter, J. Weiss, G. H. C. Macgregor, B. S. Easton, and many others, that John knew and presupposed Mark. His knowledge of Luke was not so certain. Matthew he seemed not to have known at all; so that the presumed "supplementing and correcting" of the synoptics really reduced itself chiefly to the supplementing and correcting of Mark. Now, Mark was certainly in need of supplementing—both Luke and Matthew had already undertaken independently to supply this lack; but it is impossible to see in John an avowed and purposeful supplementing of Mark, along the same general lines as those followed in the synoptics, or even a "correction" of either Mark's general outline or of his view of the content of Jesus' teaching. John of course shares Mark's view of the "stupidity" or incomprehension of the disciples, for whom the most precious truths of the gospel were often "hid from their eyes," as they also were hid from the unbelieving Jews. This point was greatly stressed by Johannes Weiss, especially in his *Aelteste Evangelium* (The Oldest Gospel), 1903. But it is really only the widespread view of the early church; Paul shared it; so did Luke (24:25, 45, Acts 1:6 f.) for all his "sparing the Twelve"; so did Matthew (28:17, "some doubted"); and hence it cannot be cited as a special bond of connection between Mark and John. In brief, the theory, when brought face to face with the facts, seems peculiarly unadapted to explain the situation. The discourses of Jesus, as John represents them, are not further material of the kind already familiar—such as Q provides in addition to the Marcan discourses. Something wholly new and different is presented in John, and it is offered not as a supplement but as a *substitute* for the Marcan discourses or sayings. This is the necessary formula, if John knew Mark. The time had come when, at least in one particular locality, the Marcan account of Jesus' life and teaching no longer sufficed, even with the possible addition of sayings and incidents from Luke or L. As Wilhelm Bousset said in his *Kyrios Christos* (p. 159; cf. Bauer's commentary, p. 239), "The figure of Jesus of Nazareth thus delineated [i.e., in the synoptics] was much too earthly and concrete, much too human and Jewish and limited, too little glorified and dogmatically interpreted. A comparison of the gospels shows what positive difficulties they presented. But the mere revision of minor details was hardly sufficient. What *might* be done, the Gnostics soon demonstrated; and the life of Jesus as presented in the synoptics could of course be allegorized, as men had learned to allegorize the Old Testament. Then came the author of the Fourth Gospel and undertook to meet the need with a wholly new construction of the life of Jesus."

This is perhaps the best possible solution, on the assumption that the author of John knew and used Mark—or all three Synoptic Gospels. But a far simpler solution is at hand, and one now more widely held as a result of the influence of Gardner-Smith's little book, viz., that John wrote down "the" gospel as it was known in his time and place, without regard to the earlier "gospels." He made use of the earlier gospel *tradition*—three of his great "signs" are also found in the synoptics. But it is a strange and unaccountable phenomenon, upon the theory of dependence, or of the revision and supplementing of the earlier gospels, that John's parallels with these earlier gospels are found only in peripheral, inconsequential words, those which would be used in any telling of the stories, or in only occasional key words from the sayings, not the great shining utterances which unveil their inner meaning or sparkle like jewels at the heart of the tale.

The clue to the author's purpose is not to be discovered by comparing incident with incident and saying with saying, on the theory that the author of John is revising the synoptic narrative; it is to be seen, rather, in the work as a whole, viewed not as a supplement to the synoptics but as an independent and comprehensive presentation of the life and teaching of Jesus. If a supplement to the earlier gospels had been in the author's mind, John would have taken far more thorough account of the details presented in Mark —plus whatever other sources were available. But he is not interested in history as such—only in the divine manifestation which for him characterized the life of Jesus as a whole, and which was evidenced by the seven great "signs" or proofs of Jesus' divine nature which form the bulk of his "historical" material (outside the Passion Narrative). History as history had little meaning for John, but only as philosophy of history: it is exhausted in its inner significance, so to speak, and not much is left of the outward, factual, concrete course of events. *Alles Vergängliche ist nur ein Gleichniss!* The past is not "prologue"—as in a popular modern quotation— but only a "parable," an illustrative story. He combines the mystical with the dramatic view of the past. As Aeschylus or Euripides seized upon an incident—Agamemnon's tragic homecoming or the Titan Prometheus overwhelmed by injustice and suffering at the hands of Zeus or Hecuba in the midst of her unbearable grief —and found all the tragedy and pathos of human existence summed up in that one moment; as the medieval ascetic found in Jesus' temptation and passion the deepest meanings in the gospel and the supreme guide to that *via negativa* which he himself pursued; so John looks back upon the life of Christ as a whole, or summed up in a few selected incidents, and sees its real significance in the manifestation of divine power, wisdom, and love which he effected. Thus the inner meaning of Christ's life has all but crowded the external events off the stage! Before the supreme fact of the revelation which he has made, the bare historical data of his outward life fade almost into insignificance—with the exception of the few selected incidents which are retained on account of their profound symbolic value.

For this reason the theory that the discourses in John were a later insertion into an older historical framework (e.g., the theory of A. T. Olmstead) is quite impossible: the discourses are the indispensable explanation of the whole narrative. A better theory, if discourses must be separated from narrative, is Rudolf Bultmann's, according to which the *Redequelle* (Discourse Source) is an old Gnostic poem, perhaps originally existing in Syriac or Aramaic, and to it has been added the setting of narrative derived from the current early Christian tradition—though with many resulting dislocations in the order of the *Redequelle*. The traces of the Semitic origin of the RQ are very faint and difficult to isolate: for the Greek of the Fourth Gospel, as Ernest C. Colwell demonstrated in his book by that title (1931), is a good *koinē*, i.e., Hellenistic, Greek. But one wonders if either theory is necessary. The ancient view that John's Gospel is itself a "seamless robe" has much to commend it. In all the gospels the deeds and the words of Jesus are those of the exalted, heavenly Christ, during his brief sojourn here upon earth, preliminary to his "coming" in glory. This is the *theological* setting of the whole primitive Christian tradition, and it is not in the least a secular tradition, belonging to the world's "great historical records of the past." What John did was to carry this principle to its full conclusion: the deeds and the discourses in John are those of the cosmic, eternal Christ, the divine Logos, manifesting himself here upon earth for a brief time, gathering to himself those whom the Father "had given" him (i.e., the elect), and then returning once more to the "glory" which he shared with the Father before the creation of the world. Unless this point of view is understood and accepted by the reader, he will have great difficulty in recognizing the genuinely historical element in John and the completely transcendental purpose of the author in writing what appears to be a "gospel," like the others, but is really a sacred drama of the Life, Death, and Glorification of the divine Logos incarnate upon earth.

What the author purposed to do, accordingly, was to set forth in terms of his own and his readers' deepest spiritual needs the gospel of their divine satisfaction in the life, teaching, and redemptive work of the Logos manifest in human flesh. He may have been a Gnostic—a "converted" Gnostic, perhaps; a Gnostic like Clement of Alexandria's ideal of the perfect Christian; at the least, it is from a Gnostic Christian or quasi-Gnostic point of view that this book is best understood. (See the commentary in Harper's Annotated Bible Series.) The men and women of his circle were strongly influenced by the growing movement of this name which surrounded them—a movement much older than we have ordinarily assumed, and much more widespread in Jewish and Hellenistic Christian circles even in the first century. Indeed, the origin of the Gnostic movement as a fringe sect on the periphery of

Judaism, as a kind of syncretistic, paganized Judaism, is not only supported by the tradition—the church fathers traced it to Simon Magus (Acts 8:9–24), the Samaritan goēs—but also by the actual content of the later systems, for which we are now at last beginning to obtain firsthand documentation, thanks to the manuscripts discovered at Nag Hammadi in 1945. Along with this incipient Gnosticism, and as a ready corollary to it, went the movement known as Docetism, against which Ignatius of Antioch protested in vehement terms.

Not Judaism but *Gnosticism* was now the enemy of Christianity. Even though its origins may have been Jewish, i.e., in the Graeco-Jewish-Oriental syncretism of Samaria or of Syria, its earliest adherents certainly were found far outside the pale of Judaism. It met and answered a widespread mood in Graeco-Roman religious thought, one which had been growing since the end of the second century B.C., or even since the middle of the third century, and which was also reflected in Neo-Pythagoreanism, Hermetism, the philosophy of Philo of Alexandria, and the revival of Orphism under the early empire. Its varying types of cosmology, ontology, epistemology ranged from primitive myths to a refined and abstract metaphysics (see p. 22). It was fundamentally dualistic, matter and spirit being in complete opposition—as in Orphism, where the formula was found, *sōma* (body) = *sēma* (tomb, i.e., of the soul). It also included elements from popular astrology, with its iron mechanism of unyielding fate, and it assumed that the material universe is evil, the creation of wicked or fallen or downward-tending spirits, inflamed with wicked passions or in revolt against the Supreme Being, who was the One as opposed to the Many. Hence birth is evil, for it means the entrance of an originally spiritual being into this lower realm of matter; hence marriage is evil, as it leads to procreation and further enslavement within the cycle of existence; hence marriage is to be avoided, and the pure soul must live as little contaminated by the flesh as is possible in this present life. Echoes of such teachings are to be found even in the New Testament (e.g., I Tim. 4:3). The "heresies" of the second century produced more than echoes. And if Gnosticism is technically only the name—a modern name at that —for a movement largely limited to the Christian church, the explanation of this view is the fact that Christian *gnōsis* is far better documented than pagan. The eminent historian of Greek religion, Martin P. Nilsson, views Hermetism and Gnosticism as fundamentally the same religious philosophy, one in pagan terms, the other in Christian.

On the basis of such religious views as these, salvation must consist in release from enslavement to evil—i.e., to evil matter—and deliverance from the dark dungeon of the material world. This can come about only by knowledge (gnōsis), i.e., the soul's realization that its true nature is heavenly and divine. This knowledge is imparted either by a message (as in Hermetism—the pagan Gnosticism) or by a messenger (as in the Christian form of the doctrine, the heavenly Messenger being identified with Christ). The messenger has come down from the realm of light, of true or pure being, into this dark dungeon of matter and has roused the soul from its condition of drugged somnolence and lethargy. Awaking from its dull state of life-in-death, the soul cries out, "I will arise to go to my Father." Thus the heavenly messenger becomes, in the Christian systems, in effect a Redeemer, a Saviour—the terms are retained, though the emphasis is different from that of the New Testament: for the salvation effected is only a "salvation by knowledge," not by repentance or an atonement for sin.

Among the many different types of early Gnosticism, the one which most seriously affected Christian teaching in the area from which the Fourth Gospel came, or at least to which it was addressed, is that known as Docetism. Here the "heavenly messenger" or "witness" who brings the "saving knowledge" is Christ, and his gospel consists in the truths about creation, the nature of the soul, and the way of escape from this dark realm of matter. But, although he entered the world, he himself was never contaminated by its physical material. He was the "true light," and the darkness never overcame him (cf. John 1:5)—hence he returned to the supreme realm as pure as when he left it. The explanation of this is simple: he did not really adopt a body of flesh, but only a phantom shape resembling one. Like a Greek god, he could adopt any disguise he chose—e.g., a vulture, an old woman, a Trojan prince, an Achaean warrior—and so he chose that of a Galilean carpenter. His flesh was unreal—as the apostle John is made to testify in one of the Gnostic books of Acts (Acts of John, § 89, 96). And had not Paul described him as coming only "in the likeness of sinful flesh" (Rom. 8:3)?—not "in the flesh" or as flesh. (Contrast John 1:14, which boldly states that "the word became flesh.")

It is against this particular type or phase of gnōsis (though all Gnostics would be inclined to agree with it) that the Fourth Gospel is directed, a type which "denied that Jesus Christ has come in the flesh." It was clearly recognized and identified by the early Paulinists—"the gnōsis falsely so called" (I Tim. 6:20).

Ignatius of Antioch referred to it repeatedly, and rejected it—long before the tremendous apologetic and polemical works of Irenaeus, Hippolytus, Tertullian, and Epiphanius. But the battle with this subversive creed lasted for a long time—the better part of two centuries. Had the church succumbed to this "theology of syncretism," as Paul Wendland called it, the Christian religion might easily have gone the way of all the other pagan and syncretistic creeds. Instead, as we have seen (in ch. III), the church threw up three powerful lines of defense: (1) the old Roman baptismal creed, enshrining the truly "apostolic" faith, (2) the apostolic tradition handed down in succession by the teachers and leaders in the great Christian centers, and (3) the apostolic writings—especially our present New Testament.

Among all the New Testament books, the most powerful opposition to Gnosticism is found in the Gospel and First Epistle of John. From beginning to end of the gospel, John stresses the reality of Jesus' human nature. He was the Incarnate Logos who had not merely "taken our nature upon him," as the church was content to say, in later ages, but who "became flesh" and "dwelt among us"; his physical body was as real as any man's; he was hungry and thirsty, weary and exhausted, he even wept at the grave of a friend, he was flogged by Roman soldiers, he suffered on the cross, he died there, and when dead his body—no phantom! —was pierced by a soldier's spear, and out of it came water and blood (19:34). The four Roman soldiers did not nail either a phantom or a corpse to the cross, but a living man; nor had his human nature been merely "assumed," and then at last laid aside "like a soiled garment." In the Gnostic Gospels, before the first nail was driven into his hands or feet, the aeon Christ left his temporary house of the "body," and only an empty shell was left on the cross. Or his final cry was—not "My God, my God, why hast thou forsaken me?" but "My power, my power (*Khayil*, not *El*), why hast thou left me?" And although John does not quote this cry, but substitutes the far more appropriate final word, "It is finished" (19:30), there is no question that John's major emphasis, throughout the Passion Narrative as everywhere else in his gospel, is upon the simple, natural, undeniable reality of Jesus' physical body. And for the best of reasons. Had the plain historical reality of Jesus' life, death, and resurrection been abandoned in favor of the speculative fantasia of the Gnostic interpretation, the whole meaning of the gospel would have been perverted, and Christianity would eventually have sunk without trace in the quicksands of some highly imaginative system of metaphysical speculation.

Now, it was probably from within this circle of early Christian Gnostic mysticism, sharing in considerable measure its presuppositions but at the same time, and thus all the more effectively, protesting against its extravagances, that the author of the Fourth Gospel wrote his marvelous book. Some of these presuppositions— e.g., the mystical-devotional view of religion and the use of profound symbolic or allegorical terms—seem to be reflected in the *Odes of Solomon*, an early Christian collection of hymns with a strongly Jewish basis or bias. Others—on the theological side—are clear from the cognate Epistles of John, especially I John, probably by the same writer. The language of the gospel and that of the epistles have almost everything in common, and both are clearly influenced by the "hieratic" style one finds also in such different writings as the Hermetic literature, the Mandaean sacred books, and the works of Philo of Alexandria. But it is not the style that is most significant, or was most significant for the gospel's earliest readers; what was significant was the appearance in such a milieu, and written to a considerable degree in the familiar language of contemporary Gnostic mysticism, of a book which insisted so strongly on the actual historical manifestation, life, passion, and death of the divine Logos, the Son of God, the highest being in the universe next to God, the One who dwelt in the bosom of the Father, and in whom all life, all knowledge, indeed, all the fullness of the godhead dwelt. That this being, who was in the presence of God from the beginning, "*became flesh* and tabernacled among us, and we beheld his glory, as of the only begotten Son of the Father"—this was the author's real and most astonishing contribution to the religious thought of his time and place. As Augustine explained (*Confessions*, VII. 21), no Platonist—and, he might have added, no Gnostic—could possibly have described this divine being as born in flesh or dying on a cross. It was as if a Christian Hindu, his mind steeped from childhood in the profound ideas of the *Bhagavad Gita*, were to compose a philosophical and devotional meditation on the life of Christ in the language of that ancient sacred book of his own people; or as if some disciple of Plotinus, let us say, rather than Theocritus,

> Had come upon the Figure crucified,
> And lost his gods in deep Christ-given rest.

In fact, substitute "the early Gnostics" for "Plotinus" and the parallels exactly merge. The Fourth Gospel was the first—at least it is the earliest surviving—attempt to rewrite the life of Christ from a point of view, or for a point of view, which was widespread in the Hellenistic world at that time and was destined to grow ever more influential and more philosophical until it rose to the heights of the Valentinian and Ptolemaic systems. The wonder is, not that the Gospel of John contains Gnostic or quasi-Gnostic elements, but that it contains so few, or, rather, so much else—so much that went beyond Gnostic mysticism in retaining a real grasp upon the genuinely historical element in the church's faith.

These historical elements are easily recognizable. (1) Jesus' relations with John the Baptist were longer and more intimate than the synoptics allow (following Mark's brief note); but John's presentation has much to be said for it, as Maurice Goguel and others have shown. (2) Jesus visited Judea more than once—what could be more probable? (3) His ministry in Samaria also is probable— though all but ignored by the synoptists. (4) The "cleansing" of the temple took place earlier than in the synoptics, and the "triumphal entry" also is apparently earlier, in John. (5) The Last Supper was not a Passover meal—to which there are at least fourteen objections, which seem to dispose of the Marcan dating. (6) There was no Jewish "trial," but only an examination before the high priest. (7) Jesus was put to death by the Romans, not the Jews. (8) The resurrection appearances took place at various places, not exclusively in Galilee or Jerusalem. (9) The "Messianic secret" is also reflected (cf. 2:22, 12:16), but in more thorough fashion and in less doctrinaire terms than in Mark. (10) The Zealot danger also is recognized and emphasized (6:15). (11) The lowly beginnings of faith in Christ are stressed repeatedly (6:14, 7:12, 40, etc.; as in L, Jesus is a "prophet").

On the other hand, certain unhistorical—or at least questionable—elements also are present. (1) Jesus' self-proclamation begins at the outset of his ministry. (2) His teaching is given a *theological* formulation in anti-Gnostic, anti-Docetic terms. (3) The tension and controversy between the church and the synagogue, at the point reached ca. A.D. 100, is carried back into the lifetime of Jesus. (4) There is a bitter hatred of "the Jews" (i.e., the Jewish leaders) which would have been impossible for the Jesus of the Synoptic Gospels. (5) The order of events is so rearranged that the reader gains the impression that Jesus' headquarters was Jerusalem, not Capernaum or Galilee. (6) The very language, ideas, style, thought, and diction of the synoptic Jesus are all but unrecognizable in the words of the divine being who walks the earth incognito in the Gospel of John.

Another change in the interpretation of John which has taken place during the past half century is the widespread abandonment of the theory that the Fourth Gospel was dependent upon Paul. Bousset set forth the older view in an epigram, "John stood on the shoulders of Paul" (*Kyrios Christos*, p. 180). But we by no means appraise the gospel aright if we assume that it was some private or individual composition, written outside the Christian community or for purposes other than those of the church in which the author lived. What lies behind John is not merely Paul—let alone "Paulinism"—but the whole of early Hellenistic-Roman Christianity, as Bultmann has demonstrated in his *New Testament Theology*. The "Gnostic" strain in the author's neighborhood was no doubt found within the church. And the Christ he describes is really the Christ of the church's tradition and worship, the "Lord" of the Hellenistic Christian communities founded by Paul and other missionaries from Antioch or elsewhere outside Palestine. Yet there is a difference. Paul always retained the language of the primitive Hellenistic church from which, and within which, he had learned the gospel. "Jesus is Lord" is still his creed—though he advanced beyond this to the identification of Jesus with the divine "Logos" in whom "all things consist" (Rom. 10:9; I Cor. 12:3; Phil. 2:11; Col. 1:17)— while John, on the other hand, consistently avoids the use of the title "Lord." Bousset assumed (p. 155) that it was because he had a conception of the relation of Christians to Christ which ruled out its use: "I have called you friends—not slaves" (15:15). But an equally good reason may have been the distinction he wished to draw between Christ and the "Lords many and gods many" of the contemporary Hellenistic-Roman religious world; Christ stands on an infinitely higher plane than these empty figures. The saying, "All who came before me are thieves and robbers" (10:8), may refer to the cult-gods of the Graeco-Roman world quite as probably as to the prophets and wise men of the Jews. Count W. von Baudissin has shown, in his great work, *Kyrios als Gottesname im Judentum und seine Stelle in der Religionsgeschichte* (Kyrios [= Lord] as a Name for God in Judaism and its Place in the History of Religions, Giessen, 1929), that *kyrios* did not connote absolute deity but, rather, cult-deity, and implied a personal relationship based ultimately on that of the tribe to its god. It is essentially a Semitic conception, and reached its clearest expression about the beginning of the Christian era. Nevertheless, John uses it rarely (e.g., 4:1, 20:28).

On the other hand, the title "Son of Man" (which Paul never uses) is retained by John, and, indeed, with all its primitive Palestinian connotations of final judgment (5:27), pre-existence (3:13), and exaltation (6:62). Yet these connotations are emphasized only in passing and may simply reflect some of the older material available in the church's tradition. He has no intention of taking Jewish eschatology seriously and confining (as Matthew had done) the "work" of Jesus to the preparation for the Judgment and the messianic kingdom. The Kingdom is definitely "not of this world" (18:36); and the Judgment is a continuous one: "This is the judgment, that the light has come into the world, and men loved darkness rather than light, because their deeds were evil" (3:19).

The messianic or apocalyptic element is stripped in passing, as a miner scoops up the golden sands before he opens the lode-bearing rock whence these precious bits have been washed. The title which John uniformly prefers is "Son of God" or, more briefly, "the Son"—and this no longer in the popular and undefined sense in which he perhaps read it in Mark, but as the most significant and meaningful title of the Christ whom he knew through his own and the church's faith and worship. There was no danger of misunderstanding this title as there was the title "Lord." For the old mythological cults of "Sons of God" and public heroes, divine "saviours" and "helpers" of mankind still provided the noblest of divine titles and descriptive terms available to the early gentile church, even though the simple, unquestioning belief in their presence and power had lost, for many persons, much of its ancient realism; the new mystery cults with their far more primitive deities—old vegetation spirits, for the most part—had not yet become the church's real rivals in the first or the early second century. Moreover, the title "Son of God" possessed for John and his readers a sense—possibly derived from Paul but more probably from primitive Hellenistic Christianity generally—a meaning which no one who examined the gospel with sympathy could fail to grasp: Jesus is "the Son of God" in a unique and exclusive sense, as the "Only Son" (Monogenēs), and the title emphasized not his relation to his followers or to the church (as did the title "Lord") but his relation to the Father, the Fons et Origo of his divine nature, which was derived immediately from God. John's language is not exactly or explicitly that of the later church; but there can be no question that the Catholic creeds carry on this interpretation of the nature of Christ in the identical line of theological evolution, though using still later terminology. Thus the basis of John's theology—i.e., of his Christology—is not Paul's teaching but the whole broad foundation of early gentile Christianity, which was also, at a much earlier stage, the basis of Paul's teaching.

It has often been insisted that the Hymn to the Logos, with which the book opens, is not the key to its interpretation as a whole. Some have even concluded that the hymn is a later interpolation; and, indeed, it seems clear that if we remove the hymn we are left with a series of verses that form an admirable opening for a gospel: "There was a man sent from God, whose name was John. . . . And this is his testimony, when the Jews sent priests and Levites." Such a beginning would parallel those in Mark and the other synoptics. But the description of John the Baptist in 1:7, 8 has been added in order to bring the statement in v. 6 into relation with the hymn in which it has been inserted; it forms a parenthetic comment introductory to the whole treatment of John in the opening chapters, where his subordination to Christ is clearly emphasized. And it need not follow that the hymn has been interpolated into the gospel. On our view, precisely the opposite course has been pursued. The hymn is the author's text, so to speak, and it sets his meditative exposition in the very loftiest key. As he slips away from it into the historical narrative—or what represents historical narrative for him—he interjects the description of John, and prepares for the conclusive demonstration of the Baptist's inferiority to Christ. Its relation to the Johannine discourses is even closer. The hymn (at least the first five verses) may well have existed long before the gospel was written, i.e., it existed in the author's own mind; and it is not beyond the bounds of possibility that the author himself had first composed the hymn (or had at least added the Christian supplement, e.g., vv. 9–14, 16–18, to the philosophical hymn in vv. 1–5) as a clue to his interpretation of the whole tradition of the life of Christ, as known to him and his fellow believers.

1   In the beginning was the Word,
        And the Word was with God,
        And the Word was God.

2   He was in the beginning with God.

3   All things were made through him,
        And without him was not anything made [the
                rest of this line is a textual gloss].

4   In him was life,
     And the life was the light of men.

5   The light shines in the darkness,
     And the darkness has not overcome it.

9   The true light that enlightens every man
     Was coming into the world.

10   He was in the world,
     And the world was made through him,
         Yet the world knew him not.

11   He came to his own [people],
     And his own [people] received him not.

12   But to all who received him [i.e., who believed in his
         name],
     He gave power to become children of God,

13   Who were born, not of blood
     Nor of the will of the flesh
     Nor of the will of man,
         But of God.

14   And the Word became flesh
     And dwelt among us, full of grace and truth.

     We have beheld his glory,
         Glory as of the Only Son from the Father.

16   And from his fullness have we all received,
     And grace upon grace.

17   For the Law was given through Moses,
     But grace and truth came through Jesus Christ.

18   No one has ever seen God;
     The Only Son, who is in the bosom of the Father,
         He has made him known.

Omitting vv. 6–8, 15, which appear to have been interpolated
as historical comments, there remains a fairly homogeneous and

consecutive hymn. Its first four stanzas set forth a religious-philo-
sophical conception of the Logos similar to the conceptions found
in a number of Near Eastern cults and philosophies about the beginning of our era. The fourth stanza (v. 5) may be based upon
Gen. 1; though the symbols of light and darkness are common
to many of the old Oriental religions, as far apart in time and place
as India and Egypt, Zoroastrianism and Mithraism, the Hermetic
writings and the Neoplatonic religious philosophy. Even Paul
makes use of them, as in II Cor. 4:6, Col. 1:12, etc. The remain-
ing stanzas, forming the specifically Christian part of the poem,
reach a noble climax, and show how the fundamental postulates
of the Logos-philosophy, on the Christian interpretation, lead
naturally to the doctrine of the Incarnation. (The translation of
v. 14 is important; the order of the Greek must be changed if we
are to make the meaning clear in English.)

Thus the hymn sets forth the significance which early Christianity found in the Logos-doctrine as the interpretation of the
historical appearance of Christ, his revelation of the Father, and
his rejection at the hands of his own people. As a substitute for
the Jewish messianic category, which was unacceptable to wide
circles of Gentiles, it was wonderfully well adapted to provide a
clue to the interpretation of Christ's nature and mission, on a par
with the highest reaches of Jewish messianism and, indeed, superior to it in many ways; at the same time it related the Christian
faith in Christ not only to the tenets of a particular and widely
influential philosophy, but also to the world's age-old quest for a
Revealer of God, a Redeemer from sin and death, a Truth-bringer
and a Grace-bestower. Incidentally, it enabled the author to point
the superiority of Christ to Moses, the Lawgiver of the Jews. The
use made of this interpretation by the early apologists and by the
Alexandrian theologians is familiar to every student of the history
of Christian thought.

Further, a close study of the hymn helps us to understand far
more clearly the antecedents of the author of the gospel. Though
he makes little use of philosophical terminology, either here or in
the body of the gospel, it is clear that he is familiar with one form
of the popular Stoic-Platonic cosmogony—i.e., a popular religious
version of it; and at the same time he is in touch with sectarian
Judaism, perhaps with the Jewish Gnosticism of which we have
traces elsewhere in the New Testament, though he is full of scorn
for actual, concrete, contemporary Judaism. (This may have been
characteristic also of some of the *illuminati* of Jewish Gnosticism.)
In this he reminds us of the author of the Epistle of Barnabas, in

whose view Jewish religious institutionalism was only a superb illustration of the folly of literalism. God never intended that the laws governing the Sabbath, the rite of circumcision, the temple and its sacrifices, the public cultus and its ministers, should be taken literally—their only significance was symbolic, as the outward and visible hieroglyphs of an esoteric message of eternal life (cf. John 5:39, 46).

The rhythmic prose style of the hymn, as well as its contents, speaks strongly, I believe, against an Aramaic original. It was too palpably written in Greek: though if it could be translated from Greek into Aramaic, obviously it could also have been translated from Aramaic into Greek! The hieratic, mystagogic style, which Bousset recognized in such cognate religious writings as the later Hermetica, and which can be seen likewise in the perhaps contemporary Odes of Solomon, one can discern for himself by reading the hymn aloud (in Greek), slurring the syllables wherever possible, and making such elisions as would naturally be made in chanting. The hymn, I believe, was a real hymn, written to be sung. Verses 6–8, e.g., appear upon such a method of examination to be not only structurally unnecessary but also to lack the rhythmic style of the rest—note the frequent use of *pi* and *sigma* even in juxtaposition! Some readers may question v. 13, perhaps as too "Pauline." But the idea, and the language, are sufficiently Johannine—see 3:5, 6. Paul had no exclusive right to the doctrine of the second birth! Verse 15, which is balanced in structure, shows how easily the author echoes the style of the hymn, his thought

> . . . subdued
> To what it works in, like the dyer's hand.

This is, of course, not strange if the hymn was his own earlier creation. Verse 16 cannot be a continuation of John's testimony in v. 15, but carries on the thought of v. 14.

We cannot claim finality for the details of this reconstruction; we have only endeavored to point out what seem to be fairly certain traces of the original structure of the hymn. It probably could have been sung or chanted, or at least recited with solemn liturgical effect, supposing its author intended such use. And I believe this is what he aimed at—a hymn for liturgical use. If a purely imaginary hypothesis may for a moment be advanced, I should like to substitute for Canon Streeter's suggestion of "an old man's farewell" (*The Four Gospels*, pp. 465 ff.) the picture of a fairly young man, at most middle aged, one who was gifted with poetic

and mystic insight and schooled to some degree in current philosophy, especially the late mystical type of Platonism, but more
strongly swayed by the more popular Gnostic and theosophic religious speculation of his time. His mind had always been deeply
and genuinely religious, and in the hymn, begun some while before
he became a Christian, he had preserved the rich fruitage of
thought from the days before he had discovered Christ, but when
none the less he had been steadily drawing nearer to the true Light
that "lighteth every man." Now he makes it his point of departure
for the interpretation of the work and teaching of Christ and of
the meaning of Christ for all mankind. That the earlier part of
the hymn contains teaching not specifically Christian is evident
from the remark attributed to a later Neoplatonist that "the first
chapter of John should be written in letters of gold" (Augustine,
City of God, X. 29 ad fin.). It has been suggested that the author
is indebted to Philo, or perhaps to some Graeco-Jewish "Hymn to
Wisdom"; but its affiliations seem far more direct with the Platonized Stoicism upon which Philo himself drew, as did also in some
measure the writers of the Jewish Wisdom literature. Only, it is an
"orientalized" Platonic-Stoic mysticism, of the kind lying back of
early Gnosticism and (on the philosophical side) back of popular
Hellenistic mysticism.

   If this is the author's true background, there can be little room
for the hypothesis that Mandaean concepts underlie the Fourth
Gospel. For the Mandaean religion, as far as we can make out, had
no vital contact with Greek philosophy—certainly not in the first
or second century (supposing it even existed that early!). As that
Oriental religion spread, it eventually came in contact and conflict
with Christianity, and—through Christianity—with the Hellenistic
world at large, in Byzantine times. But the fact of its Christianiza-
tion tells against any possible earlier contacts with Greek thought:
when it comes into contact with the latter, it meets it in Christian
form. As F. C. Burkitt demonstrated, "Mandaean hostility to Jesus
is hostility to the fully developed Nicene Church," while its "Jewish ideas were most probably derived from the Peshitta," i.e., the
"authorized version" of the later Syriac-speaking Christians. (See
"The Mandaeans" in Journal of Theological Studies, XIX, No.
115, and E. A. Graham in Church Quarterly Review, No. 226, p.
237.) It may of course be true that, as Walter Bauer has said,
both Mandaeism and the Fourth Gospel "spring from a common
circle of ideas, and share a common fund of concepts, symbols,
illustrations, religious views and language generally." But the one
religion fronted eastward, and has continued to do so through all

its long and obscure history; while the other, Christianity, has faced steadily westward, and has gone forward in this direction from the day when it first crossed the borders of Palestine and advanced toward "the wide prospect"—the vast world of Greek-speaking Graeco-Roman culture, Europe, and the still undiscovered lands beyond the western sea. The probability is that the "Mandaean parallels," of which Bauer has given such a fine collection in his commentary, illustrate the common religious background of both Mandaeism and Hellenistic Christian mysticism, and indicate a common source for much of their language; but they scarcely prove any fundamental or essential dependence of the one upon the other. And the same is true of parallels and proposed "sources" in other areas, e.g., the Hermetica, whose religious and quasi-philosophical ideas and terminology may long antedate the actual writing of the tractates.

The question, though difficult to answer, is bound to be asked: Where was this gospel written? It is much easier to describe the ideas it takes for granted, and the religious situation in which it arose, than to localize it definitely. The contacts with Mandaeism, formerly so widely discussed—or, rather, the contacts with the circle of ideas which Mandaeism likewise presupposes—no doubt support the theory of an Eastern origin of the gospel, possibly at Antioch, as Walter Bauer and the late C. F. Burney have maintained. Ephrem Syrus also held this view: *Johannes scripsit evangelium graece Antiochiae*—"John wrote the gospel in Greek at Antioch." But Ephrem was a Syrian, and a pardonable local pride may account for his opinion, unsupported as it is by any earlier, or, indeed, any other ancient, ecclesiastical tradition. Burney's predilection is perhaps accounted for by his theory of "the Aramaic origin of the Fourth Gospel" (the title of his book published in 1922): Syria, next to Palestine, was the most likely region for the appearance of an Aramaic gospel. But this theory, as Ernest Colwell has shown, is "not proven": the Greek of the Fourth Gospel is *not necessarily* "translation Greek" based on a Semitic original. Bauer's arguments are stronger: (1) John must have been written in a neighborhood saturated with Oriental mysticism and Gnosticism—and Syrian Gnosticism had an early beginning. (2) A locality near Palestine is suggested by the author's violent antagonism toward the Jews. Anti-Semitism presupposes a region where Jews were in a position not only to make Christians uncomfortable, but to threaten them with actual danger. (3) Here also were to be found disciples of John the Baptist and of other Oriental prophets

and "sons of God," as Celsus said—rivals of the new religion and
its Lord—in sufficient numbers to make necessary an answer to
their claims. (4) Moreover, Ignatius of Antioch proves himself a
contemporary with strong spiritual affinities for the writer of our
gospel; while (5) the slightly Semitic tone of both the gospel and
the epistles points equally clearly in this direction.

But it could not have taken Oriental mysticism or Gnosticism
much longer to reach Ephesus—the traditional place of origin of
the book—than Antioch; and the Jews were all but ubiquitous in
the Mediterranean world of the first century—see Adolf Deissmann's map printed at the end of his *Paulus* (2d ed., 1925).
Alexandria was as likely a place, on all these grounds, as was
Antioch—witness IV Maccabees, Philo, the use made by Origen
(and even by Clement?) of the earliest commentary on John,
written by the Gnostic Heracleon, and the Christian Gnostic
teachers in that city. John's disciples were to be found in Ephesus,
according to the book of Acts (19:3), and they were doubtless
found elsewhere in Jewish centers throughout the Mediterranean
world. Apollos of Alexandria is an example of one who "knew
only the baptism of John" (i.e., the Baptist; Acts 18:24 f.). And
Ignatius presupposes an acquaintance with his ideas and sympathy with his warm feelings on the part of readers in the cities of
western Asia Minor to whom he writes. As for the Semitic "tone"
of the Johannine writings, that is still somewhat debatable—not
all authorities are agreed upon it, though both Bultmann and Dodd
have laid stress upon the indubitable Semitic parallels. So also
have other modern commentators, e.g., Bauer and Barrett, not to
mention Westcott and the older writers. But there seem to be
serious difficulties in the way of locating the gospel in Antioch, or
even in Ephesus. An insuperable obstacle is the almost certain
ignorance of the Gospel of Matthew on the part of the author of
John. That Matthew, of all three synoptists, should be unknown
or unused by a gospel writer living in Antioch seems improbable
in the extreme. And for a writer in Ephesus to disregard Paul's
teaching as completely as John does, even fifty years later, seems
equally unaccountable.

As a matter of fact, there is nothing in the Gospel or Epistles
of John to locate this literary group geographically. The hypothesis
that their ecclesiastical background was Egypt, probably Alexandria, seems to be gaining adherents—though certainly no one
would stake his life or even his reputation on its truth. Probability
is our only guide, and it seems most probable (a) that the Christian religion reached Alexandria at an early date, long before the

beginning of the second century, and (b) that the peculiar type of Christian doctrine reflected in John, its confrontation with Gnosticism and its repudiation of that philosophy along with the traces of Gnostic influence which it bears, would be appropriate to an early type of Christian teaching to be found there—the evidence may be seen in ch. II of Walter Bauer's *Rechtgläubigkeit und Ketzerei in ältesten Christentum*, 1934, in spite of his own preference for Antioch as the place of origin of the gospel. But we simply do not know. As Adolf Jülicher said, "The son of Zebedee was imported into Asia Minor by later legend" (*Einleitung*, new ed., 1931, p. 419). Similarly, Mark was imported into Alexandria—a legend that survived as late as the building of San Marco in Venice in the days of the commercial rivalry between that city and the Greek East. The "patristic traditions" of gospel origins which have come down to us are often, as Kirsopp Lake insisted, little more than "patristic guesses," good, bad, or indifferent. The very existence of the "elder" John in Asia is now questioned—it has been questioned ever since Theodor Zahn's famous article appeared in Herzog-Hauck's *Realencyklopädie für protestantische Theologie und Kirche*, Vol. XI, pp. 272 ff., especially 281–285 (1901).

But it does not greatly matter where the gospel was written: Antioch, Ephesus, Alexandria, even Rome is a possible location. Every one of these cities was a world center for religious propaganda in the first two centuries, and they were all in constant intercommunication. It is a great mistake to assume, as some writers do—especially in discussing the text of John—that a book written in Ephesus would take twenty-five years to reach Alexandria or Rome; a copy could have been taken there in less than twenty-five days! But the discovery of the tiny Roberts Fragment of John (see *An Unpublished Fragment of the Fourth Gospel*, by C. H. Roberts, Manchester University, 1935), the oldest surviving fragment of New Testament manuscript, dated by the experts between A.D. 130 and 150, at least points to Egypt as a field for the very early dissemination of the Fourth Gospel. (It contains John 18:31b–33, 37b–38.)

As for the date of John, Professor Walter Bauer has excellently summed up the evidence. "None of the Apostolic Fathers can be cited as certain evidence of familiarity with John. On the other hand, Irenaeus recognizes its canonical authority as one of 'the four'; Tatian combined it with the synoptics in his famous *Diatessaron*; the Montanist movement presupposes it; while for the younger Valentinians, Ptolemaeus and Heracleon, it was a favorite book. . . . Justin and Papias apparently presuppose it. In view of all these facts it is surely unwise to bring the book down too far into the second century." (See his commentary in Lietzmann's *Handbuch*, p. 235, and Jülicher's *Einleitung*, new ed., pp. 390 ff.) The assumed use of John by Ignatius of Antioch cannot be said to be proved. Accordingly, a date early in the second century seems best to suit the requirements of the case. Incidentally, this has the advantage of Irenaeus' (apparent) support. He seems to have thought that John was written under Trajan (A.D. 98–117); see his work *Against Heresies*, II. 33. 3, III. 3. 4. An earlier date, sometime prior to the close of the first century, is assumed by those who find themselves reluctant to abandon the possibility that John the son of Zebedee was, if not the author of the gospel, at least— as Harnack maintained—in some sense responsible for it. But this view now seems less probable every year. As we grow more familiar with the background of ideas and religious aspirations, roughly classified under the designation "Hellenistic mysticism," the more certain it seems that no Palestinian Jewish writer could have produced this book. For it abandons not only the form and in large measure the dominant ideas of Jesus' own teaching, but also those of contemporary Judaism, in the period prior to or immediately following the Fall of Jerusalem. There is nothing tentative about this transposition of the gospel into another key: it is positive throughout, and entirely dogmatic. The author has lived with some of his ideas for a fairly long time, probably most of his life. They form the very fiber and fabric of his mind.

The theory that, in view of certain parallels found in the Dead Sea Scrolls, the gospel must have been written in Palestine, preferably southern Palestine, and at a fairly early date, perhaps shortly before or after the Fall of Jerusalem, and by an apostle, presumably John the son of Zebedee, is surely an example of the wish fathering the thought. Included in the vast array of parallels found in Hellenistic religious literature, especially Greek, Egyptian, and Near Eastern (see Dodd's great work, or the commentaries, especially Bauer's and Bultmann's), the few which are found in the Dead Sea Scrolls are really minor and only "more of the same." They simply testify to the widespread religious syncretism which existed in that period and influenced the most diverse types of religious life and thought, even Jewish, even Essene—or "sectarian Jewish"—especially in their religious imagery. One and all these groups shared a widely used store of ideas, concepts, and vocabulary, as well as a common or at least a very similar religious experience. As Edwyn Bevan insisted in his great Gifford Lectures, *Symbolism and Belief* (1938), and as G. van der Leeuw and others have demonstrated (see *Phänomenologie der Religion*, 1933, Engl. tr. 1952), even the use of identical terms and images does not prove the dependence of one writer or group upon another. There are realities of the religious life which can be described only in certain universal, age-old, perfectly natural images.

The evidence contained in the tradition has been gone over repeatedly, and I do not wish to repeat it here. No one has studied it more closely than G. H. C. Macgregor, in the Introduction to his commentary in the Moffatt series. The view there set forth is a good example of the compromising type of interpretation popular a generation ago. There were many similar views, temporary halting places in a long rearguard action covering the slow retreat. As a conclusion, or, rather, as a defensible hypothesis, he proposed three successive figures, each of whom had a hand in the composition of the gospel: (1) the *Witness*, "the disciple whom Jesus loved," "a young Jerusalemite disciple, outside the number of the Twelve, but admitted to the inner circle during the closing days"; (2) the *Evangelist* himself, afterward "John the elder" of Ephesus, "a younger contemporary and disciple of the Witness," who made use of the latter's testimony, though he was himself "almost certainly a Jew, and in all probability, at least by birth and early training, a Jew of Palestine." He wrote the gospel in his old age, in Ephesus, and after his death (3) the *Redactor* of the gospel revised its order, interpolated certain "anti-Baptist" sections, and added the appendix (ch. 21).

This hypothesis is perhaps the best possible one under the circumstances, from the conservative viewpoint, and motivated by the desire to retain as much as possible of the early ecclesiastical tradition. But its weakness lies in the assumption of the "memoirs" or recollections of "the Witness." A man whose memory retained as much as he is supposed, on this hypothesis, to have remembered would certainly have remembered much more; and he would scarcely have remembered so much that conflicts with the earlier evangelic documents. I do not mean only that his memory played false, e.g., as to the time of the temple cleansing—quite conceivably the Marcan tradition may be entirely wrong on this point, and the presumed use of the charge, at the time, that Jesus had threatened to destroy the temple, was only an editorial afterthought. But surely Mark, Q, L, and the other synoptic sources or strands of tradition, not to mention a responsible author like Luke, were not all of them dead wrong in the accounts they gave of the form, contents, subjects, interests, aims of the teaching of Jesus!

For John, Jesus wears the garb of a Hellenistic mystagogue, and speaks in the "hieratic" style appropriate to the mystery which he discloses, oracularly, mysteriously, sublimely. What John gives us

is an artistic, devotional creation—not history; his scenes are ex-
quisite, symbolic altar-panels—not transcripts of past events; like
the mystagogue, he is interested in the spiritual and eternally
valid *present meaning* of the past, not in the realistic portrayal of
events as they actually occurred (cf. II Cor. 5:16–21). Even if
some traces of Hellenistic religious thought and vocabulary are to
be found in the earlier sources (e.g., Luke 10:21–24, Matt. 11:25–
30, 13:16, 17), there is nothing like the continuous discourse in
this style which we find in John. So, too, in the even remoter documents, the recently discovered Dead Sea Scrolls, which some writers would have us accept as proof of the existence and currency
of such terminology in pre-Christian Judaism. For example, one
transcriber and editor reads "when God begets the Messiah"—a
phrase which cannot possibly have been meant in either a physical
or a metaphysical sense, but only figuratively, as in Ps. 2:7. The
hiphil form of the Hebrew root *yld* does not necessarily mean
"beget," but also means "cause to be born," "cause to exist," or
even "create," which are certainly ideas far more consonant with
all Jewish messianism, early and late, orthodox and sectarian. As
one later rabbi said, "God has no son" (R. Abin II, ca. A.D. 370)
—a statement which was certainly correct, understanding sonship
as he did, i.e., in the mythological sense. This statement is one
more evidence that "Son of God" was *not* a Jewish messianic title
(see Gustav Dalman's study in *The Words of Jesus*, 1901, and
also the more recent works of Paul Volz, Joseph Klausner, and
Sigmund Mowinckel listed in the Bibliography, on p. 204), and
points away *from* rather than toward any supposed connection between the Dead Sea Scrolls and the Gospel of John. The teaching
of the historical Jesus of Nazareth was sublime—but it was not
delivered in Johannine language or in the language of popular
Hellenistic mysticism. Even in the letters of Paul, who stood in
fairly close contact with this type of religious thought and was
himself by no means unaffected by it, when the words of Jesus are
quoted or his teaching alluded to, their form and structure are
entirely Palestinian Jewish, not Hellenistic, and classify easily with
the synoptic traditions rather than with the Johannine discourses.

What we have in John, in other words, is an apologetic statement of Christian faith and practice in wholly new terms; and
there is as little evidence for a continuous Palestinian-Ephesian or
Palestinian-Alexandrian type of historical tradition as there is for
a Johannine document, or *Grundschrift*, which Macgregor rightly
rejects (p. xl). The basic material of the discourses, which Bult-

mann assigns to a *Redequelle,* is something else. The structure of the gospel (see the Outline on pp. 198 ff.) shows only the slightest indication of any underlying sources or of development in composition. As the older scholars used to say, it is the "seamless robe" (19:23) and its materials have been closely woven together "from the top throughout." The Prologue cannot be separated from the rest of the gospel, nor can the Appendix in ch. 21—it has the same vocabulary and style as the main document. Apparently, (a) the "Book of the Seven Signs" (not merely the narrative), (b) the Supper Discourses, including the High Priestly Prayer, and also (c) the Passion Narrative all represent blocks of material which may have been written down, by the author himself, prior to his writing of the gospel; but the hypothesis cannot be proved. What we have in John is more probably a series of *strands of tradition,* all carefully worked over and knit together into a compact unity.

In outward form the Gospel of John appears to be historical; but history, in the strict sense, was the last thing in the world its author thought he was writing. It was not even Jewish midrash or haggadah; it was Hellenistic religious mystery-drama brought down to earth and forced to make terms with a tradition—not extensive or exhaustive—of the kind that underlies the earlier Gospel of Mark. This is the tradition which Professor Dodd identifies with the outlines of Jesus' ministry presupposed in the addresses contained in the earlier chapters of Acts, i.e., in a stratum of good older Palestinian tradition. By "Hellenistic religious mystery-drama" we do not mean something non-Christian; "mystery-drama" was the native heath of this writer, but he was a Christian, and the church of his time and place already, no doubt, set forth its faith in this perfectly normal way; and, moreover, he was a Hellenist—probably not a Jew, but a Levantine or Greek. There are no tears in his eyes when he writes of the self-condemnation of "the Jews," as there were in the eyes of the old scribe who wrote "Matthew." Nor could he have shared Paul's readiness to be "anathema" for his people's sake. He was a daring speculative genius in religion, and his identification of Christ with the eternal Logos who became incarnate is something no ancient Jew could have accepted. Certainly Philo of Alexandria would have repudiated this speculation, instantly. What "John" did, whoever he was, wherever he lived and wrote, was to give creative expression to a type of Christian faith and piety without which Europe might never have become even outwardly Christian.

It is perhaps true that he was in large measure responsible for bringing into the church a one-sided and self-centered mysticism, for setting up an academic and superficial criterion of orthodoxy, for legitimizing a type of emotional piety diametrically opposed to that enjoined by our Lord—who had no patience with those who "said but did not." For it is perfectly evident that John, despite his glowing paragraphs about "love" in the abstract, nevertheless hates "the Jews"—i.e., the Jewish leaders—with all his heart. Such orthodoxy and spirituality of profession, contradicted by actual performance, was a bad heritage for the Hellenistic church, and one destined to survive for a long time. However, this is only one aspect of his achievement—its darker side; and the main fact still holds true, viz., that no one contributed more toward the evolution of Catholic Christianity than this early second-century mystic. All the future lay before him, as he wrote his new and revolutionary account of the life of Christ, transposing and transforming it into a dramatic exposition of the inner meaning of Christ for the world, in place of the bare facts enshrined in the traditional narratives. All the future lay before him—the Greek church fathers and apologists with their elaborate exposition and defense of the faith; the elaborate liturgies of the Oriental churches; the devout hymnology of the early ages; the Catholic creeds with their subtle definitions and thunderous anathemas; the art and architecture of the Great Church, with its solemn services, its celestial music, its multitude of ministers, its sacraments, and the grace of heaven streaming through it like the sap of that Living Vine our author himself described. The future of Catholicism, the Great Church of East and West, of Orient and Occident, uniting Palestine and Greece and fusing Hebraism and Hellenism into one compact and indissoluble spiritual unity—all this future lay before him as he put pen to paper to draw his picture of the glorified Christ of the Hellenists.

Outlines of the Gospels

OUTLINE OF MARK

Title, 1:1

I. Introduction. Jesus and John the Baptizer, 1:2–13
John the Baptizer, 1:2–6
John's messianic preaching, 1:7, 8
Jesus is baptized, 1:9–11
Jesus is tempted, 1:12, 13

II. Jesus in Galilee, 1:14–9:50

A. About the Sea of Galilee, 1:14–5:43

Jesus begins his preaching of the Kingdom of God, 1:14, 15
A day in Capernaum, 1:16–38
    (a) Jesus calls his first disciples, 1:16–20
    (b) Jesus heals a demoniac, 1:21–28
    (c) Jesus heals Peter's wife's mother, 1:29–31
    (d) Jesus heals the multitude at Capernaum, 1:32–34
    (e) Jesus leaves Capernaum, 1:35–38
Jesus heals a leper, 1:39–45
A series of controversies, 2:1–3:6
    (a) Jesus heals a paralytic, 2:1–12
    (b) Jesus calls Levi, 2:13, 14
    (c) Jesus eats with publicans and sinners, 2:15–17
    (d) The question about fasting, 2:18–20
    (e) The new patch and the new wine, 2:21, 22
    (f) The disciples pluck grain on the Sabbath, 2:23–28
    (g) Jesus heals a withered hand, 3:1–6
Jesus' popularity and his cures, 3:7–12
Jesus appoints twelve apostles, 3:13–19a
Further controversies, 3:19b–30

(a) The charge of the scribes, 3:19b–22
(b) The Beelzebul controversy, 3:23–30
Jesus' true family, 3:31–35
A collection of parables, 4:1–34
    (a) The parable of the different soils, 4:1–9
    (b) The purpose of parables, 4:10–12
    (c) The meaning of the parable, 4:13–20
    (d) The right use of parables, 4:21–25
    (e) The parable of the seed growing secretly, 4:26–29
    (f) The parable of the mustard seed, 4:30–32
    (g) Jesus' use of parables, 4:33, 34
A group of miracle stories, 4:35–5:43
    (a) Jesus quiets a storm, 4:35–41
    (b) Jesus cures a maniac, 5:1–20
    (c) Jesus is called to heal Jairus' daughter, 5:21–24
    (d) Jesus heals a woman who touches his garment, 5:25–34
    (e) Jesus restores Jairus' daughter, 5:35–43

B. More distant journeys, 6:1–9:50

Jesus visits Nazareth, 6:1–6a
The mission of the disciples, 6:6b–29
    (a) Jesus sends out his disciples, 6:6b–13
    (b) Herod Antipas' opinion of Jesus, 6:14–16
    (c) The murder of John the Baptizer, 6:17–29
Further miracle stories, 6:30–56
    (a) Jesus feeds the multitude (5000), 6:30–44
    (b) Jesus walks on the water, 6:45–52
    (c) Jesus heals the multitude at Gennesaret, 6:53–56
Jesus rejects the tradition of the elders, 7:1–23
    (a) The controversy over defilement, 7:1–8
    (b) The case of corban, 7:9–13
    (c) The truth about defilement, 7:14–16
    (d) Explanation of the saying about defilement, 7:17–23
Further miracle stories, 7:24–8:26
    (a) Jesus heals a gentile girl, 7:24–30
    (b) Jesus heals a deaf stammerer, 7:31–37
    (c) Jesus feeds the multitude (4000), 8:1–10
    (d) The Pharisees demand a sign from heaven, 8:11–13
    (e) The saying about leaven, 8:14–21
    (f) Jesus heals a blind man at Bethsaida, 8:22–26
Messiahship and suffering, 8:27–9:13
    (a) Peter confesses his faith that Jesus is the Messiah, 8:27–30
    (b) Jesus foretells his own death, 8:31–33

(c) Jesus announces the conditions of discipleship, 8:34–9:1
(d) Jesus is transfigured, 9:2–8
(e) The prophecy of Elijah's return, 9:9–13
Jesus heals an epileptic boy, 9:14–29
Jesus again foretells his own death, 9:30–32
Jesus settles the disciples' dispute over greatness, 9:33–37
Jesus forbids intolerance, 9:38–41
The sin of causing others to stumble (fall into sin), 9:42–48
Sayings about salt, 9:49, 50

III. Jesus in Judea, 10:1–15:47

A. On the way to Jerusalem, 10:1–52

The question about divorce, 10:1–12
Jesus blesses the children, 10:13–16
The meaning of discipleship, 10:17–31
(a) Jesus and the rich young man, 10:17–22
(b) The handicap of riches, 10:23–27
(c) The reward of renunciation, 10:28–31
Jesus once more foretells his own death, 10:32–34
The request of James and John, 10:35–45
Jesus heals Bartimaeus, 10:46–52

B. Jesus in Jerusalem, 11:1–12:44

Jesus enters Jerusalem, 11:1–10
Jesus returns to Bethany, 11:11
Jesus curses a fig tree, 11:12–14
Jesus cleanses the temple, 11:15–19
The lesson of the withered fig tree, 11:20–26
A second series of controversies, 11:27–12:34
(a) Jesus' authority is challenged, 11:27–33
(b) The parable of the wicked vineyard tenants, 12:1–12
(c) The question about tribute to Caesar, 12:13–17
(d) The question about the resurrection, 12:18–27
(e) The question about the great commandment, 12:28–34
Jesus questions the scribes, 12:35–37a
Jesus warns against the scribes, 12:37b–40
Jesus praises a widow's offering, 12:41–44

C. The Discourse on the Last Things, 13:1–37

Jesus predicts the destruction of the temple, 13:1, 2
The signs of the Parousia, 13:3–8

The disciples will be persecuted, 13:9–13
The "abomination of desolation," 13:14–20
False Messiahs and false prophets will appear, 13:21–23
The Parousia of the Son of Man, 13:24–27
The date of the Parousia, 13:28–37

D. *The Passion Narrative, 14:1–15:47*

The plot against Jesus, 14:1, 2
Jesus is anointed at Bethany, 14:3–9
Judas agrees to betray Jesus, 14:10, 11
The disciples prepare for the Passover, 14:12–16
Jesus foretells the betrayal, 14:17–21
The Last Supper, 14:22–25
Jesus foretells Peter's denials, 14:26–31
Jesus in Gethsemane, 14:32–42
Jesus is arrested, 14:43–52
Jesus is examined before the high priest, 14:53–65
Peter denies that he knows Jesus, 14:66–72
Jesus is tried by Pilate, 15:1–5
Jesus is condemned to be crucified, 15:6–15
Jesus is mocked by the soldiers, 15:16–20
Jesus is crucified, 15:21–32
Jesus dies on the cross, 15:33–41
The burial of Jesus, 15:42–47

IV. The finding of the empty tomb, 16:1–8
[The longer conclusion of Mark, 16:9–20]
[Another ending.]

OUTLINE OF LUKE-ACTS

Part One: *The Gospel*

The Prologue to Luke-Acts, 1:1–4

I. The birth and early years of Jesus, his preparation and divine commission, 1:5–4:13
The infancy and childhood of John the Baptist and Jesus, 1:5–2:52
   (a) John's birth foretold, 1:5–25
   (b) Jesus' birth foretold, 1:26–38
   (c) Mary visits Elizabeth, 1:39–56
   (d) The birth of John, 1:57–80
   (e) The birth of Jesus, 2:1–20

(f) The naming of Jesus and his presentation in the temple, 2:21–40
    Simeon's thanksgiving, 2:25–35
    Anna's thanksgiving, 2:36–38
(g) The boy Jesus in the temple, 2:41–52

The mission of John the Baptist, 3:1–20
(a) John's call and message, 3:1–6
(b) John's preaching of repentance, 3:7–9
(c) John's message to special groups, 3:10–14
(d) John's messianic announcement, 3:15–18
(e) John imprisoned by Herod Antipas, 3:19, 20

The baptism and temptation of Jesus, 3:21–4:13
(a) The baptism of Jesus, 3:21, 22
(b) The genealogy of Jesus, 3:23–38
(c) The temptation of Jesus, 4:1–13

II.   The ministry of Jesus in Galilee, 4:14–9:50
The beginning of Jesus' ministry, 4:14–44
(a) Jesus teaches in the synagogues of Galilee, 4:14, 15
(b) Jesus visits the synagogue at Nazareth and is rejected, 4:16–30
(c) Jesus visits the synagogue at Capernaum and cures a demoniac, 4:31–37
(d) Jesus heals Peter's wife's mother, 4:38, 39
(e) Jesus heals the sick at evening, 4:40, 41
(f) Jesus leaves Capernaum for other towns, 4:42, 43
(g) Jesus travels about Galilee, preaching in synagogues, 4:44

The call of the disciples, 5:1–6:16
(a) Jesus calls Simon, 5:1–11
(b) Jesus heals a leper, 5:12–16
(c) Jesus heals a paralytic, 5:17–26
(d) Jesus calls Levi, 5:27–32
(e) The question about fasting, 5:33–39
(f) The disciples pick grain on the Sabbath, 6:1–5
(g) Jesus heals a man on the Sabbath, 6:6–11
(h) Jesus chooses the twelve apostles, 6:12–16

The Sermon on the Plain, 6:17–49
(a) Jesus heals the multitudes, 6:17–19
(b) Jesus pronounces blessings upon the poor and the persecuted, 6:20–23
(c) Jesus pronounces woes upon the rich and the self-satisfied, 6:24–26
(d) Jesus' disciples must love their enemies, 6:27–36
(e) Jesus' disciples must not judge others, 6:37–42
(f) The test of true piety is active goodness, 6:43–45
(g) Jesus' disciples must keep his sayings, 6:46–49

Scenes from the ministry in Galilee, 7:1–8:3
  (a) Jesus heals a centurion's slave, 7:1–10
  (b) Jesus raises a widow's son at Nain, 7:11–17
  (c) John's question: Is Jesus the Messiah? 7:18–23
  (d) Jesus' words about John, 7:24–30
  (e) Jesus' criticism of his contemporaries, 7:31–35
  (f) Jesus is anointed by a penitent woman, 7:36–50
  (g) Jesus' women disciples, 8:1–3
Jesus teaches by parables, 8:4–18
  (a) The parable of the different soils, 8:4–8
  (b) Jesus' reason for using parables, 8:9, 10
  (c) The explanation of the parable of the soils, 8:11–15
  (d) The right use of parables, 8:16–18
A group of miracles, 8:19–56
  (a) Jesus' true family, 8:19–21
  (b) Jesus calms a tempest, 8:22–25
  (c) Jesus cures a maniac in Gadara, 8:26–39
  (d) Jesus raises the daughter of Jairus, 8:40–42a, 49–56
  (e) Jesus heals a woman who touches his garment, 8:42b–48
Jesus and the twelve disciples, 9:1–50
  (a) Jesus sends out his twelve disciples, 9:1–6
  (b) Herod Antipas' opinion of Jesus, 9:7–9
  (c) Jesus feeds the multitude, 9:10–17
  (d) Peter confesses his faith in Jesus the Messiah, 9:18–22
        Jesus foretells his own death, 9:21, 22
  (e) The conditions of discipleship, 9:23–27
  (f) Jesus is transfigured, 9:28–36
  (g) Jesus heals an epileptic boy, 9:37–43a
  (h) Jesus again foretells his own sufferings, 9:43b–45
  (i) The disciples' question: Who is greatest? 9:46–48
  (j) The strange exorcist, 9:49, 50

III. Jesus on the way to Jerusalem, 9:51–19:27
Jesus in Samaria, 9:51–10:37
  (a) The Samaritan villagers reject Jesus, 9:51–56
  (b) Three tests of discipleship, 9:57–62
  (c) The mission of the Seventy, 10:1–24
        Jesus sends out seventy disciples, 10:1–16
          Woes pronounced on the Galilean cities, 10:13–15
        The seventy disciples return, 10:17–20
        Jesus' exultation and thanksgiving, 10:21, 22
        A blessing pronounced upon the disciples, 10:23f.
  (d) The lawyer's questions, 10:25–28, and the story of the Good Samaritan, 10:29–37

Jesus' teaching on prayer, 10:38–11:13

    (a) Mary and Martha, 10:38–42

    (b) The Lord's Prayer, 11:1–4

    (c) The parable of the friend at midnight, 11:5–8

    (d) The certainty of answer to prayer, 11:9–13

Jesus is criticized by the Pharisees—and his criticism of them, 11:14–54

    (a) Jesus is accused of collusion with Beelzebul, 11:14–23

    (b) The lapsed demoniac, 11:24–26

    (c) A blessing is pronounced upon Jesus' mother, 11:27, 28

    (d) No sign shall be given but that of Jonah, 11:29, 30

    (e) Jesus' criticism of his contemporaries, 11:31, 32

    (f) Jesus' sayings about light, 11:33–36

    (g) Jesus' criticism of the Pharisees, 11:37–44

    (h) Jesus' criticism of the lawyers, 11:45–54

Jesus and his disciples, 12:1–48

    (a) Jesus warns his disciples against hypocrisy, 12:1

    (b) Jesus exhorts his disciples to fearless proclamation of the gospel, 12:2–7,
    and to fearless confession of the Christian faith, 12:8–12

    (c) Jesus warns his disciples against covetousness, 12:13–21
       The parable of the rich fool, 12:16–21

    (d) Jesus exhorts his disciples to trust in God, 12:22–34

    (e) Jesus exhorts his disciples to be vigilant, 12:35–40, and to be faithful, 12:41–46

    (f) Different degrees of responsibility, 12:47, 48

The seriousness of the time, 12:49–13:9

    (a) The tragic aspect of Jesus' mission, 12:49, 50, and its consequences in family life, 12:51–53

    (b) Signs of the time, 12:54–56

    (c) Prudence in litigation, 12:57–59

    (d) Tragic warnings seen in current events, and the call to repent, 13:1–5

    (e) The parable of the unfruitful fig tree, 13:6–9

The end of the Galilean ministry, 13:10–35

    (a) Jesus heals a crippled woman on the Sabbath, 13:10–17

    (b) The parables of the mustard seed and the leaven, 13:18–21

    (c) Few will be saved, 13:22–24

    (d) Casual acquaintance with Christ will not avail in the Judgment, 13:25–27

    (e) Reversals of fortune in the Kingdom of God, 13:28–30

    (f) Jesus leaves Galilee, deliberately, for Jerusalem, 13:31–33,

        whose tragic fate he foresees, 13:34, 35

Jesus' table talk, 14:1–35

    (a) Jesus heals a man with dropsy, on the Sabbath, 14:1–6

    (b) Jesus teaches humility, 14:7–11

    (c) Jesus teaches charity, 14:12–14

    (d) The parable of the Great Supper, 14:15–24

    (e) The cost of discipleship, 14:25–33

    (f) The saying about salt, 14:34, 35

Jesus and the outcast, 15:1–32

    (a) Jesus is criticized for mingling with sinners, 15:1, 2

    (b) The parable of the lost sheep, 15:3–7

    (c) The parable of the lost coin, 15:8–10

    (d) The parable of the lost son, 15:11–32

Jesus' teaching about wealth, 16:1–31

    (a) The parable of the clever steward, 16:1–13

    (b) Jesus' criticism of the Pharisees, 16:14–18

    (c) The story of the rich man and Lazarus, 16:19–31

The duties of disciples, 17:1–10

    (a) The seriousness of causing others to sin, 17:1, 2

    (b) Jesus' saying about forgiveness, 17:3, 4

    (c) Jesus' saying about faith, 17:5, 6

    (d) Slaves do not claim either thanks or wages, 17:7–10

Jesus heals ten lepers, 17:11–19, and only one returns to thank him, 17:15–19

Jesus' teaching about the latter days, 17:20–18:8

    (a) The date of the arrival of the Kingdom cannot be calculated, 17:20, 21

    (b) The sudden coming of the Son of Man, 17:22–37

    (c) The parable of the widow pleading for justice, 18:1–8

The story of the Pharisee and the tax collector, 18:9–14

Jesus blesses little children, 18:15–17

The rich man who failed to meet the test of renunciation, 18:18–30

Jesus a third time foretells his own death, 18:31–34

Jesus in Jericho, 18:35–19:27

    (a) Jesus heals Bartimaeus, 18:35–43

    (b) Zacchaeus welcomes Jesus, 19:1–10

    (c) The parable of the entrusted funds, 19:11–27

IV.   Jesus in Jerusalem, 19:28–21:38

    Jesus enters Jerusalem and cleanses the temple, 19:28–46

        (a) Jesus enters Jerusalem, 19:28–38

(b) Jesus foretells the destruction of Jerusalem, 19:39–44
(c) Jesus cleanses the temple, 19:45, 46
Jesus teaches in the temple, 19:47–21:38
   (a) Jesus' authority is challenged, 19:47–20:8
   (b) The parable of the wicked husbandmen, 20:9–19
   (c) The question about tribute to Caesar, 20:20–26
   (d) The question about the resurrection, 20:27–40
   (e) The question about the Son of David, 20:41–44
   (f) Jesus warns against the scribes, 20:45–47
   (g) Jesus praises the widow's offering, 21:1–4
The discourse on the end of the age, 21:5–36
   (a) Jesus foretells the destruction of the temple, 21:5, 6
   (b) The signs to precede the Parousia, 21:7–11
   (c) The disciples to be persecuted, 21:12–19
   (d) The coming siege and capture of Jerusalem, 21:20–24
   (e) The Parousia of the Son of Man, 21:25–27
   (f) The parable of the fig tree, 21:28–31
   (g) The date of the Parousia, 21:32, 33
   (h) The disciples must keep watch, 21:34–36
Jesus teaches daily in the temple, 21:37, 38

V. The Death of Jesus, 22:1–23:56
The conspiracy against Jesus, 22:1, 2
Judas agrees to betray Jesus, 22:3–6
The Last Supper, 22:7–38
   (a) The preparation for the Passover meal, 22:7–13
   (b) The Last Supper, 22:14–20
   (c) Jesus foretells the betrayal, 22:21–23
   (d) The question of greatness, 22:24–30
   (e) Jesus foretells Peter's denial, 22:31–34
   (f) The two swords, 22:35–38
The arrest and trial of Jesus, 22:39–23:25
   (a) Jesus in Gethsemane, 22:39–46
   (b) Jesus is arrested, 22:47–53
   (c) Peter denies that he knows Jesus, 22:54–62
   (d) Jesus is mocked by his captors, 22:63–65
   (e) Jesus before the Sanhedrin, 22:66–71
   (f) Jesus before Pilate, 23:1–7
   (g) Jesus before Herod Antipas, 23:8–12
   (h) Jesus is sentenced to die, 23:13–25
The crucifixion of Jesus, 23:26–49
   (a) Jesus is led to Calvary, 23:26–32
   (b) Jesus is crucified, 23:33–38
   (c) The penitent robber, 23:39–43
   (d) Jesus dies on the cross, 23:44–49
The burial of Jesus, 23:50–56

VI. The Resurrection of Jesus, 24:1–53
The empty tomb, 24:1–12
Jesus appears to his disciples, 24:13–49
- (a) The appearance of the risen Jesus at Emmaus, 24:13–35
- (b) The appearance to the disciples at Jerusalem, 24:36–49

The ascension of the risen Christ, 24:50–53

Part Two: The Acts of the Apostles

I. The early church in Jerusalem, 1:1–5:42
Introduction, 1:1–5
The disciples in Jerusalem, 1:6–26
- (a) The Ascension, 1:6–11
- (b) The upper room, 1:12–14
- (c) The speech of Peter and the election of Matthias, 1:15–26

The coming of the Spirit on the day of Pentecost, 2:1–42
- (a) The coming of the Spirit, 2:1–4
- (b) The impression on the multitude, 2:5–13
- (c) Peter's sermon, 2:14–36
- (d) The conversion of three thousand, 2:37–42

The communal life of the disciples in Jerusalem, 2:43–47
The healing of the lame man at the Beautiful Gate, 3:1–4:31
- (a) The healing, 3:1–10
- (b) Peter's address in Solomon's portico, 3:11–26
- (c) The arrest of Peter and John, 4:1–4
- (d) Peter's address before the high priest, 4:5–12
- (e) The apostles warned and released, 4:13–22
- (f) They return and report to the other disciples: the prayer of the community, 4:23–31

The story of Ananias and Sapphira, 4:32–5:11
- (a) Communal life of the disciples, 4:32–35
- (b) The gift made by Barnabas, 4:36, 37
- (c) Ananias and Sapphira: their lie and its punishment, 5:1–11

Renewed opposition of the high priests, 5:12–42
- (a) Miraculous healings by the apostles, 5:12–16
- (b) The apostles arrested, miraculously released, and haled before the Sanhedrin, 5:17–28
- (c) Peter's address to the Sanhedrin, 5:29–32
- (d) Gamaliel's advice, 5:33–39
- (e) The apostles scourged and released, 5:40–42

II. The spread of the church throughout Palestine, 6:1–12:24
     The martyrdom of Stephen, 6:1–8:3
         (a) The appointment of the Seven, 6:1–6
         (b) The growth of the church in Jerusalem, 6:7
         (c) Stephen's preaching and arrest, 6:8–7:1
         (d) Stephen's defense, 7:2–53
         (e) The stoning of Stephen, 7:54–8:3
     The mission of Philip, 8:4–40
         (a) Philip's preaching in Samaria, 8:4–13
         (b) Peter and John in Samaria: Simon Magus, 8:14–25
         (c) Philip and the Ethiopian, 8:26–40
     The conversion of Paul, 9:1–31 [cf. 22:3–21 and 26:9–23]
         (a) On the road to Damascus, 9:1–9
         (b) Paul's baptism, 9:10–19a
         (c) Paul's preaching, 9:19b–22
         (d) The plot against Paul and his escape, 9:23–25
         (e) Paul returns to Jerusalem and goes to Tarsus,
             9:26–30
         (f) The peace of the church, 9:31
     Peter's pastoral ministry in Judea, 9:32–11:18
         (a) Peter at Lydda: Aeneas, 9:32–35
         (b) Peter at Joppa: Tabitha, 9:36–43
         (c) Cornelius' vision, 10:1–8
         (d) Peter's vision, 10:9–16
         (e) Peter goes to Cornelius, 10:17–33
         (f) Peter's address in the house of Cornelius, 10:34–43
         (g) The baptism of Cornelius' household, 10:44–48
         (h) Peter's return to Jerusalem and defense of his ac-
             tion, 11:1–18
     The beginnings of the church in Antioch, 11:19–30
         (a) The gospel spread by persecution, 11:19–26
         (b) The famine relief mission to Jerusalem, 11:27–30
     Peter's imprisonment and the death of Herod Agrippa I,
         12:1–24
         (a) The martyrdom of James and the arrest of Peter,
             12:1–5
         (b) Peter released by an angel, 12:6–11
         (c) Peter's return to the disciples, 12:12–17
         (d) Herod's anger over Peter's escape, 12:18, 19
         (e) The death of the persecutor, 12:20–24

III. Christianity is carried to Cyprus and Galatia, 12:25–15:35
     The Antiochene mission: Paul and Barnabas, 12:25–14:28
         (a) Paul and Barnabas return from Jerusalem, 12:25
         (b) Paul and Barnabas commissioned by the church,
             13:1–3
         (c) Paul and Barnabas in Cyprus, 13:4–12

(d) Paul and Barnabas at Pisidian Antioch, 13:13–15

(e) Paul's sermon, 13:16–41

(f) The favorable response of the synagogue congregation, 13:42, 43

(g) Paul and Barnabas turn to the Gentiles, 13:44–47

(h) The outbreak of persecution in the new field, 13:48–52

(i) Paul and Barnabas at Iconium, 14:1–7

(j) Paul and Barnabas at Lystra, 14:8–18

(k) Renewed persecution: The apostles retrace their steps, 14:19–23

(l) Paul and Barnabas return to Antioch, 14:23–28

The council at Jerusalem, 15:1–35

(a) The question of admitting Gentiles without circumcision, 15:1–5

(b) Peter's address, 15:6–11

(c) The testimony of Paul and Barnabas, 15:12

(d) The address of James, 15:13–21

(e) The decision and the pastoral letter, 15:22–29

(f) The letter delivered, 15:30–35

IV. Christianity is carried to Macedonia and Achaia (Paul's Second Missionary Journey), 15:36–18:22

(a) Paul's plan to revisit the churches in Asia Minor, 15:36–41

(b) Paul revisits Derbe, Lystra, and Iconium, 16:1–5

(c) Paul at Troas, 16:6–10

(d) Paul and Silas at Philippi, 16:11–40

The conversion of Lydia, 16:11–15

Paul and Silas in prison, 16:16–40

The exorcism of a slave girl, 16:16–18

The complaint of her owners, 16:19–24

An earthquake and the conversion of the jailer, 16:25–34

The apostles are released, 16:35–40

(e) Paul and Silas at Thessalonica, 17:1–9

(f) Paul and Silas at Beroea and Athens, 17:10–15

(g) Paul's address at Athens, 17:16–34

Paul led before the Areopagus, 17:16–21

Paul's address, 17:22–31

The results of Paul's address, 17:32–34

(h) Paul at Corinth, 18:1–17

Paul stays with Aquila and Priscilla, 18:1–4

Paul preaches in Corinth for eighteen months, 18:5–11

Paul is accused before Gallio, 18:12–17

(i) Paul returns to Antioch, 18:18–22

V. Christianity in the province of Asia (Paul's Third Missionary Journey), 18:23–21:16
   (a) Paul revisits Galatia and Phrygia, 18:23
   (b) Apollos visits Ephesus and Corinth, 18:24–28
   (c) Paul arrives at Ephesus, 19:1–7
   (d) Paul preaches in Ephesus for two years, 19:8–41
      Preaching to Jews and Gentiles, 19:8–10
      The success of the mission, 19:11–20
      Paul's further plans, 19:21, 22
      The riot at Ephesus, 19:23–41
   (e) Paul revisits Macedonia and Greece, and returns to
Troas, 20:1–12
      Paul preaches at Troas, 20:7–12
   (f) Paul at Miletus, 20:13–38
      Paul's address to the Ephesian elders, 20:18–35
   (g) Paul returns to Jerusalem, 21:1–16

VI. Paul in Jerusalem, Caesarea, and Rome, 21:17–28:31
Paul in Jerusalem, 21:17–23:35
   (a) Paul's report to James and the elders, and their proposal, 21:17–26
   (b) Paul is arrested in the temple, 21:27–36
   (c) Paul is permitted to address the mob, 21:37–40
   (d) Paul's address, 22:1–21 [cf. 9:1–31]
   (e) Paul is threatened with scourging, but claims Roman
citizenship, 22:22–29
   (f) Paul's address before the council, 22:30–23:10
   (g) Paul's encouraging vision, 23:11
   (h) The plot against Paul's life, 23:12–22
   (i) Paul is transferred to Caesarea, 23:23–35
Paul in Caesarea, 24:1–26:32
   (a) The case against Paul, 24:1–9
   (b) Paul's defense before Felix, 24:10–21
   (c) Paul's trial is postponed, 24:22–27
   (d) Paul's trial is taken up by Festus, 25:1–12
   (e) A special hearing before Agrippa II, 25:13–27
   (f) Paul's defense before Festus and Agrippa, 26:1–23
[cf. 9:1–31]
   (g) The end of the hearing, 26:24–32
Paul in Rome, 27:1–18:31
   (a) The journey by sea and shipwreck, 27:1–44
   (b) Paul is safe on Malta, 28:1–10
   (c) The final stage of the journey, 28:11–16
   (d) Paul meets with the Jewish leaders in Rome,
28:17–28
   (e) Paul preaches in Rome for two years, 28:30, 31

OUTLINE OF MATTHEW

The Infancy Narrative, 1:1–2:23
    The genealogy of the Messiah, 1:1–17
    The birth of Jesus, 1:18–25
    The visit of the Magi, 2:1–12
    The flight into Egypt, 2:13–15
    The death of the innocents, 2:16–18
    The return from Egypt, 2:19–23

I.   Discipleship, 3:1–7:29

A. Narrative, 3:1–4:25

The mission of John the Baptist, 3:1–12
    (a) John's appearance and message, 3:1–6
    (b) John's preaching of repentance, 3:7–10
    (c) John's messianic preaching, 3:11, 12
The baptism of Jesus, 3:13–17
The temptation of Jesus, 4:1–11
The beginning of Jesus' ministry, 4:12–25
    (a) Jesus begins preaching in Galilee, 4:12–17
    (b) Jesus calls his first disciples, 4:18–22
    (c) A preaching tour through Galilee, 4:23–25

B. Discourse, 5:1–7:29. The Sermon on the Mount

Introduction, 5:1, 2
The Beatitudes, 5:3–12
Salt and light, 5:13–16
The reinterpretation of the ancient Law, 5:17–48
    (a) Jesus' attitude toward the Law, 5:17–20
    (b) The law forbidding murder, 5:21, 22
    (c) On reconciliation with friends, 5:23, 24, and enemies, 5:25, 26
    (d) The law forbidding adultery, 5:27–30
    (e) The law about divorce, 5:31, 32
    (f) The law about oaths, 5:33–37
    (g) The law about revenge, 5:38–42
    (h) On love for one's enemies, 5:43–48
The true practice of pious works, 6:1–18
    (a) Almsgiving, 6:2–4
    (b) Prayer, 6:5–15
        The Lord's Prayer, 6:7–15
    (c) Fasting, 6:16–18

The requirement of singlehearted devotion, 6:19–24, and trust in God, 6:25–34
    (a) On true treasure, 6:19–21
    (b) On seeing clearly, 6:22, 23
    (c) On undivided loyalty, 6:24
    (d) On trust in God: against anxiety, 6:25–34
On judging others: against censoriousness, 7:1–5
On prudence in presenting the gospel, 7:6
The assurance of answer to prayer, 7:7–11
The Golden Rule, 7:12
The test of true discipleship, 7:13–27
    (a) The narrow way, 7:13, 14
    (b) The test of goodness, 7:15–20
    (c) The criterion at the Judgment, 7:21–23
    (d) Hearers and doers of the word, 7:24–27
Jesus astonishes his hearers, 7:28, 29

II.   Apostleship, 8:1–10:42

A.   Narrative, 8:1–9:34

Jesus' ministry of healing, 8:1–17
    (a) Jesus heals a leper, 8:1–4
    (b) Jesus heals a centurion's slave, 8:5–13
    (c) Jesus heals Peter's wife's mother, 8:14, 15
    (d) Jesus heals the sick at evening, 8:16, 17
The tests of discipleship, 8:18–22
Further miracles and healings, 8:23–9:8
    (a) Jesus calms a tempest, 8:23–27
    (b) Jesus cures two demoniacs at Gergesa, 8:28–34
    (c) Jesus heals a paralytic, 9:1–8
The call of Levi (Matthew), 9:9–13
The question about fasting, 9:14–17
The climax of Jesus' healing ministry, 9:18–34
    (a) Jesus raises a ruler's daughter and heals a woman who touches the hem of his garment, 9:18–26
    (b) Jesus heals two blind men, 9:27–31
    (c) Jesus heals a dumb demoniac, 9:32–34

B.   Discourse, 9:35–10:42. The mission of the disciples

Jesus has compassion on the multitudes, 9:35–38
Jesus sends out his disciples to preach and to heal, 10:1–15
The disciples will be persecuted, 10:16–25
They must be fearless in confessing Christ, 10:26–33
Divisions in families will result from persecution, 10:34–39
The reward for receiving the missionaries, 10:40–42

III.   The hidden revelation, 11:1–13:52

A. Narrative, 11:1–12:50

Jesus goes about Galilee preaching, 11:1
The question of John the Baptist: Are you the Messiah?
11:2–6
Jesus' words about John, 11:7–15
Jesus' view of his own mission, 11:16–30
    (a) Jesus' criticism of his contemporaries, 11:16–19
    (b) Jesus pronounces woes on the Galilean cities,
        11:20–24
    (c) Jesus' thanksgiving and invitation, 11:25–30
Jesus and the law of the Sabbath, 12:1–14
    (a) The disciples pick grain on the Sabbath, 12:1–8
    (b) Jesus heals a withered hand on the Sabbath, 12:9–14
Jesus heals the multitudes, 12:15–21
The Pharisees' charge against Jesus, and his refutation of
    it, 12:22–37
    (a) Jesus heals a blind and dumb demoniac, 12:22, 23
    (b) The charge of collusion with Beelzebul, and Jesus'
        reply, 12:24–30
    (c) On blasphemy against the Holy Spirit, 12:31, 32
    (d) The tests of goodness, 12:33–35
    (e) On responsibility for idle words, 12:36, 37
The Pharisees demand a sign from Jesus, 12:38–45
    (a) The sign of Jonah, 12:38–40
    (b) Jesus criticizes his contemporaries, 12:41, 42
    (c) The return of an evil spirit: the lapsed demoniac,
        12:43–45
Jesus' true family, 12:46–50

B. Discourse, 13:1–52. The Hidden Teaching of the Parables

The parable of the different soils, 13:1–9
The reason for teaching in parables, 13:10–15
The disciples' blessings, 13:16, 17
The meaning of the parable of the soils, 13:18–23
The parable of the tares, 13:24–30
The parable of the mustard seed, 13:31, 32
The parable of the leaven, 13:33
Jesus teaches publicly by parables, 13:34, 35
The meaning of the parable of the tares, 13:36–43
The parable of the hidden treasure, 13:44
The parable of the costly pearl, 13:45, 46
The parable of the dragnet, 13:47–50
The instructed scribe or teacher, 13:51, 52

IV.   The Church, 13:53–18:35

A.   Narrative, 13:53–17:23

Jesus visits Nazareth, 13:53–58
The death of John the Baptist, 14:1–12
    (a) Herod Antipas' opinion of Jesus, 14:1, 2
    (b) Herod's murder of John, 14:3–12
Jesus feeds the multitude (5,000), 14:13–21
Jesus walks on the water, 14:22–33
Jesus heals the multitude at Gennesaret, 14:34–36
Jesus rejects the tradition of the elders, 15:1–20
Jesus heals a demoniac girl in Phoenicia, 15:21–28
Jesus heals a multitude on a mountain, 15:29–31
Jesus feeds the multitude (4,000), 15:32–39
The Pharisees demand a sign, 16:1–4
The discourse on leaven, 16:5–12
Peter's confession of faith and the transfiguration of Jesus,
    16:13–17:13
    (a) Peter confesses his faith that Jesus is the Messiah,
        16:13–20
            The future founding of the church, 16:17–19
    (b) The first passion announcement, 16:21–23
    (c) The disciples' pathway of suffering, 16:24–28
    (d) The transfiguration of Jesus, 17:1–8
    (e) The coming of Elijah, 17:9–13
Jesus heals an epileptic boy, 17:14–21
The second passion announcement, 17:22, 23

B.   Discourse, 17:24–18:35. On Church Administration

The temple tax, 17:24–27
The question of greatness: rank in the Kingdom, 18:1–5
Responsibility for leading others to sin, 18:6–10
The parable of the lost sheep, 18:11–14
On rebukes and reconciliation, 18:15–20
The rule of unlimited forgiveness, 18:21, 22
The parable of the unmerciful creditor, 18:23–35

V.   The Judgment, 19:1–25:46

A.   Narrative, 19:1–22:46

Jesus in Peraea, 19:1, 2
The question about divorce and remarriage, 19:3–9
Renunciation of marriage for the sake of the Kingdom of
    God, 19:10–12
Jesus blesses the children, 19:13–15

Renunciation of wealth for the sake of the Kingdom of God, 19:16–30
  (a) Jesus and the rich young man, 19:16–22
  (b) The hindrance of riches, 19:23–26
  (c) The reward of complete renunciation, 19:27–30
The parable of the day laborers in the vineyard, 20:1–16
The third passion announcement, 20:17–19
Jesus and the two sons of Zebedee, 20:20–28
Jesus heals two blind men, 20:29–34
Jesus enters Jerusalem and cleanses the temple, 21:1–22
  (a) Jesus enters Jerusalem, 21:1–11
  (b) Jesus cleanses the temple, 21:12–16
  (c) Jesus curses a fig tree, 21:17–22
Controversies in the temple court, 21:23–22:46
  (a) Jesus' authority is challenged, 21:23–27
  (b) The parable of the two sons, 21:28–32
  (c) The parable of the wicked husbandmen, 21:33–46
  (d) The parable of the marriage feast, 22:1–14
  (e) The question about tribute to Caesar, 22:15–22
  (f) The question about the resurrection, 22:23–33
  (g) The question about the great commandment, 22:34–40
  (h) The question about the Son of David, 22:41–46

B. *Discourse, 23:1–25:46. The doctrine of the Judgment and the Parousia*

1. The discourse against the scribes and Pharisees, 23:1–39
  (a) Their hypocrisy, heartlessness, and ostentation, 23:1–12
  (b) The seven woes, 23:13–33
  (c) The impending Judgment, 23:34–36
  (d) The lament over Jerusalem, 23:37–39
2. The apocalyptic discourse, 24:1–25:46
Jesus predicts the destruction of the temple, 24:1, 2
  (a) The signs of the Parousia, 24:3–8
  (b) The disciples will be persecuted, 24:9–14
  (c) The abomination of desolation and the final woes, 24:15–28
  (d) The Parousia of the Son of Man, 24:29–31
  (e) The parable of the fig tree, 24:32, 33
  (f) The date of the Parousia, 24:34–41
  (g) The duty of watchfulness: the parable of the watchful householder, 24:42–44
  (h) The parable of the faithful servant, 24:45–51
  (i) The parable of the ten maidens, 25:1–13
  (j) The parable of the entrusted talents, 25:14–30
  (k) The Last Judgment, 25:31–46

The Passion and Resurrection Narratives, 26:1–28:20

The preparation for the passion, 26:1–46
    (a) Jesus once more foretells his own death, 26:1, 2
    (b) The plot against Jesus, 26:3–5
    (c) Jesus is anointed at Bethany, 26:6–13
    (d) Judas agrees to betray Jesus, 26:14–16
    (e) The preparation for the Passover, 26:17–19
    (f) Jesus foretells the betrayal, 26:20–25
    (g) The Last Supper, 26:26–29
    (h) Jesus foretells Peter's denial, 26:30–35
    (i) Jesus in Gethsemane, 26:36–46

Jesus is tried, condemned, crucified, and buried, 26:47–27:66
    (a) Jesus is arrested, 26:47–56
    (b) Jesus before the Sanhedrin, 26:57–68
    (c) Peter denies that he knows Jesus, 26:69–75
    (d) Jesus is led before Pilate, 27:1, 2
    (e) Judas hangs himself, 27:3–10
    (f) Jesus is tried before Pilate, 27:11–14
    (g) Pilate orders Jesus put to death, 27:15–26
    (h) Jesus is mocked by the soldiers, 27:27–31
    (i) Jesus is crucified, 27:32–44
    (j) Jesus dies on the cross, 27:45–56
    (k) The burial of Jesus, 27:57–61
    (l) The guard at the tomb, 27:62–66

The Resurrection, 28:1–20
    (a) The empty tomb, 28:1–8
    (b) The risen Jesus appears to the two Marys, 28:9, 10
    (c) The bribing of the guard, 28:11–15
    (d) The risen Jesus appears to the eleven disciples, 28:16, 17
    (e) The great commission, 28:18–20

OUTLINE OF JOHN

Prologue: The Incarnation of the Word, 1:1–18
The existence of the Word before Creation, 1:1–5
    (a) His relation to God, 1:1, 2
    (b) His relation to the world, 1:3–5
The Word the revealer of God in history, 1:6–18
    (a) His presence in the world, 1:6–13
    (b) The Incarnation of the Word, 1:14–18

I. Jesus, the Heavenly Messenger: His work in the world, 1:19–12:50

The testimony of John, the forerunner, 1:19–34
   (a) John's words about himself, 1:19–23
   (b) John's words about his mission, 1:24–28
   (c) John's recognition of Jesus, 1:29–34
The call of the first disciples, 1:35–51
   (a) The call of Andrew, Peter, and one other, 1:35–42
   (b) The call of Philip and Nathanael, 1:43–51

The Book of the Seven Signs, ch. 2–12
The revelation of the Divine Glory to the world
   (a) The marriage feast at Cana, 2:1–12 (Sign I)
   (b) The cleansing of the temple, 2:13–22
   (c) The visit of Nicodemus, 2:23–3:36
         Jesus' miracles, 2:23–25
         The mystery of rebirth, 3:1–8
         The mystery of the Son of Man, 3:9–21
            The heavenly witness, 3:9–13
            The crisis of his coming, 3:14–21
         (Interlude: The final testimony of the Baptist, 3:22–30)
         The mystery of the heavenly testimony, 3:31–36
   (d) Jesus and the Samaritans, 4:1–42
         Jesus rests beside the wall of Sychar, 4:1–6
         Jesus' dialogue with the woman of Samaria: the Living Water, 4:7–15
         True worship is in spirit, 4:16–26
         The Samaritans come to Jesus, 4:27–30
         Jesus' true food, 4:31–34
         The mission of the disciples, 4:35–38
         The conversion of the Samaritans, 4:39–42
   (e) Healing the nobleman's son, 4:43–54 (Sign II)
   (f) The healing at the Pool of Bethzatha, 5:1–16 (Sign III)
         The traditional story, 5:1–9a
         The controversy over healing on the Sabbath (5:9b–16)
   (g) The Christological Discourse, 5:17–47
         Jesus' reply to the charge of Sabbath-breaking, 5:17, 18
         The revealer of God is the final Judge, 5:19–30
         The testimony to the revealer, 5:31–40
         Why the revealer is not honored, 5:41–47
   (h) The feeding of the five thousand, 6:1–13 (Sign IV)
   (i) Jesus walks on the water, 6:14–21 (Sign V)

Martha goes to meet Jesus, 11:17–27
The raising of Lazarus, 11:28–44
Conclusion, 11:45, 46
(r) The authorities decide to put Jesus to death, 11:47–57
(s) The anointing at Bethany, 12:1–8
(t) The authorities decide to put Lazarus to death, 12:9–11
(u) The triumphal entry, 12:12–19
(v) Jesus and the Gentiles, 12:20–36
(w) Conclusion of the "Book of the Seven Signs": a review of the public ministry of Jesus, 12:37–50

II. Jesus, the Heavenly Messenger: His return to the Father, 13:1–20:29

The Johannine Passion Narrative, 13:1–19:42
(a) The Last Supper, 13:1–30
Jesus washes his disciples' feet, 13:1–11
The meaning of Jesus' act, 13:12–20
The prediction of the betrayal and designation of the betrayer, 13:21–30
(b) Farewell Discourse I, 13:31–14:31
Jesus anticipates his death as glorification, 13:31–33
The New Commandment, 13:34, 35
The prediction of Peter's denial, 13:36–38
The disciples are to follow Christ, 14:1–4
Christ is the way to the Father, 14:5–14
The promise of the Spirit, 14:15–17
The promise of Christ's return, 14:18–21
The real Presence of God and of Christ, 14:22–24
Summary and conclusion, 14:25–31
(c) Farewell Discourse II, 15:1–16:33
"Abide in me," 15:1–8
"Continue in my love," 15:9–17
The world's hatred of Christ and of his disciples, 15:18–20
The sins of the world, 15:21–25
The mission of the disciples in view of the world's hatred, 15:26–16:4a
The Spirit and the church's testimony, 15:26f.
Jesus predicts the persecution of his disciples, 16:1–4a
The Spirit will come if Jesus goes away, 16:4b–7
The Spirit's judgment upon the world, 16:8–11

For Further Reading: A Selected Bibliography

A Bibliography of Bible Study for Theological Students, published in 1948 by Princeton Theological Seminary, Princeton, N.J., contains useful lists of books for further study. See also the Index to Articles on the New Testament and the Early Church Published in Festschriften, compiled by Bruce M. Metzger, published by the Society of Biblical Literature in 1951. A supplement appeared in 1956. The Introductions to the Gospels and Acts in The Interpreter's Bible, Vols. VII–IX (1951–54), contain good selected bibliographies. See also the introductory articles in Vol. I and Vol. VII. The following titles are recommended for further study of the Gospels and Acts.

GENERAL AND INTRODUCTORY

Barr, Allan, A Diagram of Synoptic Relationships, 1938.

Bauer, Walter, Rechtgläubigkeit und Ketzerei in ältesten Christentum, 1934.

Black, Matthew, An Aramaic Approach to the Gospels and Acts, 1946.

Bundy, W. E., Jesus and the First Three Gospels, 1955.

Burkitt, F. C., The Gospel History and its Transmission, 1906; 3d ed., 1911. Earliest Sources for the Life of Jesus, 1910; 2d ed., 1922.

Brandon, S. G. F., The Fall of Jerusalem and the Christian Church, 1951.

Cullmann, Oscar, and Menoud, P. H., eds., Aux Sources de la Tradition Chrétienne, 1950.

Davies, W. D., and Daube, D., eds., The Background of the New Testament and its Eschatology, 1956.

Dibelius, Martin, A Fresh Approach to the New Testament and Early Christian Literature, 1936. Botschaft und Geschichte, ed. by G. Bornkamm, 2 vols., 1953, 1956.

Dodd, C. H., The Apostolic Preaching and its Developments, 1936. New Testament Studies, 1952.

Eltester, W., ed., Neutestamentliche Studien fur Rudolf Bultmann, 1954.

Filson, F. V., Origins of the Gospels, 1938.

Goodspeed, E. J., Introduction to the New Testament, 1937.

Grant, F. C., The Growth of the Gospels, 1933. The Gospel of the Kingdom, 1940.

Harnack, Adolf, The Sayings of Jesus, 1908.

Heard, Richard, An Introduction to the New Testament, 1950.

Hawkins, J. C., Horae Synopticae, 2d ed., 1909.

Jülicher, Adolf, An Introduction to the New Testament, 1904; 7th German ed., 1931.

Klausner, Joseph, The Messianic Idea in Israel, 1955.
Knox, John, Criticism and Faith, 1952.
Knox, W. L., The Sources of the Synoptic Gospels, ed. by Henry Chadwick, 2 vols., 1953, 1957.
Lightfoot, R. H., History and Interpretation in the Gospels, 1935. Locality and Doctrine in the Gospels, 1937.
Manson, T. W., The Teaching of Jesus, 1931.
McNeile, A. H., Introduction to the Study of the New Testament, 1927; new ed., 1953.
Moffatt, James, Introduction to the Literature of the New Testament, 2d ed., 1912.
Mowinckel, Sigmund, He that Cometh, 1956.
Redlich, E. Basil, The Student's Introduction to the Synoptic Gospels, 1936.
Richardson, Alan, The Gospels in the Making, 1938.
Riddle, D. W., The Gospels: Their Origin and Growth, 1939.
Sanday, William, ed., Studies in the Synoptic Problem, 1911.
Scott, E. F., The Literature of the New Testament, 1932.
Stanton, V. H., The Gospels as Historical Documents, 3 vols., 1903–20.
Streeter, B. H., The Four Gospels, 1924; rev. ed., 1930.
Taylor, Vincent, The Gospels: A Short Introduction, 1930. Behind the Third Gospel, 1926.
Volz, Paul, Die Eschatologie der judischen Gemeinde im Neutestamentlichen Zeitalter, 1934.
Wendland, Paul, Die Urchristlichen Literaturformen, 2d ed., 1912.
Wernle, Paul, Die Synoptische Frage, 1899.
Zahn, Theodor, Introduction to the New Testament, 3 vols., 2d ed., 1917.

FORM CRITICISM

Albertz, M., Die synoptischen Streitgespräche, 1921.
Bertram, Georg, Die Leidensgeschichte Jesu und der Christuskult, 1922.
Bultmann, Rudolf, Geschichte der synoptischen Tradition, 1921; 2d ed., 1931. The Study of the Synoptic Gospels, in F. C. Grant, Form Criticism: A New Method of New Testament Research, 1934.
Dibelius, Martin, Die Formgeschichte des Evangeliums, 1919; 2d ed., 1933; Engl. tr., From Tradition to Gospel, 1935. The Message of Jesus Christ, 1939. Gospel Criticism and Christology, 1935.
Easton, B. S., The Gospel before the Gospels, 1928.
Fiebig, Paul, Der Erzählungsstil der Evangelien, 1925.
Grobel, Kendrick, Formgeschichte und Synoptische Quellenanalyse, 1937.
Kundsin, Karl, Primitive Christianity in the Light of Gospel Research, in Grant, Form Criticism, as above.

McGinley, L. J., Form-criticism of the Synoptic Healing Narratives, 1944.

Redlich, E. Basil, Form Criticism, Its Value and Limitations, 1939.

Richardson, Alan, The Miracle Stories of the Gospels, 1941.

Schmidt, K. L., Der Rahmen der Geschichte Jesu, 1919.

Taylor, Vincent, The Formation of the Gospel Tradition, 1933.

COMMENTARIES ON THE GOSPELS AND ACTS

Harper's Annotated Bible Series: New Testament, 1952 ff.

The Interpreter's Bible, Vols. VII–IX, 1951–54.

Holtzmann, H. J., Die Synoptiker, 1889; 3d ed., 1901.

Loisy, Alfred, Les Evangiles Synoptiques, 1907–08.

Major, H. D. A., Manson, T. W., and Wright, C. J., The Mission and Message of Jesus, 1937. Also separately, Part II, The Sayings of Jesus, by T. W. Manson, 1949.

Montefiore, C. G., The Synoptic Gospels, 2d ed., 1927.

Strack, H. L., and Billerbeck, Paul, Kommentar zum Neuen Testament aus Talmud und Midrasch, 4 vols., 1922–28; Index vol., 1956.

Weiss, Bernhard and Johannes, Commentaries on Matthew, Mark, Luke in the Meyer-kommentar (in German), 2 vols., 1901.

Weiss, Johannes, Die Schriften des Neuen Testaments, 2 vols., 1906; 3d ed., 4 vols., 1917.

Wellhausen, Julius, Einleitung in den Evangelien, and separate commentaries, 1903 ff.

MATTHEW

Bacon, B. W., Studies in Matthew, 1930.

Kilpatrick, G. D., The Origins of the Gospel according to St. Matthew, 1946.

Commentaries on Matthew by W. C. Allen, 1907; F. C. Grant in Harper's Annotated Bible Series, 1955; F. W. Green, 2d ed., 1945; Sherman Johnson in The Interpreter's Bible, Vol. VII, 1951; E. Klostermann (in German), 2d ed., 1927; M. J. Lagrange (in French), 4th ed., 1927; A. H. McNeile, 1915; P. A. Micklem, 1917; Alfred Plummer, 1909; T. H. Robinson, 1928; B. T. D. Smith, 1927.

MARK

Bacon, B. W., Is Mark a Roman Gospel? 1919. The Gospel of Mark, 1925.

Cadoux, A. T., The Sources of the Second Gospel, n.d.

Carrington, Philip, The Primitive Christian Calendar, Vol. I, 1952.

Dibelius, Martin, Jesus, 1949.

Grant, F. C., The Earliest Gospel, 1943.

Guy, H. A., The Origin of the Gospel of Mark, 1955.
Lightfoot, R. H., The Gospel Message of St. Mark, 1950.
Weiss, Johannes, The History of Primitive Christianity, 2 vols., 1937, ch. 22. Das Aelteste Evangelium, 1903.
Wendling, E., Die Entstehung des Marcusevangeliums, 1908.
Werner, Martin, Der Einfluss Paulinischer Theologie im Markusevangelium, 1923.
Commentaries on Mark by W. C. Allen, 1915; B. W. Bacon, The Beginnings of Gospel Story, 1909; B. H. Branscomb, 1937; F. C. Grant, in The Interpreter's Bible, 1951; F. C. Grant, in Harper's Annotated Bible Series, 1952; E. Klostermann (in German), 2d ed., 1926; M.-J. Lagrange (in French), 1920; 5th ed., 1929; Engl. tr., 1930; Ernst Lohmeyer (in German), 1937; Allan Menzies, The Earliest Gospel, 1901; A. E. J. Rawlinson, 1925; H. B. Swete, 1902; Vincent Taylor, 1952; C. H. Turner, in Charles Gore's New Commentary on Holy Scripture, 1928; also separately.

LUKE–ACTS

Cadbury, H. J., The Making of Luke–Acts, 1927. The Style and Literary Method of Luke, 1920.
Harnack, Adolf, Luke the Physician, 1907.
Commentaries on Luke by J. M. Creed, 1930; B. S. Easton, 1926; S. M. Gilmour, in The Interpreter's Bible, 1952; A. J. Grieve, in Peake's One Volume Bible Commentary, 1919; Erich Klostermann (in German), 2d ed., 1929; M.-J. Lagrange (in French), 1921; 5th ed., 1927; H. K. Luce, 1933; W. Manson, 1930; Alfred Plummer, 1896; Lonsdale Ragg, 1922.

ACTS (alone)

Cadbury, H. J., The Book of Acts in History, 1955.
Dix, Gregory, Jew and Greek, 1953.
Easton, B. S., "The Purpose of Acts," in Early Christianity, ed. by F. C. Grant, 1954.
Dibelius, Martin, Studies in the Acts of the Apostles, ed. by Heinrich Greeven, 1956.
Harnack, Adolf, The Acts of the Apostles, 1909. The Date of Acts and the Synoptic Gospels, 1911. Luke the Physician, 1907.
Meyer, Eduard, Ursprung und Anfänge des Christentums, 3 vols., 1921–23.
Ramsay, William, St. Paul the Traveller and Roman Citizen, 1896; 7th ed., 1903; Luke the Physician, 1908.
Weiss, Johannes, The History of Primitive Christianity, tr. and ed. by F. C. Grant, A. H. Forster, P. S. Kramer, and S. E. Johnson, 1937. Ueber die Absicht und den literarischen Charakter der Apostelgeschichte, 1897.
Wellhausen, Julius, Kritische Analyse der Apostelgeschichte, 1914.

Wikenhauser, Alfred, *Die Apostelgeschichte und ihr Geschichtswert*, 1921.

Commentaries on Acts by A. W. F. Blunt, 1922; F. F. Bruce, 1951; H. J. Cadbury and Kirsopp Lake, in *The Beginnings of Christianity*, ed. by F. J. Foakes-Jackson and Kirsopp Lake, 5 vols., 1920–33; F. J. Foakes-Jackson, 1931; Ernst Haenchen (in German), 1956; H. J. Holtzmann (in German), 3d ed., 1901; Rudolf Knopf (in German), in *Die Schriften des Neuen Testaments*, 3d ed., 1917; G. H. C. Macgregor, in *The Interpreter's Bible*, 1954; Erwin Preuschen (in German), 1912; R. B. Rackham, 1906; 10th ed., 1925; H. H. Wendt (in German), 1880, last ed., 1913; Alfred Wikenhauser (in German), 2d ed., 1951; Theodor Zahn (in German), 3d ed., 1927.

JOHN

Bacon, B. W., *The Gospel of the Hellenists*, 1933.

Colwell, E. C., *The Greek of the Fourth Gospel*, 1931.

Colwell, E. C., and Titus, E. L., *The Gospel of the Spirit*, 1938.

Dodd, C. H., *The Interpretation of the Fourth Gospel*, 1953.

Gardner, Percy, *The Ephesian Gospel*, 1916.

Gardner-Smith, P., *St. John and the Synoptic Gospels*, 1938.

Hoskyns, E. C., and Davey, F. N., *The Fourth Gospel*, 2 vols., 1940.

Howard, W. F., *Christianity according to St. John*, 1946. *The Fourth Gospel in Recent Criticism and Interpretation*, new ed., 1955.

Redlich, E. Basil, *An Introduction to the Fourth Gospel*, 1939.

Roberts, C. H., *An Unpublished Fragment of the Fourth Gospel in the John Rylands Library*, 1935.

Sanders, J. N., *The Fourth Gospel in the Early Church*, 1943.

Scott, E. F., *The Fourth Gospel, its Purpose and Theology*, 2d ed., 1908.

Strachan, R. H., *The Fourth Evangelist, Dramatist or Historian*, 1925. *The Fourth Gospel, its Significance and Environment*, 1941.

Commentaries on John by C. K. Barrett, 1955; Walter Bauer (in German), 3d ed., 1933; J. H. Bernard, 2 vols., 1929; Rudolf Bultmann (in German), 1941; F. C. Grant, in *Harper's Annotated Bible Series*, 1956; W. F. Howard, in *The Interpreter's Bible*, 1952; M.-J. Lagrange (in French), 1921; 5th ed., 1936; G. H. C. Macgregor, 1928.

All these books contain references to other works; some provide extended bibliographies. See also the modern Bible Dictionaries, such as T. K. Cheyne and J. S. Black, *Encyclopaedia Biblica*, 4 vols., 1899–1903; James Hastings, *Dictionary of the Bible*, 5 vols., 1905–09; *Dictionary of the Apostolic Church*, 2 vols., 1916–18; *Dictionary of Christ and the Gospels*, 2 vols., 1909; *Dictionary of the Bible* (in one vol.), 1909; M. W. Jacobus, E. C. Lane, A. C. Zenos, and E. J. Cook, *A New Standard Bible Dictionary*, 3d ed., 1936; M. S. and J. L. Miller, *Harper's Bible Dictionary*, 1952.

Index

I. SUBJECTS

Abomination of desolation, 53
Acts of the Apostles, 124
   Outline of Acts, 189 ff.
   Sources, 125 ff.
Apocrypha, 13
Apologetic interest, 35
Apostles, 84
Aramaic, 34
Aramaic originals, 69

Baptismal formula in Matt., 147, 150 f.
Baptism of Jesus, 56 f.
Beelzebul, 90
Bible study, 7 f.
Bibliography, 203 ff.
Bibliolatry, 8
Biographical interest, 33
Biographies, 26 f.
"Blocks," 56, 76, 86; see Sequences

Caligula's statue, 100
Canon law, 37
Catholic Apostolic writings, 18
chreias, pros tas, 77
Church books, 3, 6, 11 ff., 16, 19 f.
Church history, 17, 73
Controversy, 34
Controversies in Mark, 81 ff., 98 ff.
Cost of materials, 29

Data of the gospels, 30
Dead Sea Scrolls, 135, 175
Discipleship, 85, 95
Docetism, 161

Edification, 32
Editorial additions, 49
Elijah, 95

Fasting, 89

Form Criticism, vii, 12, 27, 52 ff.
Formgeschichte, see Form Criticism
Form History, see Form Criticism
Gilyōn, 70 f.
Gnosticism, 22 ff., 159 ff.
Gospels, why written, 25 ff.
Greek, 34
Groups of writings, 17, 20

Hellenists, 154 ff.
Hieratic style, 176
Historical origins of Christianity, 9
Historical study of the New Testament, 15
History in the Hellenistic age, 119
Hymn to the Logos, 167 ff.

Interpretation, 14
Interrelationship of the Synoptics, 39

Jerusalem, Fall of, 135
John the Baptist, 84
Johannine literature, 18
John, 154 ff.
   Author of John, 176
   Christology of John, 166, 177
   Date, 174 f.
   Discourses in John, 158 f., 177 f.
   History in John, 158, 164, 178
   John and the Dead Sea Scrolls, 175 ff.
   John and Paul, 165
   John and the Synoptics, 6, 155 ff.
   John, where written, 172
   Messianic and Apocalyptic elements, 165 ff.
   Outline of John, 198 ff.
   Purpose of John, 159
Judaism, 124, 137, 152

II. PERSONS

III. TEXTS